AF600610

MEDIEVAL ROMANCE

The Aesthetics of Possibility

Medieval Romance

The Aesthetics of Possibility

JAMES F. KNAPP AND PEGGY A. KNAPP

UNIVERSITY OF TORONTO PRESS
Toronto Buffalo London

Toronto Buffalo London
www.utorontopress.com

ISBN 978-1-4875-0191-4

Library and Archives Canada Cataloguing in Publication

Knapp, James F., author
Medieval romance : the aesthetics of possibility / James F. Knapp and Peggy A. Knapp.

Includes bibliographical references and index.
ISBN 978-1-4875-0191-4 (cloth)

1. Romances, English – History and criticism. 2. English literature – Middle English, 1100–1500 – History and criticism. I. Knapp, Peggy Ann, author II. Title.

PR321.K63 2017 821′.109353 C2017-903276-3

University of Toronto Press acknowledges the financial assistance to its publishing program of the Canada Council for the Arts and the Ontario Arts Council, an agency of the Government of Ontario.

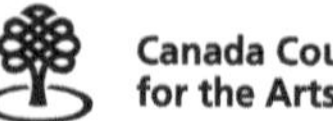

Conseil des Arts du Canada

Funded by the Government of Canada Financé par le gouvernement du Canada

For Jim and Kate

Contents

Preface

It's tense and thrilling when Orfeo in the early-fourteenth-century poem *Sir Orfeo* enters a narrow cleft in a mountain, risking the dangers of an uncharted realm armed only with his lyre in order to follow his much-loved wife after a ten-year separation. It's painfully perplexing when Dorigen in Chaucer's *Franklin's Tale* and Gawain in *Sir Gawain and the Green Knight* see themselves tangled in conflicting promises. Nobody believes anymore in fairy strongholds under mountains or green horsemen who, having been beheaded, pick up their heads by the hair and ride off. Why, then, do we ourselves and many of our students over the years feel the immediacy of these old stories and ponder their implications? *Medieval Romance: The Aesthetics of Possibility* is our attempt to wrestle with that issue by asking new questions about old questions.

Medieval Romance: The Aesthetics of Possibility is the first book we have co-authored, although for decades we have collaborated on all our intellectual projects and in recent years written articles together. Many of our discussions concerned the curious fact that medieval texts, so distant in historical time, seem so close to thought and feeling in the present. All texts are historically situated, and the rich historicizing scholarship about medieval literature has always been indispensible to our teaching as well as our writing. But we wanted to find a way to think about the very long timeline of medieval writing as well, how it makes the past new for its own era, but also encodes the future, inscribing questions that might seem vital in entirely new ways to generations to come. We knew we wanted to write a book about medieval romance, and we knew that romance as a genre, whether medieval or modern, is often regarded as delightful, but not terribly serious. We see it as serious indeed, in that part of its appeal over so many centuries is its power to incorporate complex ideas delightfully, to invite reflection on the very nature of perceived reality, to communicate the lived experience of social structures such as those of gender and class, and to deploy counterfactual fiction to imagine alternative potential futures.

A beautiful image of the fairy Mélusine, from a fifteenth-century manuscript, looking for all the world like a construction foreman as she directed workers building a great castle, became for us an icon of the way incompatible worlds often interpenetrate in romance fiction. To help us step aside from our own familiar discourse of literary history, and shape our questions as rigorously as possible, we turned to philosophy. Three philosophers in particular contributed to our emerging project: G.W. Leibniz, Immanuel Kant, and Hans-Georg Gadamer. Each has been fundamental to some aspect of our argument, but we make no pretense of intervening in the immense philosophical literature surrounding these figures. Our book is finally about the awesome power of art, and our argument is our own.

Nevertheless, we discussed our thesis (and occasionally the resonance of key German words) with philosophers at a number of universities, in particular Andrew Cutrofello, Anja Jauernig, Nicholas Rescher, Daniel Selcer, and Wilfried Sieg, all of whom helped us through the many difficulties of these formidable authors. We thank Jonathan Arac, director of the Humanities Center at the University of Pittsburgh, for sponsoring a colloquium on one of our early chapters that allowed us to interact with colleagues from across the humanities. As our project moved closer to its final form, we benefited greatly from the support of Suzanne Rancourt at the University of Toronto Press, and from the careful and pointed critiques we received from her readers. Jon Klancher, Ryan McDermott, Andreea Ritivoi, and Christopher Warren generously shared their remarkable and remarkably different stores of learning with us. We particularly want to thank James A. and Kate Knapp, who have patiently read and discussed our developing thoughts for some years now and to whom this book is dedicated.

The publication of this book was made possible in part by support from the Richard D. and Mary Jane Edwards Publication Fund at the University of Pittsburgh and by the Department of English of Carnegie

Mellon University. English versions of passages from *The Lais of Marie de France*, translated by Robert Hanning and Joan Ferrante, are reprinted by permission of Baker Publishing Group. Cover art is from Le Roman de Mélusine, ou "la noble histoire de Lusegnen," par Jehan d'Arras, Arsenal MS-3353, 22v, by permission of the Bibliothèque nationale de France.

MEDIEVAL ROMANCE

The Aesthetics of Possibility

Introduction

> The world can never take a holiday
> From metaphysical first principles.
> Even the raving, bolted in their cells,
> Have not the files to file these chains away.
>
> Gladys Schmitt, *Sonnets for an Analyst*, #10

The Serious Pleasure of Romance

A lonely lady, confined by her jealous husband, stands looking out the window in her tower when a hawk suddenly flies into the room, transforms itself into a handsome knight, and becomes her lover. A young man in fear for his life encounters a beautiful lady in the forest; she marries him, and without letting on that she is a fairy, makes him the wealthy lord of a vast realm. Medieval romance is an extravagant form. Widely heard and read throughout the Middle Ages, persisting for centuries, and in our own time re-emerging with particular force as speculative fiction, romance invites its readers to step out of the actual world and experience the intriguing pleasure of possibility. This is a book about the seriousness of that pleasure, why it has continued to intrigue for so many centuries, and why, in its invitation to understanding as well as imagination, it deserves to be called beautiful. It is our contention that, while romance elicits wonder through its marvellous adventures, it is at the same time deeply philosophical, as it asks us to imagine other worlds, to gather perception out of an infinity of tiny detail, to enter into fictions that evade conceptual closure by containing some mysterious surplus.

In discussing medieval romance, we will reflect on a number of philosophical ideas that we believe to be unusually powerful, ideas drawn from the writings of G.W. Leibniz, Immanuel Kant, and Hans-Georg Gadamer in particular. We make no pretence of intervening in current philosophical debates about these philosophers, nor do we intend to lay philosophical patterns over literary ones in order to demonstrate some kind of structure of ideas across history. By reflecting on philosophical and literary texts together, we hope that each will open the other in significantly new ways. But the pleasurable seriousness of literary romance is our topic, and the questions that brought us to this study are literary. Foremost among these questions is the one that troubles all of us who teach the literature of the past in a time of radical contemporaneity, when technological "ideation" threatens to replace learning: not so much "why read old books," but why, when students do read a 700-hundred-year-old romance, they love it and take it seriously. Much common wisdom speaks against this response. Romance writing is customarily regarded as a genre starkly opposed to the real and devalued as escapist. Modern instances are associated with books sold cheaply in airports, offering readers exciting, fantastic, predictable, and often lurid gratifications. Medieval instances were banished from serious thinking about the real on authority as early as Augustine's self-reproach for his youthful fascination with Dido's suffering and consequent neglect of mathematics. The best known, perhaps, of the rejections of romance in the Middle Ages appears in Dante's *Inferno*, canto 5. Francesca's admission that her indiscretion with Paulo began as they *read* together of Lancelot's passion triggers a disquieted swoon by Dante the pilgrim, but he recovers in canto 6, apparently reconciled to the justice of this charge against the moral effects of romance writing. Nevertheless, its prevalence and influence in the Middle Ages is undeniable. In Helen Cooper's words, romance remained for five hundred years "the major genre of secular fiction" in spite of censure from the church. Cooper acknowledges that scholarship still often characterizes medieval romances as both unrealistic and unrealistically pleasant (charges she demonstrates are off the mark).[1] Although both comedies and romances may contain an undercurrent of wish fulfilment, Fredric Jameson distinguishes the serious nature of the wishes: "Comedy is social; romance metaphysical."[2]

Further complicating the reception, and teaching, of romance is the notion that a great chasm of alterity separates us from the distant past, threatening to make these texts seem historically impenetrable.

In order to address this paradox of how literary works could be thought to be too popular and at the same time too distant from the readers of later generations, we will consider two further questions. Marie de France posed the first when she recognized the openness of texts both to writers and to readers. Texts are always open to translation (in the fullest sense) by subsequent writers, but also by readers, who might find new meanings hidden in intentionally difficult texts, or else might apprehend a tale in ways only possible to someone reading under new historical circumstances. In our own time romances still speak to readers who have never been locked in a stone tower or ridden a horse to battle, and the old stories are retold by novelists and filmmakers. So occasionally we will look to some of these modern versions to try to understand better how textual details invisible to readers in one era may rise into perception for a later audience. The persistence of a work over time is one of our concerns, and we believe the power of literary art is not well served by a notion of the past as continuously receding from us towards some distant vanishing point. A remote detail may sometimes be made vividly present to us, and while this has little to do with the indefensible idea that art is eternal, the experience of art from an earlier era cannot be understood without some way of imagining time folded back upon itself, allowing distant moments to exist together.

Finding pleasure or emotional impact in a tale first told centuries ago is only the beginning, however. With Kant, we hold that an object can only be called beautiful when it engages the intellect as well as eliciting pleasures of extended imagination. That old romances remain pleasurable for later generations is perhaps not a difficult argument to make, but we contend that romance is intellectually serious as well, because in its fanciful narratives are posed deeply philosophical questions. Most fundamental for the men and women of romance, whose stories are told as movement through time, as successive moments of choice or fate, is the issue of possibility and necessity. Leibniz gave us the most memorable image of possibility, and we will discuss his version at some length, but the philosophical issue remains important to modern philosophy as well in the sphere of modal logic, as it deploys the notion of possible worlds. While science fiction, a late emergence of the romance genre, may use possible worlds to reflect on a post-human future, medieval romance uses the same trope to suggest escape from the social and intellectual constraints of its own time. Both elicit thought about questions that are rarely posed in other kinds of writing.

The genre of romance may have pleased readers for centuries, but part of the pleasure lies in its capacity for metaphysical probing.

In order to examine these contentions we will reflect on some time-honoured medieval narratives in dialogue with the philosophical work of Kant, Leibniz, and Gadamer and their heirs. Leibniz on time, perspective, and possibility intersects with Kant's criterion for beauty, the simultaneous "quickening of imagination and understanding." And Gadamer, writing in the twentieth century, was above all a philosopher of knowledge over time. In reflecting on their arguments, however, we hope as well to further a conversation about philosophical work and its relation to the work that art has always performed.

We are treating romance as a genre and regarding generic sorting as helpful to hermeneutics in enabling the examination of like objects, but the genre is notoriously difficult to define in spite of its wide use over centuries. Of course, many genres are known to evolve over time, but even in the case of medieval romance, there is little consensus about the breadth of the category. Scholars disagree about whether fictionalized historical accounts, saints' lives, and didactic exempla and the like should be included, whether it was primarily an oral or a written form, and whether it always included women.[3] Our solution is to link our chosen fictions through a Wittgensteinian array of "family resemblances": "The various resemblances between members of a family: build, features, color of eyes, gait, temperament, etc., overlap and crisscross."[4] Among their most prominent overlapping features are these: (1) Romance story arcs consist of *aventures*, involving a particular blend of causality and unpredictability that confers suspense, gathering its surprises into coherence, but not into so fixed a causal chain as to be foreseeable.[5] (2) They are often conceived through an intricate structuring of space-time, allowing moments separated in linear time to be experienced simultaneously, what we are calling "folded time." (3) Of central concern is the representation of characters' perceptions as they pursue their *aventures*, signalling an increasingly strong attention to subjectivity in the Middle Ages.[6] (4) "Other worlds" are possible, intruding on, and often disrupting, the posited world of the fiction.[7]

The alignment of romance plots with philosophical issues asserts the weight of the genre as a whole, but our focus is on a few instances that have echoed across culture with particular vitality and which reflect internally on romance itself.[8] These case studies begin with Marie de France's *Lais*, written in French (but on English soil) late in the twelfth century. Marie's practice introduces our inquiry for its groundbreaking graceful sophistication, telling detail, and close attention to personal subjectivity. From the *Lais* we move to the Middle English *Sir Orfeo* early in the fourteenth century, then to Chaucer's *Troilus and Criseyde*, Jean d'Arras's French prose romance *Melusine*, several *Canterbury Tales*, and finally to the gem of the medieval romance tradition, *Sir Gawain and the Green Knight*. Each of them is an aesthetically impressive narrative, uniting sensible detail with a provocative form of intelligibility.

The fascination these particular fictions continue to exert and the wonder they continue to inspire is our overarching concern. Storytelling itself is basic to all social formations; without it we are reduced to "the most primitive mode of existence – a life without imaginary alternatives," as Lubomír Doležel puts it.[9] Some stories, romances in particular, invite elucidation from the fundamental questions about time, perception, and possibility raised by philosophers. Such questions are radical, literally rooted like perennial plants in a garden that may seem to disappear for decades, but show up later, perhaps taller or with white rather than purple blossoms. While the stories benefit from explication from philosophy, so too may philosophical issues be posed freshly by the fictions; the two kinds of writing are reciprocally enlightening.[10] Although neither Kant nor Leibniz is contemporary with us or our medieval texts, their reflections on certain perennial questions address both past (especially Augustine and Boethius) and future. Both the texts we explicate and the philosophers we consult in doing so are "filled with the future and laden with the past," as Leibniz says of the present.[11] Leibniz is celebrated in many branches of philosophy, but rarely consulted by aestheticians. We think he should be, and thus weave one thread of his legacy – his views on modality, including subsequent versions practised by those who, like Doležel and Marie-Laure Ryan, are interested in fiction – together with Kant's and Gadamer's.

Folded Time

As Augustine pondered how to explain time in book 11 of the *Confessions*, his explication made measured, linear time – past/present/future – evaporate from being, while at the same time acknowledging that everyone recognizes and refers to this kind of measured time. "O Lord, we perceive intervals of time," he writes, but then asks:

> How, then, can these two kinds of time, the past and the future, be, when the past no longer is and the future as yet does not be? But if the present

> were always present, and would not pass into the past, it would no longer be time, but eternity ... If any point in time is conceived that can no longer be divided into even the most minute parts of a moment, that alone it is which may be called the present. It flies with such speed from the future to the past that it cannot be extended by even a trifling amount. For if it is extended, it is divided into past and future. The present has no space.[12]

Yet we routinely remember the past and expect the future, as if they are folded into the present. The mystery of Augustine's present as both vanishingly small and yet all-encompassing speaks to our concern for the persistence of literary works. When we read medieval literature in the present, our perception is constrained by traces of the past, and from the moment a medieval author begins to write, she addresses a future audience. Asked to discuss the history of literary texts, a critic might find a quite straightforward answer: Boccaccio and Petrarch were sources for Chaucer's *Clerk's Tale*. Or perhaps the conclusion might be that the story of Orpheus is a classic, and therefore recurs throughout the ages. But what if *Troilus and Cressida* is significantly different than *Troilus and Criseyde*, altering its tone and import? A familiar modern example would be the numerous adaptations of Sherlock Holmes. Our approach to the echoes that reverberate across centuries is to imagine time as a fabric infinitely folded. Augustine's paradox carries in embryo something like this metaphor of a fold in time: since the memory of the past and anticipation of the future meet in the intuition of the present, time has folded in upon itself in individual thought.

For G.W. Leibniz, who first used the metaphor, the notion of linear time folded in upon itself means even more: that time itself can fold. Leibniz's work is infused throughout with the insight that the soul's knowledge of the world is "all there" but not all perceived; much of it is *folded away* from immediate view so as not to be clearly seen until sought and reflected upon. Each subject is a monad, a soul that contains every true thing that can be said about it; every soul capable of self-reflection is a spirit. In the *Monadology* §61 we find: "He who sees all can read in each thing what happens everywhere, and even what happened or will happen by observing in the present what is remote in time as well as space ... But a soul can read in itself only what is distinctly represented there; it cannot unfold all its folds at once, because they go to infinity." In the *Discourse on Metaphysics* he writes: "But these perceptions even provide a way of recovering the memory, as needed, through periodic unfoldings which may occur one day" (55).[13]

In *The Fold*,[14] Gilles Deleuze uses the idea of folded perceptions, potentially brought into distinctness, as the keystone of his analysis of Leibniz's thought, initiating his exploration of the notion of the "fold" with this quotation from Leibniz's *Placidus Pilalethi*: "The division of the continuous must not be taken as of sand dividing into grains, but as that of a sheet of paper or of a tunic in folds, in such a way that an infinite number of folds can be produced, some smaller than others, but without the body ever dissolving into points or minima."[15]

The fold is to be understood temporally as well as materially: "The matter-fold is a matter-time" (7). Michel Serres, often cited in Deleuze's account of Leibniz, multiplies the metaphoric vehicles to include the pleat – "An object, a circumstance, is thus polychronic, multitemporal, and reveals a time that is gathered together, with multiple pleats" – and the baker kneading bread – "folding, stretching, possibly cutting, but usually ending with the same square."[16] All of these figures deny the smooth historical progression we usually take for granted: time as a straight line carrying us ever further from the past.[17] Bruno Latour uses a different image to capture a related notion of time:

> Let us suppose, for example, that we are going to regroup the contemporary elements along a spiral rather than a line. We do have a future and a past, but the future takes the form of a circle expanding in all directions, and the past is not surpassed but revisited, repeated, surrounded, protected, recombined, reinterpreted and reshuffled. Elements that appear remote if we follow the spiral may turn out to be quite nearby if we compare loops.[18]

The spiral also appears as a "healthy, rather than vicious circle" in Ricoeur's explication of mimesis.[19] More recently, and from a different set of concerns, Carolyn Dinshaw provides a useful term for these "collisions between points in time," by referring to "a denser, more crowded now."[20]

The fold enables contiguity without identity: A and B can be close to each other while remaining distant at the same time, and yet A need not be an adaptation of the distant B. The two are in some sense genuinely close. So what if we push this metaphor a bit further and say, as Liebniz did, that each soul, into which time is so intricately folded, is filled with the future and laden with the past? (*Preface*, 55). Then the folds do not simply bring distant moments close, but reveal mysteriously deep connections among them. Physicists speak of the quantum entanglement of particles, or what Einstein (who was not convinced) called "spooky action at a distance." This is only an analogy, but it is suggestive of something equally spooky that happens when an old text suddenly seems shockingly familiar, when a modern reader sees herself in a Breton lai, or, put another way, when Marie's counterfactual becomes credible many centuries later. Entanglement simply means that something is shared, that a textual event distant in time can make something new happen in the future. Literature is also an immensely complex body of code that may be deciphered in unpredictable ways over the centuries, but it is more as well, because it is read by embodied individuals who in empathy may recognize in old texts a strangely familiar struggle between freedom and constraint. The idea that cultural contiguities obscured or disguised by temporal distance can be reclaimed imaginatively serves us well as we consider the use medieval writers made of the past, and the *present* beauty of medieval writing for us. This is where Gadamer's *Truth and Method* comes in.[21]

Gadamer credits language with allowing communication between life-worlds across time: "Being that can be understood is language" (*TM*, 474). Influential arguments against his position raise the spectre of a radical alterity between us and the past. Prominent among them is Jürgen Habermas's position that we can never be certain what implications the words carried in the life-world of their author and early audiences because of the "deforming" effects of ideology.[22] One response to this might be to undertake as full a restoration of the text's "world" as possible, forsaking any immediate impression we might have "from our point of view," and perhaps as a result turning linguistic art into an impressive relic, admirable but inert. The opposite tactic is to seek our own preoccupations in the text and marginalize what doesn't fit them, letting us tell our own story over and over. Gadamer embraces neither, rejecting both "presentism" and a historicism that allows the "past" to perform the work of interpretation (*TM*, 218–31). Gadamerian interpretation is a negotiation between horizons, each of which is itself an unfixed social and ideological ground. Ricoeur's *Time and Narrative* relies heavily on this "fusion of horizons," and it is widely used in literary criticism.[23] While some feminist philosophers (e.g., Marie Fleming)[24] see too little opportunity for historical rupture in Gadamer's use of tradition, others regard the fusion of horizons as quite compatible with feminist insistence on the embodiment of knowledge. In particular, Linda Martin Alcoff[25] argues that the openness to the other is "nascently feminist."[26] Silja Freudenberger[27] contends that Gadamer's "prejudice" is not unlike "feminist concepts of the situatedness of all knowledge" (266).[28]

Full detail of the author's situatedness within a limited horizon of possibility is not *completely* knowable, and it was never entirely conscious in the creation of the work: "Even knowledge of oneself can never be complete" (*TM*, 302–6). Neither meaning nor aesthetic effect, however, is limited by that horizon: "Not just occasionally but always, the meaning of a text goes beyond its author" (*TM*, 300). In this scenario, instead of being the victim of historical deformation, language is the conduit through which meaning flows from generation to generation. Both creation and reception belong to "effective history" (*Wirkungsgeschichte*) – an acknowledgment that our own life-world is inflected by what has happened and been conveyed through us. Although a later generation does not see everything as it was seen when a text was written, an interpretation based on a newer mental encyclopedia has a validity of its own. Because it acknowledges that all language requires a kind of translation over time (certainly medieval texts with their various dialects), Gadamerian hermeneutics provides a slower path to aesthetic pleasure than Kant's immediate-sounding excitement of imagination and understanding. Some works produce aesthetic thrills on first encounter; for others exacting study may be needed.

Art is a special case, although it too needs hermeneutic attention. While acknowledging the historical situatedness of language and its susceptibility to historical change, Gadamer argues for the immediacy, indeed the intimacy, of the experience of art, even that which is distant in time:

> The mode of being of a text has something unique and incomparable about it ... The written word and what partakes of it – literature – is the intelligibility of mind transferred to the most alien medium. Nothing is so purely the trace of the mind as writing, but nothing is so dependent on the understanding mind either. In deciphering and interpreting it, a miracle takes place: the transformation of something alien and dead into total contemporaneity and familiarity. That is why the capacity to read, to understand what is written, is like a secret art, even a magic that frees and binds us. (*TM*, 163)

"Miracle," "secret," and "magic" in this passage resonate with much that is written about aesthetic effects. Gadamer is specific about how the magic plays out, positing that texts from the past connect with us through a fusion of the horizon of the author with that of the reader, linear time acknowledged but folded, so that old texts are *present* to us, seeming both temporally relevant and emotionally imposing. Sometimes artworks from our own world activate this process of cultural memory by appropriating the aesthetic ideas, shapes, or rhythms of earlier fictions, as in A.S. Byatt's recreation of Melusine's story in *Possession*, or the remediation of Orfeo's in the film *Black Orpheus*. For the way such perceptions take shape, we turn to Leibniz.

Perception and Perspective: "The Immense Subtlety of Things"

However we might imagine moments of history in mutual communication, whether through overlapping horizons of expectation, or folded time, an audience, reader or viewer, is always present. A crucial question, then, is how the world is known, or for our more limited purposes, how a literary text is perceived by readers long removed from the original creation. Leibniz presents a world of objects that are extremely complex, as are the mental operations that intuit them. The mind receives a vast confusion of "tiny perceptions," though each one might potentially be clarified ("Preface to the New Essays" 55). "All this can allow us to judge that noticeable perceptions arise by degrees from ones too small to be noticed. To judge otherwise is to know little of the immense subtlety of things, which always and everywhere involves an actual infinity" (*Monadology* §57). And in "New Essays": "These tiny perceptions are therefore more effectual than one thinks. They make up this I-know-not-what, those flavors, those images of the sensory qualities, clear in the aggregate but confused in their parts; they make up those impressions the surrounding bodies make on us, which involve the infinite, and this connection that each being has with the rest of the universe" (55). In this striking passage one can find a meditation on Augustine's paradoxes, which involve the difference between God's perception of the whole in the "smallest of substances" and the difficulty of human perception in bringing to consciousness what it always already has folded within it.

The manner in which insensible details may ground the higher levels of perception that Leibniz calls apperception has consequences as crucial to individual subjects as they are to the movement of history. Recent philosophers use the term "novel emergent" to describe a distinct perception which cannot be reduced to the confused infinity of insensible perceptions on which it is founded – perceiving as green a multitude of tiny dots of blue and yellow, for example.[29] The principle, however, allows more openness than the predictability of this example would suggest. Robert McRae puts it like this: "As qualitatively simple these sensible perceptions are not aggregates of insensible perceptions. Rather, they are novel emergents from a mass of insensible perceptions, emergents for an apperceptive mind which is incapable of distinguishing components."[30] That is, any perception, whether of a face, or a tree, or a work of art, is novel. It is not simply the sum of its insensible details, but emerges out of those details in the act of perception.

In *Monadology*, Leibniz uses the further metaphor of a pond; the eye that sees its serene surface at a distance finds it empty, but up close finds it to reveal a teeming multiplicity of life forms and forces beneath the surface, "a world of creatures ... in the least part of matter" (§§66–7). Perspective is everything. Perception has too much to take in, like the sound of individual waves breaking which is heard as the roar of the sea.[31] Deleuze describes these echoes, traces, and folds as the basis of psychic life: he calls these tiny movements of mind "microperceptions or representatives of the world" that make up our macroperceptions, our conscious, clear, and distinct apperceptions."[32] However, they are gathered into an apperception that can never account for all of them. The notion of insensible perceptions leads Leibniz to a further contention: "It can even be said that as a result of these tiny perceptions, the present is filled with the future and laden with the past, that everything conspires together (*sympnoia panta*, as Hippocrates said), and that eyes as piercing as those of God could read the whole sequence of the universe in the smallest of substances" ("New Essays" 55). In *Monadology* Leibniz uses a biological image: "And since every present state of a simple substance is a natural consequence of its preceding state, the present is pregnant with the future" (§22).

The history of every literary work that continues to be read across generations is a history of persistence entangled with change. Textual details call forth innumerable microperceptions – sensations, memory traces, images – all prior to any possible articulation. But infinite tiny perceptions join, rising to higher levels of perception ("Ah, the roar of the sea"), and they may finally produce those apperceptions that seek to make meaning (in Chaucer's Franklin's Tale, "Dorigen's is a story about the moral dilemma of a woman who makes a rash promise"). This way of thinking about a reading recognizes the fundamental openness of art to endlessly new understanding, and so to the possibility of new readers suddenly finding themselves in an old tale. It also acknowledges that, however complex, perception is not solipsistic, it does not imagine a world out of nothing. History is there, folded into the details, and it constrains, even if the future is there as well.

This crowded psychic landscape resembles Bergson's discussion of duration in *Time and Free Will*: "The intensity of a psychic state" has a qualitative shading, "its characteristic colouring," rather than a measurable span.[33] The role of what Leibniz calls tiny perceptions is captured in Bergson's discussion of novel reading, with its "infinite permeation of a thousand different impressions which have already ceased to exist the instant they are named"; he may be seen as elucidating Leibniz on this point, as Deleuze remarks at some length.[34] Adorno's discussions of "micro- and macro-perceptions" in *Aesthetic Theory* make a similar point.[35] Doležel widens the circle of perceptions by ascribing the phenomenon of emergence within literary tradition to the structuring play of intertextuality, both within and among individual works. He contrasts intertextual analysis with unidirectional influence study, in which a younger text can have no influence on a text from the past. Intertextuality, by contrast, is "bidirectional," as semantic traces may be shared "in texts irrespective of their chronological order," consequently bringing distant texts together "in a relationship of mutual semantic illumination."[36] We may see Jean d'Arras's *Melusine* differently after reading Byatt's *Possession*. This understanding of intertextuality is akin to the Leibnizian image of linear time folded in such a way that past and future may touch. It is our contention that literary emergence, the unforeseeable novelty arising out of old words, is central to understanding how the aesthetic power of literary works may persist over generations. In every act of reading, and every retelling of an old story, perceptions of the past ground the emergence of the future.[37]

Leibniz's analysis of perception deeply informs our attention to the intricate patterning of the inner lives of romance characters, their subjectivity (in the current sense). A good deal of medieval studies ink has been spent on debating whether or not medieval mental lives resemble our own or even whether medieval characters should be imagined as having individual subjectivity at all.[38] Actually, medieval romances often represent subjective states as Robert Solomon has described them; it is through the tiny details that distinguish one story from another that we can recover their "engagements in the world," and see them as "*grappling with the world*" (italics in original), as we still do.[39] When we take the long view of Orfeo and Heurodis in *Sir Orfeo*, as if we were seeing Leibniz's pond from a distance, they look a lot like their ancestors in Virgil, Ovid, or Boethius, but a closer perspective on their seeming simplicity reveals the far more complex representation of feeling and understanding that we will examine in the chapters to follow.

Structuring Wonder: Possible Worlds

Medieval romance is not alone among literary genres in its availability to many kinds of readers over a long period of time. Moments when a structure of feeling seems to be shared across history are enabled by a richness of textual detail that may be shaped again and again through individual acts of perception. But the textual surplus that all literary works offer to perception is given to us in romance in a form that is uniquely powerful, and beautiful in the Kantian sense, because it is speculative in deep and serious ways. The main characters make promises that come to be seen as inviolable in almost all the works we will discuss. Any promise is inherently bound up with time in that it attempts to project a certain future out of a present commitment. However, in the course of their *aventures*, men and women in medieval romance often cross a mysterious boundary to enter a magic space, a future that tests the very *trouthe* of their initial vow.[40] Such alternative worlds make up some part of all the fictions we will discuss, and we are indebted to Leibniz's notion of "possible worlds" for anchoring our understanding of how the familiar world might be known better when set against its irreconcilable others. Near the end of his *Theodicy* (1710), Leibniz introduces a memorable account of possible worlds through a dream vision much like that of any hero of medieval romance about to encounter another world: "Theodorus journeyed to Athens: he was bidden to lie down to sleep in the temple of the Goddess. Dreaming, he found himself transported into an unknown country. There stood a palace of unimaginable splendour and prodigious size. The Goddess Pallas appeared at the gate, surrounded by rays of dazzling majesty."[41]

Theodorus is shown a great library in which all the possible lives of Sextus Tarquinius, son of the last Roman king, are already written out. If he touches any line in the book, a moment in one possible world will open before him, as the metaphor of a book is suddenly transformed into that of a great pyramid of infinite rooms, each one holding a different world. Theodorus can follow Sextus through a life in which he never rapes his friend's wife, never is driven out of Rome, and lives a long and happy life. The pyramid's base descends through an infinity of such alternate narratives, but at its top is only one world, that which actually exists because God chose to create it – the world in which Sextus actually lived the life and suffered the fate we know.

Leibniz argued against the actuality, but not the possibility, of multiple worlds. He believed that infinite possible worlds could exist as ideas in the mind of God, and be thought by philosophers or poets as ideas. In the twentieth century, analytic philosophy revived Leibniz's notion of possible worlds as a powerful language for examining modal logic (the logic of propositions involving modifiers such as *necessary* or *possible*). While we do not intend to take sides on this decades-long and highly complex philosophical debate, we find its language, and many of its typical concerns, useful for understanding how romance storytelling can call into question the conceptual certainties of the everyday. While much recent philosophical work concerns the validity of statements, the issues at stake may be traced back to Leibniz, for example, whether the identity of a person could be preserved across worlds. In the twentieth century David Lewis shared Leibniz's realism with regard to possible worlds, though without Leibniz's resort to the mind of God: "Are there other worlds that are other ways? I say there are. I advocate a thesis of plurality of worlds, or *modal realism*, which holds that our world is but one world among many."[42] He makes a distinction about how we speak about worlds, however. For Lewis, statements about the actual world are indexical – they are grounded by words that refer to the site from which a world is observed. To say, "Now I will describe the spring flowers to you," is to define the speaker's world as actual. Others have rejected the extreme realist position, but argued for a thesis that "takes possible worlds seriously as irreducible entities, a thesis that treats possible worlds as more than a convenient myth or notational shortcut, but less than universes that resemble our own."[43]

The conceptualist position taken by Nicholas Rescher holds that possible worlds are mental constructions. Unlike Lewis's contention that actual and possible worlds are equally real, Rescher's possible worlds are ontologically distinguished from actual worlds because "Unrealized possibilities are *generated* by minds, and so they can be said to 'exist' only in a secondary and dependent sense, as actual or potential objects of thought."[44] Marie-Laure Ryan sees the usefulness of both positions for literary analysis. Rescher's emphasis on construction allows us to understand the inventions of fiction as possible worlds. But in her view, Lewis's indexical position, from which we may see a universe of possible worlds surrounding the actual world in which we are located, allows the universe to be "recentered" by changing the site from which we observe. In literary fiction, when a character travels to another possible world, then that world becomes actual, not only for the fictional character, but also for the reader who empathizes with the character.[45] This is, of course, what every reader experiences when entering the fictional world of a literary work. In several of our narratives the other world intrudes on what we will call "fictional realism," the actual world (usually a somewhat idealized feudal aristocratic setting) *within the text* of a medieval romance. The genre of romance is interesting in this respect because it typically involves a journey or quest that takes its hero to a place of otherness which we could rightly call a possible world. In his discussion of modality, Lewis writes that "possible worlds" may be used to "characterize the content of thought." The terms he invokes are particularly pertinent to the understanding of romance narrative: "The content of someone's knowledge of the world is given by his class of *epistemically accessible* worlds. These are the worlds that might, for all he knows, be his world."[46]

Allegory is one way the art of the Middle Ages considers "how the world might be, for all we know." This epistemic approach to an otherworld that interrupts the actual world within the fiction refigures the *aventure* of the protagonist(s), from a good story about something that happens to humans in a relatively recognizable setting to some sort of lesson or insight to be penetrated *through* the pattern of its events. From the eighth sphere, Troilus looks down on the world in which he had loved and suffered so much and sees it transformed into something trivial. Cases of this kind may be considered a special form of epistemic possibility, supported as they were by centuries of religious doctrine. Another wrinkle is that some fictions openly provide signals that they are to be read allegorically; Maureen Quilligan calls these instances "allegories," but provides as well the term "allegoresis" to describe an interpreter's imposition of a pattern not openly signalled within the text.[47] Obviously, fictions that contain magic and fairies are sitting ducks for allegoresis, but the problem is complicated by time: suppose we imagine a cultural context in which magic and fairies *may be believed to act* in the quotidian world. As Ryan points out, the "actual world" is differently interpreted across time, so that, for example, the invention of the submarine gives *20,000 Leagues under the Sea* different modal operators.[48] The "magic potions" of Gottfried von Strassburg's Queen Isolde and Malory's Dame Brusen are much easier for modern readers than they were sixty years ago when the pharmaceutical industry was less advanced in producing mind-altering drugs. Readers' personal encyclopedias[49] change over history. Thinking of this kind was apparent to medieval authors; Chaucer's Wife of Bath and Franklin both comment on historically distinct readings of the actual, as we shall see in chapter 5.

Lewis's indexical manner of establishing the actuality of worlds (I am here, smelling the flowers), centres one world as actual among many other possible worlds; its emphasis on the conscious subject is related to the notion of *epistemic* possible worlds, which represent ways the world might be, for all we know. Such worlds may or may not exist, but they seem to be coexistent with the actual world we know, unlike *metaphysically* possible worlds, which are clearly understood within the fiction as counterfactual, ways the world might have been, but is not. Medieval narrative often represents metaphysical possible worlds as startlingly incompatible with the laws governing the everyday, disrupting in essential ways the order of what we will call fictional reality. The fairy kingdom in which Orfeo must seek his stolen wife would seem to be such a place, but you cannot always tell – perhaps Troilus is right and this world is ephemeral. The wonder of romance often lies in the tangled epistemological dilemmas underlying the marvels of *aventure*.

The difficulty of travelling between worlds in medieval romance often depends on the fundamental ways in which the difference between worlds is conceived. It is generally assumed that everything in a possible world must be capable of existing together with everything else in that world, or to put it another way, a coherent set of laws must govern that world. In Leibniz's terms, all things in a world must be "compossible." If all human beings must die, but all fairies are immortal, for example, then there can be no place for a mortal fairy in the world of fairy. So how can a single person be imagined to exist in two worlds, or, more to the point of romance narrative, travel from one world to another and then return?[50] The problem is posed most starkly in the early Irish tale of *The Voyage of Bran* when one of Bran's companions, after spending 300 years in the land of fairy, returns to Ireland, and, disregarding the command never to dismount, does so and instantly turns to dust. Leibniz might well have been describing this ancient story when he wrote, "I call possible anything which is perfectly conceivable and which, as a result, has an essence or an idea, without raising the question of whether the rest of the world permits it to become existent."[51] In the "actual" world (actual from the point of view of the fiction) a 300-hundred-year-old man cannot be anything other than a pile of dust. However, in the counterfactual world of romance, a questing knight does sometimes enter a realm of possibility alien to his own, and then return, raising the question of whether he could be the same man and yet return altered in such a way as to effect new possibility in his own world, thereby altering the actuality of that world. The persistent power of romance to pose this question, even when the paradigm has been reversed, was made clear by the 2014 film *Interstellar*, when the hero travels to a distant star in search of a new home for the people of a dying earth. Because of gravitational dilation as he nears a black hole time slows down for him, so that when he and his daughter meet once again he has hardly aged at all, while his daughter is now an old woman on her deathbed. Like Theodorus in Leibniz's imagined library, this space traveller had been able to look back from a structure of many rooms within a black hole and see multiple moments in his daughter's life by simply touching a book.

One way to approach the difficulty of the problem would be to regard each subject as having an essence, a thisness, which cannot change.[52] Or we might argue that only some properties of each individual are essential, while others are contingent or accidental, so that Orfeo's wife Heurodis, for example, might be different in the realm of fairy, contingent upon the circumstances of that other world, and yet still retain her essential identity. Once out of the actual world (or in Ryan's terms, having "recentered" the actual world), the heroine can then look back to that world from outside, and see it as no longer actual – fixed in conceptual closure – but possible, open to a changed interpretation of its "reality." Here we are very close to Leibniz's observation about perspective in the *Monadology* §57, that "the same city viewed from different directions appears entirely different, as it were, multiplied perspectively." We want to argue that the *energeia*[53] of these romances is precisely to make us, along with the hero and heroine, feel otherness as real, and from that imagined perspective, better discern essence from accident in the actual world.

While analytical philosophy generally defines possible worlds (other than the actual one) through stipulations such as "the Napoleon who did not die on Elba," Leibniz and his contemporaries did admit mythical narrative and literary romance, with all their seeming infinity of detail, into the discussion of possible worlds. In a philosophical dispute with Louis Bourguet concerning compossibility, Leibniz rejects Bourguet's assumption that even a purely literary fiction such as the romance of *Astrea* cannot be said to be possible unless we know all of its connections to the real world. Leibniz agrees that "it would indeed be necessary to know this if it is to be compossible with the universe, and as a consequence to know if this romance has taken place, is taking place, or will take place in some corner of the world."[54] For Leibniz, however, whether or not the events of this enormously popular pastoral novel could ever take place in our world is a separate question from that of their possibility in a counterfactual world which might be as suggestive as his own deployment of the fiction of Sextus's many lives was in describing God's choice of a single world.

The Aesthetics of Possibility

The long history of fascination these romances have generated is simply explained: they are beautiful. No argument can compel agreement with the proposition that an object is beautiful, according to Kant's *Critique of the Power of Judgment*, but beauty may be gestured towards, and we will invite others to experience it in this selection of medieval romances.[55] Finding aesthetic pleasure impels one to share the discovery by replicating or explicating it,[56] which is relevant to the history of reappropriation and commentary these texts have been accorded across the intervening centuries. Kant bases aesthetic regard on the simultaneous excitement of imagination and understanding – pure fantasy may be agreeable, but logical coherence is required to arouse understanding. To justify our claim that these tales are beautiful – unique, shapely, haunting – we will attempt to demonstrate that they not only produce wonder (which they often acknowledge overtly, especially *Sir Orfeo*, *Melusine*, and *Gawain and the Green Knight*), but invoke the philosophical puzzles that stimulate cognitive frisson.

Granting aesthetic attention to medieval texts has only recently garnered much enthusiasm. The enterprise was often thought counter-intuitive because "aesthetics" had not been invented when these narratives were written and first enjoyed. It has seemed to many scholars that eighteenth-century figures like Baumgarten, Shaftesbury, Kant, Hume, Burke, and Schiller introduced the idea as well as the term, but a closer look shows a Middle Ages with plenty to say about both beauty and art, some of it congruent with Kantian and neo-Kantian thinking. Bonaventure, for example, locates beauty in the onlooker's emotional and intellectual pleasure, just as Kant does: Bonaventure insists on the beauty of fearsome gargoyles well represented, and Kant calls it the excellence of art to render "beautifully things that in nature would be ugly or displeasing (*CPJ*, 190).[57] On the other hand, beauty is valued in the Middle Ages in terms of its utility for moral inspiration, which would seem to run counter to Kant's distinction between the judgment of beauty and that of goodness. We hope to show that this tension has often been overstated, that Kant is not as far from these medieval writers as he has sometimes seemed. He connects beauty with morality at a higher level of abstraction than direct didacticism and stresses pleasure in beauty as inhering in the "proportion" of the object's unique formal features just as much medieval thinking does.[58] Rather than aesthetic pleasure, though, much medieval scholarship has concentrated on establishing philological "firsts," findings about what medieval society was like, clues to the origin of modern artistic achievements, or a kind of tourism through "otherness." These researches have all yielded important discoveries, many of which we will be taking advantage of, but our focus is on aesthetic pleasure, and for that we are sticking with Kant's *Third Critique*.

The *Third Critique* begins with an "Analytic of the Beautiful," the centrepiece of which is that aesthetic pleasure results from the simultaneous animation (*Belebung*, in Meredith's translation, "quickening") of imagination and understanding.[59] Four claims, which Kant calls "moments," draw out the implications of this animation or quickening. Each of the moments seems to us to resonate with ideas from Leibniz, without claiming him as a direct source, and to Gadamer's position, which was substantially influenced by Kant's. First moment: although it is very deeply *of interest* (intriguing, moving, compelling), pleasurable satisfaction in artistic beauty is disinterested in that it is not concerned with questions of the existence of its object or of its immediate usefulness, either for practical or sensual gratification or, like the good, for moral instruction. Although Kant himself does not invoke the Gadamerian term *energeia*, his *Lebensgefühl*, "sense of life," points up the mental activity involved in responding to beauty without interest. A fullness of life brought into sudden clarity accords with Leibniz's apperception resulting from reflection. Imagination and understanding may be stimulated differently at different historical junctures (Gadamer) and at different instantiations of a reader's personal encyclopedia of world knowledge.

Kant's second moment insists that no concept is adequate to account for the aesthetic satisfaction of a beautiful object. Concepts are always buzzing around artworks ready to capture and explain them, but they are continually found wanting, especially in romance narratives, by swerves in plotting (just when you thought you knew where things were headed), strange turns in diction that nag at attention, and even poetic rhythms. Aesthetic pleasure results from the activity of intuiting the way parts are related to each other and to the whole, rather than proving a fit between the artwork and "its" concept. Our understanding of the inadequacy of a particular concept for the work resonates with the Leibnizian idea of folds within folds and tiny perceptions curiously packed together. Foldings in the fabric of time also reveal this inadequacy. Both a text's past and future can intrude into it, setting off surmises about its precursors and legacies – say, Orfeo's resemblance to and difference from the Orpheus of antiquity, or from his later image embodied in a film. Even the reading of a single line can be overpopulated in a way that eludes final conceptual grasp.

The third moment posits that possession of form by a beautiful object implies or indicates purposiveness without purposeful closure (*Zweckmässigkeit ohne Zweck*). This intuition of a purposiveness that eludes our assigning it a conceptual end introduces his emphasis on the formal aspect of beauty: "purposiveness as to form (*Zweckmässigkeit der Form nach*)." This phrasing, however, does not establish Kant as a "formalist" in the pejorative way that term is often used now. A frequent misunderstanding of this tenet is what has given Kantian aesthetics the reputation of "formalism," a reputation disputed by his careful interpreters like Gadamer and (yes) Adorno.[60] The elusive purposiveness that Kant lodges in the work is a consequence of its form or design, but that form is itself unfixed, immanent, and unyielding to conceptual distillation. On the other hand, the ways we describe form in literary history (period styles, genres, modes) are merely abstractions, and, following Gadamer's line of thought, at any one time, products of "effective history." Later art, life-worlds, and methods of analysis may rearrange our sense of what any particular form or genre might entail, and old artworks may be seen newly in the light of that rearrangement. Aesthetic attention to a possible world – a world in which some adventures entail magic, for example – will sustain satisfaction (or not) based on form in this sense.

The fourth is the most difficult of Kant's moments (for current thought); it is his claim that an aesthetic judgment, though subjective, is necessarily universal: the necessity is "exemplary." Subjective judgment in its current sense is personal, but to Kant's generation of metaphysicians it meant something like "inherent" (*OED*). It relies on assent to "a judgment that is regarded as an example of a universal rule that one cannot produce" (*CPJ*, 121). His basis for this claim is that a *sensus communis* posits that all rational humans can, in roughly the same ways, align cognitive faculties in making judgments.[61] This brand of necessity seems substantially different from the usage of modal logic, in which the only necessarily true propositions are those whose contraries are impossible. It seems closer to Gadamer's insistence on the role of tradition, which is (like a language) always at work in our reading of both art and nature at a level below consciousness (*TM*, 358, 474). Perhaps from our point of view, folds in linear time, as Leibniz describes them, account for the recurrence of aesthetic judgments more convincingly than positing a universal human capacity. Recurrence itself is unpredictable; it blends the rigour of causality with the *aventure* of accident. The stored and restored *energeia* of whole artworks or passages within them suffuses the mind with an arresting, life-like image, with the effect of binding people who might disagree conceptually into a trans-historical community of admirers of a beautiful object and giving art its sometimes unexpected power and longevity. Kant's use of the term "moments" (*Momente*) to refer to these four tenets is worthy of note: he is referring to aspects of cognition, movements of mind, but his choice of the term suggests a relation to moments in time as well.[62]

Since the logic of possible worlds is powerfully manifested in art, the mysterious other worlds of the romance tradition are precisely where choices unavailable in the actual world can be made. The resulting extravagance of medieval romance *aventures* invites the charge of naivety and masks the sophistication with which they raise perennial questions. Among literary fictions, medieval romances in particular explore philosophical questions about time, perception, and possibility, as well as making use of the philosophers' metaphors – folds in time, stored energeia, the immensely detailed subtlety of life under the surface of the fish-pond – but no two romances in quite the same way. Different as they are in scale, language, and literary form, each implies a surplus of intellectual and emotional investment that eludes conceptual containment and prevents purposiveness from settling into purpose.

The Chapters

The *Lais* of Marie de France initiate many of the qualities we now think of as characterizing the romance tradition, and they do so with a disarmingly simple elegance that slyly masks its own sophistication. Marie's *lais* fold the past of classical Latin learning and Breton storytelling into the aristocratic French culture of her own present, while anticipating a future that will see a *surplus* of meaning in them – and John Fowles's twentieth-century novella *Eliduc* does just that. Marie's tales rely on the Leibnizian notion of possible worlds, with its attendant questions of the trans-world identity of individuals across worlds and the status of "real" or "actual" worlds in a fictional universe. We will focus primarily on three of the lais, in two of which, *Yonec* and *Lanval*, the narrative is structured around the intersection of an alternate world with that of the everyday reality of the actual (aristocratic) world. *Eliduc* would seem to be set entirely within the normal world of courtly life, with only a touch of natural magic, but it too yields a *surplus de sen* when read in light of the philosophical questions we have posed.

The Middle English *Sir Orfeo*, like Marie's *Lais* so deceptively simple on the surface, raises questions about the essential and accidental attributes of identity when challenged by the strange laws of a Celtic Otherworld. Philosophical discourse about possible worlds is especially relevant with regard to the question of whether personal identities can persist across worlds. The *aventure* of Orfeo and Heurodis is essentially a journey of inwardness, in which their growth in apperception is figured in the poet's representation of tiny, insensible perceptions finally gathered to conscious awareness for characters and reader alike. Their *aventure* takes place within a highly complex folding of the ancient past with the author's present and propelled into the future, as in the French-Brazilian film *Black Orpheus* and a novel by Salman Rushdie about the globalization of song.

Chapter 3, on Chaucer's *Troilus and Criseyde*, argues that the poem sets the story of love and loss told in books 1 to 5 in dialectical play with the concluding allegory in which beauty, Criseyde's apparently otherworldly beauty in particular, is figured as illusory. As an epistemically possible world, Troilus's final location as he looks down from the eighth sphere *might be the actual world for all we know*. The aesthetic design of the poem counterposes the *energeia* of the time-bound world of Criseyde's and Troilus's creaturely experience made present to imagination against the timeless, unchanging perspective of Boethian allegory offered to understanding.

A beautiful female connected with illusion is also featured in Jean d'Arras's *Melusine: or, The Noble History of Lusignan* (Middle French, 1393), the subject of chapter 4. Unlike Criseyde, though, Melusine really has come to the human world from elsewhere – she descends from an alluring *fée* and the human king of Scotland, marries the French knight Raymondin, founds the kingdom of Lusignan, and bears ten sons who extend its influence. This substantial prose romance/history, commissioned by the Duke de Berry and read throughout Europe, serves as a reminder that fourteenth-century English culture was bi- or tri-lingual. Melusine's name becomes generic in folklore for those otherworldly beings who marry humans and remain in the human world with their husbands. The love story comprises only about half of the narrative; the long middle sections deal with the empire-building exploits of nearly all of Melusine's sons, and these episodes fall quite close to known histories (greatly compressed) of the Lusignan dynasty. *Melusine*, therefore, posits the coexistence and interaction of two worlds with differing causal domains and different temporal regimes. The text was completed after *Troilus and Criseyde* and before the *Canterbury Tales*, but its place in our story between Chaucer's two imposing poems is not just historical; we argue that it casts light on both of them.

Chaucer's *Canterbury Tales* is not usually considered in terms of romance, but chapter 5 treats tales in which the genre is beautifully exemplified (*Franklin's Tale*), subjected to philosophical interrogation as serious as it is comic (*Wife of Bath's Tale*), threatened by allegory (*Clerk's Tale*), and undermined by critique (*Canon Yeoman's Tale*). All four are related to Jean d'Arras's narrative through the key issue of promise keeping and the trope of transformation, in that Jean's heroine takes several shapes and invites several interpretations; Melusine herself is paralleled in the crone in the Wife's tale, Griselda in the Clerk's.

In *Sir Gawain and the Green Knight*, the final chapter, the aesthetic "magic" that, according to Gadamer, transforms *energeia* into form, serves to unite the realistic specificity of the poem with the romance genre that it both enacts and violates. The poem's unusually detailed representation of the objects and practices of the actual feudal aristocratic formation leads to a distinctive twist on the usual romance scheme of possible worlds in mutual opposition and challenge. In *Sir Gawain* the wonder evoked by the intrusion of the "other world" is strangely meshed with the wonder of the real feudal world so as to blur the line between them. This anonymous late-fourteenth-century poem traces the *aventures* of a hero whose rectitude is celebrated above his prowess and yet whose triumph he himself regards as moral failure. The intruding other world is precariously balanced between the mythical Celtic forces called up by the identification of Morgan as *fée* and the Christian pattern of salvation history. The apparently seamless weaving together of the ancient Celtic and feudal Christian elements in the poem exhibit Gadamer's "fusion of horizons" and project it into the future through the "mysterious intimacy" of art that allows a work to appear fully present to readers centuries later. In spite of the many disclosures with which the poem ends, the final meaning of Gawain's *aventure* remains suspended – a remarkable instance of a coherent aesthetic object that stirs imagination and understanding, escaping concept and creating wonder.

Chapter One

The Speculative Fiction of Marie de France

I want to know how it happened that those days of bloom when
rumours of wings and sightings – always seen by
someone else, somewhere else –
filled the air.

Eavan Boland, "A Sparrow Hawk in the Suburbs"

Writing with simple elegance in the latter half of the twelfth century, Marie de France shaped the genre of romance narrative in ways that resonate to the present. She gathered her matter, as she tells us, from older traditions of Breton and Welsh storytelling, but she was familiar with the classics as well, and with the works of the medieval rhetoricians. Her importance was recognized early, and scholarship has been at work ever since attempting to untangle the linguistic and folkloric threads of those multiple traditions in the fabric of Marie's *lais*. Historical study has revealed a great deal about the legacy of the past on which so much of her writing depends. But we want to look as well to the future, which is no less embedded in her words than is the remembrance of Celtic lore and classical learning. Marie's *Prologue* is a remarkably self-reflexive enfolding of past and future. She tells us that she chose neither to compose stories herself nor to translate Latin works into *romanz* – which had already been done too many times to bring her fame. Instead, she would translate the Breton *lais* that she knew well, and by doing so she would ensure her own future fame, while honouring the futurity that the original makers had hoped to invest in their texts as well:

Ne dutai pas, bien le saveie,
Ke pur remambrance les firent

Des aventures k'il oïrent
Cil ki primes les comencierent
E ki avant les enveierent.
Plusurs en ai oï conter,
Nes voil laissier ne oblier. (34–40)[1]

[I did not doubt, indeed I knew well,
that those who first began them
and sent them forth
composed them in order to preserve
adventures they had heard
and I don't want to neglect or forget them.]

If the Breton *lais* were to be truly forgotten, it would effectively be as if they had never existed. But remembering an old work is more complicated than forgetting it. In translating the *lais* into a new medium and a new language, Marie had to perceive the old stories differently. Out of the virtually infinite detail of her sources, she perceived what we have called a "novel emergent," a form that cannot be described by simply accounting for its elements. When she composed her own *Lais* she was not only writing the past differently, but participating in the founding of a new literary genre, one which would ensure that she will not be forgotten. Future readers and authors might perceive and appropriate her writing in endlessly new ways, continuing a chain which still remained unbroken when John Fowles wrote his version of *Eliduc* eight hundred years later.

Unfolding the Future out of the Past

Marie was explicit about her strategy for seeing that her name would be remembered and used her *Prologue* to describe the way the life of a work might be extended by its own textual difficulty as successive readers sought to make sense of it. She points to the purposeful obscurity of the ancient writers, who expected those who followed to gloss their texts, after much study, in the pursuit of truth. Marie, herself well educated in the rhetorical teachings of her time, was not taking a position against writing which is intended to be read for its moral precepts; she was (ostensibly) simply stating her desire to be noticed as an innovator who wanted to be remembered for bringing a new kind of literary form to the world of Anglo-Norman writing. The Breton storytelling she brought was also old, of course, and translated, but it carried with it a new, inexhaustible strangeness that would continue to be glossed by generations to come. Rather than invoking Celtic magic to explain Marie's new literary niche, however, we want to reflect further on the famous passage in the Prologue about the obscurity of books:

> Custume fu as anciëns,
> Ceo testimoine Preciëns,
> Es livres que jadis feseient
> Assez oscurement diseient
> Pur ceus ki a venir esteient
> E ki aprendre les deveient,
> K'i peüssent gloser la lettre
> E de lur sen le surplus mettre. (9–16)
>
> [The custom among the ancients –
> As Priscian testifies –
> was to speak quite obscurely
> in the books they wrote,
> so that those who were to come after
> and study them
> might gloss the letter
> and supply its significance from their own wisdom.]

When they translate the continuation of this passage, Robert Hanning and Joan Ferrante characterize the philosophers who use their own wisdom to gloss the letter of the old texts:

> they understood among themselves
> that the more time they spent,
> the more subtle their minds would become.

In a note, however, Hanning and Ferrante point out that their translation depends on ignoring the emendation of *trespassereit* in favour of the (H ms) reading of *trespasserunt*. Had they not made this decision, the lines might be translated "the more time went by, the more difficult the sense became, and the more care they must take to find what might be overlooked."[2] The sense adopted by Hanning and Ferrante suggests that the time spent is that of an individual philosopher, working within his lifetime to understand the works he studies, and that the outcome of this labour is something that happens within the philosopher: his mind becomes more subtle. The alternative translation acknowledges the text as well as its reader.[3] Time does not so much measure the labour of an individual, but seems instead to be historical time, a medium in which the work grows more obscure as it becomes more distant. The first reading may be understood to mean that authors veil their writings in obscurity so that scholars must work very hard, and become more subtle readers as they do so. In this sense, Marie is describing the exegetical tradition of glossing texts believed to contain a determinate sense which might one day be revealed. Leo Spitzer discussed Marie's prologue in these terms, but as he did so he raised a related question of whether those still to come referred only to authors or also to readers.[4] Whether commenting around the margins of a text, translating it, or even writing a new version of an old story, authors certainly bring new sense to texts. But if we take those newcomers to be readers as well, the text is further opened, as new personal encyclopedias encounter it.[5] Less like a series of boxes within boxes waiting to be unwrapped, the text now becomes something like Leibniz's pond, a reservoir of infinite tiny details that may be gathered to perception in endlessly different ways. Thus, when Marie considers and then rejects, for herself, the philosopher's task of exegesis, and chooses to translate the Breton *lais*, she chooses to write for the future, out of the past.

Marie's introduction of the problem of textual obscurity as she begins her *Lais* is itself difficult. For Monica Brzezinski Potkay, the difficulty of the *Lais* may be viewed as "an obscurity that ultimately invites readers to add their own glosses and so become co-creators of the tales' meaning."[6] However, if given only the choice between this empowering of the reader, and the contrary notion that a text is like a puzzle to be solved, we are faced with either a single meaning waiting for its time to blossom, or a multiplicity of meanings, each potentially unique to an individual reader. Crediting both possibilities, Potkay acknowledges the value of pleasure to medieval commentators on the parables who wanted to entice readers to "learn and practice virtue." But in her view, pleasure is "an end in itself" for Marie, and she concludes by describing the difficulty of the *Lais* as essentially a strategy of delayed gratification: "To penetrate an enigma brings delight, and Marie's poetics of obscurity wraps riddles in enigmas within mysteries in order to prolong almost indefinitely the reader's pleasure in encountering her Lais."[7] While there is much to be said for this position, we want to argue that the pleasure of encountering obscurity for its own sake is very much like the pleasure of a good dinner, in Kant's formulation. A good, certainly, it nevertheless lacks the quality of understanding that must accompany pleasure in order for true aesthetic experience to take place.

In our view, the *surplus* of sense that later readers may bring to a work is made possible by a *surplus* within the text itself, an excess of tiny detail always available to new perception. In Marie, this textual *surplus* exists most strongly in the strange otherness of moments "where women are free to engage a partner of their choice in a world of sexuality without violence."[8] The social vulnerabilities of women are present throughout the *Lais,* and we want to keep in mind the core realism of this writing even though it is filled with shape-shifting lovers and mysterious other worlds. We will argue that the *energeia* at the heart of Marie's tales of courtly life is an event, or perhaps a thing (the dead nightingale of *Laüstic,* for example), which makes love visible and memorable because it somehow contradicts the actual world of the present. Like a sudden intrusion from the realm of fairy (which sometimes it is), the moment is arresting, unknowable, and beautiful. It is both powerfully attractive and dangerous, threatening disorder to the known world, but holding out a space of marvellous fulfilment before betrayal and discovery (in most but not all the tales) re-establish social law. But just as the heroes of the *Lais* seek *aventure* as escape to the openness of another world from the social and imaginative closure of the court, some critics see the textual obscurity of Marie's written words as opening a similar kind of space for herself and for her readers. Milena Mikhaïlova regards the textuality of the *Lais* as Marie's own *aventure* as a writer, inscribing an openness that exceeds all conceptual closure.[9] Contrasting the psychological and analytic style of *la Châtelaine de Vergi,* to Marie's use of *style indirect libre* in *Lanval,* Jean Rychner argues that Marie's narrative choice allows her to witness the events and characters, speak overtly to her audience, and feel the emotions she relates, rather than explain them.[10] Thus, Marie opens the interpretive space of the text rather than closing it through conceptual intervention, and so allows endless new perceptions of the narrative. Michelle A. Freeman is also concerned with Marie's writerly decisions, but specifically with the obscurity of her self-positioning as author: does she translate Breton *lais,* or tell us about the origin of those *lais,* or perhaps write *lais* herself? The deeply veiled and layered version of *translatio studii* that she practises makes it possible for Marie to draw out "the hidden and obscure meaning of word and object – a meaning that is not readily apparent on the surface, or publicly, but that eventually can be grasped by the reader-translator willing and able to retrace the line of *translatio*."[11]

Marie Unforgotten: John Fowles's *The Ebony Tower*

Translatio may occur over centuries, as with Thomas Chestre's fourteenth-century translation of *Lanval* into English, folding time in such a way as to affiliate two claims to Breton origin within a new configuration of French and Anglo-Norman power.[12] We will consider *Lanval* presently, but we begin with an instance of translation over a far longer time span. The survival of Marie's art into the twentieth century in John Fowles's recasting of *Eliduc* in his 1974 novella *The Ebony Tower* is by no means a translation of the *lai*, but his prose translation is appended to his own fiction. In remembering an ancient tale by making it new, as Marie did, he offers remarkable insight into questions central to Marie's writing: how does art persist over time? Can human identity transcend the moment of its social formation? Are the worlds I can imagine possible?

Reversing what little we know of the geography of Marie's life, a central character in *The Ebony Tower* is an English artist, Henry Breasley, who has spent most of his working life in France, first in Paris and then in an old house deep in the Breton forest. Though he is a realist, his art is difficult, and when David Williams, a young painter and critic, comes to interview him in preparation for writing an introduction to a major catalogue of his work, he finds Breasley to be "hopelessly cryptic, maliciously misleading or downright rude."[13] When David stands before one of Breasley's famous works, he sees its source in Uccello's *Night Hunt*, but "the mysteriousness and the ambiguity" (17) of the painting complicate any easy sense of a tradition being passed on. To use Marie's term, there is a *surplus* in all of his works, a kind of difficult excess that frustrates closure and invites endlessly new perception. David feels that "the picture stood up well to renewed acquaintance," and while he is not sure it is a masterpiece, its very indeterminacy seems to assure that it will keep its place in the history of modern art.

In one sense, then, *The Ebony Tower* is an extended meditation on Marie's *Prologue*. In a "personal note" appended to his fiction, Fowles acknowledges his source in the *Lais*, and *Eliduc* in particular, and the debate between Breasley and the young painter whose commentary will shape perception of the old master for new generations is in some sense a restaging of Marie's discussion of her sources. Artists like

Pisanello and Uccello are fundamental to Breasley's work, but he has seen something in their paintings that others have not, and his intense perception of details in the classic painting appears only darkly in his own works. As much as David knows that the art of Pisanello is foundational to Breasley, he finds it nearly impossible to articulate its traces. How some unperceived detail in previous art (Leibniz's "immense subtlety of things") can speak to later generations of artists or viewers and so assure that the predecessor will not be forgotten even as it is translated into a new language is the intellectual question that David ponders. But the emotional urgency of the question might well have been shared by Marie in the twelfth century as she worked into the night on her *lais*.

In Fowles's homage to *Eliduc*, Marie's plot is mirrored and doubled. Henry Breasley lives in an old manor house in a forest in Brittany, with two young women, the most recent of countless earlier lovers. He describes them as "Those two gels now. Two gels in *Eliduc*" (51), putting himself in the role of the knight with two wives, and, like Eliduc, eventually making a choice between them. The plot is mirrored when David, a moderately happily married man when he comes from London to interview the master, finds the Breton forest to be as mysterious and unsettling as it is in any of the old Celtic tales recalled by Marie. He seems to glimpse another possible world, which he characterizes as "the breaking-out of the closed formal garden of other medieval art, the extraordinary yearning symbolized in these wandering horsemen and lost damsels and dragons and wizards" (51). He falls in love with Diana as quickly as any itinerant knight might have done, and she with him, though she has already been asked by Breasley to become his wife. David is faced with the choice of discarding his own wife and rescuing Diana from a life in which she would relinquish her own possible career as an artist to live in virtual isolation with a tyrannical old man, in a place named for the medieval monastery that once had been there. She is not yet a *malmariée*, but in an ironic reversal of the lives of all the medieval ladies imprisoned in their towers, she is free to choose that life. In the end she does so, sacrificing herself to marriage and a kind of monasticism at the same time. David, having been sorely tempted in a strange land, returns to his wife.

There may be hints of the old forest of Brocéliande in the setting of *The Ebony Tower*, but no shape-shifting lovers turn into hawks, and the details of dress and attitude are realistically post-sixties. Though all the characters participate in their collective *aventure*, David's consciousness is the most explicitly self-reflective. At one moment he feels determined by emotion and at another constructed by society, but the occasion that brings him to question his identity in the first place is a romantic encounter that could alter the course of his life. Unable to decide what to do, he says to Diana, "If one only had two existences." After they kiss, he "saw himself standing there, someone else, in another life" (90–1). More than expressions of frustrated desire, these are the simplest statements of possible-worlds philosophy.[14] When philosophers question the logic of "trans-world identity," they debate whether some qualities of an individual could be different in different worlds, and they generally begin with a statement very much like David's: "What if Nixon was not the man who resigned the presidency?" Once he has begun to think about the notion of possibility itself, David's list of "what-ifs" takes the form of a series of propositions: "His mind slid away to imaginary scenarios. Beth's plane would crash. He had never married. He had, but Diana had been Beth. She married Henry, who promptly died. She appeared in London, she could not live without him, he left Beth. In all these fantasies they ended in Coët, in a total harmony of work and love and moonlit orchard" (100). These are fantasies indeed, and fantasies within a fiction. But they could not better represent the philosophical seriousness of Marie's *Eliduc*.

Eliduc: Reading a Palimpsest

Fowles does not tell the same story Marie does, at least at the level of what the characters do and how their lives turn out. But if we take his rewriting to be an authorial exploration of the part of Marie's writing that eludes closure, its obscurity or *surplus de sen*, then we might understand the obvious departures from the source to signal a deeper fidelity to Marie's apprehension of how the identity of an individual unfolds over time. Marie and her distant heir ponder a very simple proposition: any life might have been different. *Lives*, however, are seldom simple, even in fiction, and so we might begin by thinking about the most familiar way of visualizing the course of a life: as a line that begins at birth, extends through time, and finally ends with death. One way of reading the course of Eliduc's life, as Deborah Nelson has told it, goes like this:

> In Eliduc, however, the allegorical level must be made intelligible before the literal level makes sense. More than a simple account of the adventures

> of a married knight who falls in love with a princess in a foreign land, Eliduc is most meaningfully interpreted as an allegory of the temptation and fall of man and his subsequent redemption in the manner of the medieval liturgical drama, but couched in lyrical and chivalric language.[15]

In this reading, Eliduc's life is seen as a straight line in which each event is necessary, and leads directly on to the next. Travelling to another land because he has lost favour with his lord, the happily married Eliduc falls in love with Guilliadun, the young daughter of a king with whom he has taken service; after some anxiety about betraying his wife as well as Guilliadun's father, he spirits her away to his own country, and when she appears to die upon learning that he is married, Guildeluëc, Eliduc's wife, revives her with a magic herb, and, placing the happiness of others before her own, volunteers to enter the monastic life. After endowing an abbey for her, Eliduc and Guilliadun marry, live together for a long time, doing many good works, until finally the second wife joins the first in her abbey, and Eliduc retires to a nearby monastery, all three united in Christian reconciliation. As a story of a man's journey from sin to repentance to apparent salvation, this trajectory has a kind of inevitability. Nevertheless, for other readers, there are simply too many shadows in the background of this otherwise clear picture, too much narrative noise. "If *Eliduc* is meant as a reaffirmation of the primacy of spiritual over temporal values, it is a remarkably ineffectual one. For the *lai* enacts a self-generating chain of contradictory compensations."[16] Focusing on the twelfth-century conflict between Church and aristocracy over the status of marriage, Sharon Kinoshita here sees not only a reassertion of the old aristocratic privilege to discard a wife when it serves the husband's dynastic or other purpose, in contradiction of canonical law, but also a hero who cynically plays off older feudal loyalties to his lord against an emerging economy of mercenary service, apparently conforming to whichever fits his needs at the moment, even killing a sailor who dares to point out that betraying his wife is a transgression in the eyes of God. Reading the *lai* teleologically, as always moving towards its redemptive Christian resolution, has conceptual clarity, but elides many difficulties of plot and detail in the body of the telling.

At the very beginning of her *lai*, Marie complicates interpretation by telling the reader that the name of the *Lai* once called *Eliduc* has now been changed to *Guildeluëc and Guilliadun* because the *aventure* happened to the ladies (*Kar des dames est avenue / L'aventure*).[17] In what seems to be a passing remark, Marie slyly authorizes the possibility that the *lai* might be recentred by this word that virtually defines romance – *aventure* as unexpected alteration of the everyday – mysterious, exciting, and deeply uncertain of outcome. If the reader pauses for just a moment at this note of Marie's, then the tale suddenly becomes two tales, one of a man, the other of the lives of two women, but both told at the same time, through the same events, and like a palimpsest, one written over the other, obscuring untroubled perception of either. In order to think about the *aventure* as happening to Guilliadun and Guildeluëc as well as to Eliduc, we will use what is called a "branching model" of possible-worlds philosophy, first suggested by S. Kripke, and recently discussed and critiqued at some length by Penelope Mackie.[18] In attempting to understand the identity of an individual through time or across worlds, Kripke had suggested that there is a necessary origin for each individual's identity, but that over time choice points may be encountered, so that the timeline of one's life might branch, so to speak, diverging from actuality into alternative possible futures. While for Kripke the branching was always forward, out of the actuality of the past and into the future, Mackie expands the model to include branching backward to alternative pasts, which allow us to ask questions such as "What would the world be like if Eliduc had never sought to serve the king of another land?"

Describing Eliduc's life in the terms of Robertsonian allegory suggested a straightforward timeline from proper conduct, to temptation and sin, to repentance and salvation. But if we turn to the women who figure so importantly along the line of Eliduc's life, the wife's status as symbol of marital fidelity and later as exemplum of self-sacrifice, and the young woman's role as object of temptation become less clear. In the latter case it is not Guilliadun's ultimate choice of the religious life that troubles so much as her earlier assumption of the role of loving and loyal wife, doubling Guildeluëc's initial identity in the *lai*. When we first encounter Guilliadun, her father's castle is under siege by a neighbouring lord whose suit has been refused. She would seem to be facing a life without love, or worse, that of a *malmariée*, violently taken if her father's castle should fall. When Eliduc arrives to save the day, he is a bold and courteous knight, a worthy romance hero. She accordingly falls madly in love with him, and when he tells her he must return to his own land, she asks him to take her with him. After a short postponement to allow his contract with her father to expire, Eliduc does take her away, literally in the dark of night. Upon awakening from her swoon/death after hearing that Eliduc was married, Guilliadun understands that she had been deceived, and that Eliduc has sinned by not telling her he had a wife ("Pechié ad fet k'il m'enginna:/ Femme ot espuse, nel m'en dist" 1076–7). But this reproof becomes moot when the wife immediately states that she will give Guilliadun back to her lover and take the veil herself. Earlier, Guilliadun might have refused to run away with Eliduc, and now she could still go with Guildeluëc to the abbey rather than join Eliduc as he enjoys the fruits of a broken marriage vow. Instead, she marries her lover and lives with him in perfect love (parfite amur) for many days, does good works, and only then retires to the holy life.

In this telling of one thread of the *lai*'s narrative, Guilliadun's life is imagined as a straight line, an actuality that never deviates into its alternative possibilities, and as such it makes perfect sense. But no reader can read her story so simply, because the *lai* of *Guildeluëc and Guilliadun* is about two women, not one, and the logic of their mutual *aventure* is based on the premise that both cannot continue to live in the same world. At nearly every moment in the story of either, the absent other is present, complicating understanding. If we try to capture Guildeluëc's story alone, and as briefly as we did Guilliadun's, we might say that she is the wife whose husband set out on an *aventure* and returned with a young woman, though without disclosing a plan for dealing with two potential wives; however, seeing the rightness of her husband's new love, his wife solves his problem by humbly and happily choosing to abandon her marriage and retire to a convent. Even so, Marie's details are troubling. When Eliduc first leaves Brittany for Logres, his wife is said to show great sorrow (*grant dolur*), and when he briefly returns, his wife is as joyful as his friends and relatives. But his behaviour is secretive and withholding, causing his wife to blame herself:

Sa femme en ot le queor dolent,
Ne sot mie que ceo deveit;
A sei meïsmes se pleigneit;
Ele li demandot suvent
S'il ot oï de nule gent
Qu'ele eüst mesfet u mespris
Tant cum il fu hors del païs

[His wife had a heavy heart,
she didn't know why this was;

and worried about it to herself.
She asked him often
if he'd heard from anyone
that she had done something wrong
while he was out of the country.] (718–24)

Eliduc responds by lying to his wife, telling her that he must return to Logres because the king he has sworn to aid is in dire need and he must not break his vow. The king is in fact never aware of his return, because Eliduc arrives in secret, steals Guilliadun away, and immediately sets sail back to Brittany. Once again, Guildeluëc is happy at the news of his return, and prepares herself for him (*cuntre lui s'est apareilliee*). Tiny details such as these – brief moments of spontaneous joy at news of his return, inner vulnerability and self-doubt when he treats her coldly, anxious preparations for his second return home that must include anxiety about how to greet him publicly but surely more personal concerns about how to dress and how to talk to him as well – represent Marie's deep understanding of "the immense subtlety of things."[19] When Guilliadun is brought back to life and tells Guildeluëc that her husband had sinned (*pechié*) by deceiving her about his marriage, Guildeluëc attributes her own sadness (*mun quor dolent*) entirely to concern for her husband's grief, and simply announces that she will take Guilliadun back to Eliduc, and take the veil.

The coolness of this decision, which seems all surface and no depth, is very difficult to reconcile with the inner life Marie has so carefully constructed for Guildeluëc. The earlier moment when she discovers Guilliadun in the chapel, apparently dead, is telling:

"Par fei, jeo ne m'en merveil mie,
Quant si bele femme est perie.
Tant par pitié, tant par amur,
Jamés n'avrait joie nur jur."
Ele cumencet a plurer
E la meschine regreter. (1025–30)

["By my faith, I'm not surprised,
If such a lovely woman has perished.
As much for pity as for love
I shall never have joy again."
She began to weep
and to mourn for the girl.]

She has only just discovered the existence of Guilliadun, and while her sympathy rings true, she is certainly weeping for herself as well. Guildeluëc's carefully established identity as loving wife, and the emotional details that make that identity visible, destabilizes the conceptual clarity of attempts to read the *lai* as a Christian allegory of Eliduc's redemption, rather than a story about the unforgiving logic of earthly love. Like Griselda's, Guildeluëc's story may be read as saintly self-sacrifice, but the notion that a marriage vow the Church regards as inviolable could be discarded, and its consequences easily forgotten, complicates redemption by foregrounding the contested reality of marriage in the twelfth century.

Marie's remark about the *lai*'s two titles thus poses a kind of rabbit/duck puzzle for the reader, who can hear one story or the other, but not both at the same time.[20] As the trajectory of each life unfolds in relation to the others, a complex network of possibility opens up, inviting readers to reflect on characters speculating about choices they might have made, leading to futures they might or might not experience. When Guildeluëc fears that she might have done something to offend Eliduc, her emotion is accompanied by an implicit logic of possibility: if I had never offended him at some point in the past, he would not leave me in some possible future. Guildeluëc could have done something to offend her husband, for all she knows, but the reader, who knows Eliduc has already fallen in love with Guilliadun, knows that the future shadowed in Eliduc's coldness is not of her making. Although Guildeluëc says nothing about the possibility that her husband might leave her, that is one possible consequence of the offence she fears she may have given to her husband in a past moment that is itself only a possibility. For the reader who knows that the narratives of Guilliadun and Eliduc have already intersected, however, Guildeluëc's counterfactual is already inevitable.

After Eliduc returns to Brittany with Guilliadun, who has apparently died at the shock of learning that her lover has a wife, but before she is miraculously revived, their love (and its narrative inevitability) remains unconsummated. If at that moment the weasel and the magical herb it carries had not appeared, a very different future could be imagined for Eliduc and his wife. Grieving for Guilliadun's death as they both are, and confronted by the visible sign her body had become that the future in which Guilliadun is Eliduc's wife, and Guildeluëc takes the veil, is no longer possible, Eliduc might confess the wrong he was about to do to his wife, and the two might live out their lives together, untainted by a sin avoided. Or, the magic herb might indeed return Guilliadun to life, but all three, seeing how wrong it would be to discard a loyal wife, might jointly decide to seek redemption in the monastic life immediately. Either of these possible futures would be far easier to reconcile with the wife's sudden decision to take the veil, or Eliduc and Guilliadun's willingness to enjoy the fruits of Guildeluëc's sacrifice before finally embracing the religious life themselves. The other worlds of medieval romance are often physically separated from the relative realism of courtly life, *Yonec*'s magical city of silver entered through a passage in the earth, for example. In *Eliduc* Marie is no less interested in the power of counterfactual thought to critique the social lives of women in her society, but here the world of fairy is only present for a moment, in the intercession of an enchanted weasel at a crucial juncture in the lives of the three characters. For the most part, Marie employs the simple logic of alternatives: how are we to judge the choices taken, or never realized, that define the lives of two women and a man? Guilliadun briefly posits a rewritten story when she says she should never have trusted a man, and Guildeluëc also second-guesses the past when she doubts herself, but mostly Marie's invitation to the reader is subtler, the camera shot that invites the audience to tell the detective to look behind him when he enters a room. However familiar the story of sin and redemption might be to Marie's audience, the details of her telling, whether in the heavy heart of a virtuous wife, her husband's intricate lies and deceptions, or the web of possibility in which all the characters live constitute a *surplus de sen*, an elusive knowledge that undercuts allegorical closure, interrogates love as a structure of social possibility in Marie's time, and persists into an Anglo-Breton world of the future, utterly transformed, but strangely familiar.

Erotic Agency in *Lanval*

The possible lives of the characters in *Eliduc* may all be imagined as existing within a world of plausible actuality – logical alternatives but not metaphysically different spaces. In contrast, the central *aventure* of *Lanval*, the miraculous encounter of a fairy and a human knight, deploys a more familiar set of romance conventions, but it too raises profound questions about the stability of human identity and the nature of its grounding in social community. Like so many romances, this simple tale is about an *aventure* that takes place between two worlds. For Lanval, it is an *aventure* in the sense of something that happens to him. When it happens he is lying in a meadow in a blue funk, without the slightest hint that he is trying to daydream himself out of it, so that when two beautiful maidens appear out of nowhere he is just surprised, though pleasantly. The fairy he is about to meet, by contrast, has sought out her *aventure*, following desire like any knight riding out into a mysterious forest. At the end of the tale she carries him off to Avalon, said to be a beautiful Breton isle, truly the otherness of a fairy world from which she has presumably come. Put this way, we are given two worlds, one the fictional realism of Arthur and his court, the other a possible world of fairy, where none of the laws of the familiar mortal world reach. And yet the fairies of medieval romance are apparently able to cross over to the human world at will. In chapter 4, we will discuss the very notion of travel between worlds, as it is tested more urgently by the romance of *Melusine*. But unlike Melusine, the fairy heroine who fervently wishes to become a Christian wife and mother at the cost of relinquishing her immortality, Lanval's lady shows no desire to live permanently in the human world. When Lanval is carried off to Avalon at the end of the tale, he is never heard from again and presumably has left his world forever. Mounting the fairy's horse is a bit like entering the underground passages that lead to other worlds in *Yonec* or *Sir Orfeo*, and even if the travellers may return in the latter two tales, all these worlds remain utterly separate.

When Lanval and his lover meet in a kind of overlap between worlds, their encounters raise fundamental questions about the persistence of identity across worlds. Some philosophers have argued that an individual only exists in her "actual" world, though she may have "counterparts" in other worlds. Others argue that an individual has an *essence* that can be preserved across worlds, even if accidental features may differ from one world to another.[21] However we may think about this problem, it is still the case that two things, or individuals, may not exist together in the same world if the existence of one contradicts the existence of the other. This is the notion of "compossibility," which reminds us that a thing clearly conceived as possible may nevertheless not be able to exist in a world of differently possible things.[22] Lanval and his lover are not in fact permitted by Marie to live on in a perpetual liminality of secret trysts. That arrangement is unstable and it collapses when Lanval fails to honour his vow of secrecy – a narrative device entirely conventional within romance accounts of human/fairy encounters. A pledge is made, and when it is inevitably broken, the abyss that divides the human sphere from the otherness of fairy reopens to divide the lovers once more. In the case of Lanval, the loss is only temporary, as he is saved from disgrace by his lady's reappearance at the last minute. Their permanent reunion, however, takes place only when his fairy lover carries him off to Avalon, re-establishing the distinction between their two worlds as inescapably metaphysical.

At this point we might ask what is to be gained, for Marie and for the emerging genre of romance, by reflecting on possible worlds at all. We would argue that the fictional representation of alternative worlds allows the experience of social order, at most times an infinite sea of almost insensible perceptions, to be raised to the level of apperception. In using the philosophical notion of possible worlds to discuss Marie's literary strategies, we hope to further specify Bruckner's contention that "romance fictions thus allow a kind of free space for experiments – in forms and ideas – that may function as a way to redirect and change the society it mirrors. Neither simply mimetic, nor dynamically cut off from real life, romance is an integral part of the dialectic of history."[23] Since dynastic marriage practices had been challenged in clerical debate during the twelfth century, romance, in spite of its seeming wildness actually disguises real-world contentions.[24] For all its simplicity, *Lanval* is particularly striking in making visible the buried assumptions of a highly successful society that functions almost without thought.

One of King Arthur's attributes, in the conventional praise that opens the poem, is that he distributes wives and land to all his followers. All but one, however, because he "forgot" Lanval. This strangely trivial anomaly, entirely unexplained in a system in which lordly generosity is presumed to ensure social solidarity, is immediately made to seem less anomalous when we are told that none of Arthur's men favoured Lanval either, that in fact they would not mind in the least if something bad happened to him. Just beneath the surface of Arthur's incomparable world, there is an actuality of envy and competition, as might be expected when even aristocratic knights lack any agency in the two key elements of their social identity: wives and land. In a story about finding mutual love, Lanval is thus an anomaly in another sense when he leaps onto the lady's horse at the end of the *lai*, choosing his lover as no one else at Arthur's court is allowed to do.

Early in the tale, when Lanval's horse trembles at the edge of the stream, it signals the presence of another world, and when the knight is led to a splendid tent, he begins an *aventure* initiated entirely by the beautiful lady who offers to be his lover. Though evidently a fairy, her physicality is emphasized by Marie's details: she has thrown a white ermine cloak over herself for warmth, because she is dressed only in a shift, which, as we learn at the end of the poem, is laced along the sides, leaving her side and bosom bare.[25] Falling in love on the instant, Lanval makes two avowals, the first quite to be expected: he never wants to leave her. But the second is more interesting, as he says, "For you, I shall abandon everyone." In his own world Lanval already feels himself abandoned, but now he is able to speak what he had felt but never acknowledged as he lay in the meadow, unable to know what to do. To abandon everyone is to take action, but also to acknowledge that loving this lady will make it impossible for him to any longer accept the law of Arthur's court.

When Lanval returns to the city it seems that he has forgotten his second resolution, as his new wealth allows him to embrace the ethos of lordship with great enthusiasm, abandoning no one as he hosts knights without a place to stay, dresses jongleurs, and gives generous gifts to all. But having committed himself to his fairy lover, he is no longer compossible with the men and women of Arthur's world, even though he does not yet know it. Then he encounters the queen. Just as Arthur's right to distribute wives is unquestioned, so the queen presumes to be able to take any man she wants, and expects no one to speak about it. Lanval's blunt (though truthful) rejection of her advances brings the angry counter-charge that he must prefer boys. By introducing a sexual practice which is presumed to exist, but which cannot be named, the queen gives Lanval the impossible choice of either speaking what may not be spoken, or proving his insult to her own sexual desirability. What this encounter makes visible is Lanval's utter lack of erotic agency: as a knight of the Round Table he may neither choose to love boys, nor choose not to love the queen, if she asks. That Lanval's choice is counter to all the force of social law is made clear by the trial he must soon undergo. And as he awaits the outcome, another telling detail suggests that he already knows he can no longer live in his world: his friends come to visit him because they fear that he will not eat or drink, that he might even kill himself. In his anger the king vows that Lanval will be burned or hanged if he cannot defend himself against the queen's charges, but even his sureties know that if guilty he will be exiled from the land. And so the outcome is inevitable. Vindicated by the arrival of his lover, he nevertheless chooses to mount her horse and be carried away to Avalon.

Though Lanval's other world originates in a male wish fulfilment, like Eliduc's, Marie uses that world to reflect on her own. This conclusion seems to Ben Ramm to represent Marie's attempt to impose closure on her narrative through a framing statement that subordinates the *surplus de sen* available to future readers and writers to her own authorial privilege.[26] Marie is certainly concerned with her status as a writer, as the prologue makes clear, but the rhetoric of her conclusion of this *lai* suggests a rather different strategy. After invoking a famous but mysterious island which is said to be ravishing, Marie tells us that the hero has vanished, and leaves us with the further mystery that we have received no news of a man who must surely be having astonishing experiences on that strange island. Marie's final line might better be read, then, as a sly provocation of readers whose desire to hear what happens next she has shamelessly inflamed. But her conclusion also reveals a deep understanding of the aesthetic experience. As we have argued, after Kant, the instructive value of conceptual closure may be a good, but art depends on precisely the fusion of knowledge and mystery to which Marie gives such elegant form in the simple lines of her conclusion. Lanval may be a dream of desire fulfilled, but when the knight and his lady ride away, Marie leaves the reader behind in a world where mutual love is seldom a choice for women – or for men.

The Future of the Past in *Yonec*

Lanval's beautiful lady comes to him freely, impelled, as far as we are told, by her own desire, easily wins his love, and ultimately takes him out of his world and into hers. In *Yonec*, the roles are reversed. This time a beautiful lady has been married to a jealous old man who keeps her locked in a tower, away from all human contact except that of his aged sister, whose task it is to watch her. This lady's desire is irrelevant, and her freedom to act is unthinkable. In her loneliness and misery she thinks about the storytelling of times past, when courageous knights rescued young women like her, and loved them. No sooner has she wished to be the heroine of such a tale, than a great hawk flies into her window and is transformed into a handsome knight who becomes her lover. Later the knight is betrayed and killed by her jealous husband, but not before the lovers conceive a son who many years later will avenge the death of his father.

A simple story of love, betrayal, and eventual revenge, but at the same time the details of Marie's telling are so full of significance that they tantalize the reader with occasional obscurity. The prelude to her *aventure* is conventional in its presentation of a *malmarriée*, cruelly confined by her jealous husband. But when she concludes a lament for her plight with a curse, she does not curse her husband, but rather her parents, and everyone who assented to this forced marriage:

Maleeit seint mi parent
E li autre communalment
Ki a cest gelus me donerent. (81–3)

[A curse on my family,
and on all the others
who gave me to this jealous man.]

Although she earlier laments her fate and questions her husband's sanity, her curse is reserved for something far more systemic: the social consensus supporting her father's right to choose his daughter's husband. Extending the implicit social critique of *Lanval*, Marie's language in framing the lady's curse as she does is significant because, as noted above, the aristocratic and secular marriage practices assumed by her curse were under pressure during the twelfth century from emerging attempts to formulate a Christian notion of marriage. Clerical authors, drawing on sources in Roman marriage law, increasingly came to stress *consent* and *marital affection* as requisite foundations for legitimate marriage.[27] Thus, even as the lady is about to wish for an escape into the fictional past of storytelling, Marie allows her to question the basis of her husband's behaviour by subtly reminding us of the late twelfth century's very real debate over marriage reform. This debate over how marriage ought to be defined and sanctioned by church or state stands behind the *lai* as a level of realism that serves to deepen the implications of the lady's encounter with her hawk/lover. But Marie inscribes the reality of unjust marriage on the lady's body as well, in details that are visceral, that speak of lived experience, and that cannot be captured by a legal concept such as "consent." After seven years of lonely confinement, weeping and sighing, this lady (about whom, as a conventional heroine of romance, we would know little more than that she is "beautiful") loses her beauty. Social structure, so very abstract a notion, restructures her skin, her eyes, her hair, and when she gains a secret lover and once more blooms, the change is so striking that her husband immediately guesses that something is up.

In some respects then, *Yonec* is an exercise in social realism. And even when the lady's imagination turns to the old stories of handsome knights rescuing young women in distress, her escape is not so much into pure fantasy as it is into a reality that she believes to have once existed. A number of critics have shown that in her *transitio* of Breton sources, Marie makes visible the complex fabric of linguistic, cultural, geographical, and power relations among French, Anglo-Norman, English, Breton, Welsh, and Irish spheres.[28] The lady's immediate concern, of course, is less with the shifting politics of the Anglo-Norman borderlands than it is with the conditions of her life were she to have lived at an earlier time in the Celtic realms of her literary memories. Those realms were still patriarchal, certainly, but in history as in their fictions they did allow far greater space for female *aventure* and, upon occasion, even dominance.[29]

Although we have traced a note of unmistakable social awareness in *Yonec,* we locate the power of Marie's writing elsewhere than in realistic narrative or persuasive rhetoric. Consider the vexed question of where the hawk/knight's kingdom really is, an issue on which there is little critical agreement. Sharon Kinoshita provides a detailed political as well as fictional account of Caerleon, the city to which the lady and her husband and son ride to celebrate a feast day, only to be surprised by finding there the tomb of her lover as well as his still grieving subjects. For Kinoshita this discovery ends the husband's line and initiates "the resurgence of Muldumarec's kingdom," as the son is proclaimed king of his father's realm. She sees the murder of the husband as "the 'surplus' – the constitutive excess – that enables the reimposition of traditional rule."[30] Mathieu Boyd, by contrast, discounts any significant difference between the two lands, writing that "the abbey where Muldumarec is buried happens to be in his own kingdom, and Yonec inherits this more or less Otherworldly realm as well as the lands that belonged to his mother's husband."[31]

That Muldumarec's realm first appears when the lady enters a passage into the earth and emerges to see a city apparently made all of silver seems to other critics to be a very otherworldly place indeed, even radically incompossible with the human world of the lady and her husband. For Sylvia Huot, "in this story, contact between the human and the magical realms is fatal for both sides. And although the half-blood son survives, he is integrated into the magical kingdom only, decisively rejecting his human heritage."[32] Seeta Chaganti, however, simply sees the location of the tomb as obscure in Marie's narrative, concluding that "even in his tomb, he remains mysterious, the location of his kingdom defying identification."[33] In our view, Marie's intended and celebrated obscurity is what is at issue here, rendering moot all attempts to determine the "correct" locations of the two kingdoms in the fiction. The *lai*'s obscurity reaches far beyond one spatial enigma, however, to the very heart of Marie's aesthetic in the *Lais*. Denyse Delcourt points out that the bird/lover first reveals himself to the Lady through his shadow, and that his appearance is destined to remain an "obscure" mystery to her. She sees the creative force of the lady's desire that calls forth Muldumarec as congruent with Marie's own art: "Marie writing her lais in the middle of the night and the lady in *Yonec* have this in common: the courage necessary to make room in their lives for a mysterious and intoxicating 'shadow' of which the origin is always and only 'obscure.'" [Marie écrivant ses lais au milieu de la nuit et la dame dans *Yonec* ont donc ceci en commun: le courage nécessaire pour faire place dans leur vie à une "ombre" mystérieuse et enivrante dont l'origine n'est toujours qu'"obscure."][34]

Marie translates the strangeness of Breton storytelling into detail that may justly be called "intoxicating," because it excites at the very moment that it challenges explanation. She is not simply introducing new matter into courtly context, but practising a new kind of aesthetic in which moral concept continues to exist, but supplemented by a representation which exceeds the articulations of reason. Kant puts it this way:

> In a word, the aesthetic idea is a representation of the imagination, associated with a given concept, which is combined with such a manifold of partial representations in the free use of the imagination that no expression designating a determinate concept can be found for it, which therefore allows the addition to a concept of much that is unnameable, the feeling of which animates the cognitive faculties and combines spirit with the mere letter of language. (*CPJ*, 194)

Particularly important here is the distinction between a "determinate concept" and the notion of "manifold partial representations," the second a recognition that artistic representation must always exceed conceptual closure, and yet may still be related to a concept as something additional, what Kant elsewhere calls an "attribute." Thus, when Guigemar, in another of Marie's *lais*, encounters an ambiguously gendered white hart that speaks his language, we might well invoke the concept of growing up and read the moment as an instance of Guigemar's resistance to leaving his adolescence and embracing full maturity. And yet the hero's irrational behaviour – first sending his squire to summon his men to him and then leaving before they can arrive, to embark instead on a journey he could not possibly explain to anyone – is of the essence of romance *aventure*. Marie is representing an experience of change which cannot be named, but which can be felt in the details of magical boats and of actually perceiving a lady for the first time. As a result, the cognitive faculties are stimulated to supplement concept with a manifold of newly distinct perceptions. This is precisely the experience of the lady in *Yonec*, who, from the moment she accepts her changeling lover, accepts an *aventure* filled with a wealth of detail previously unimaginable to her.

Scholars of medieval French romance have argued that romance fiction opens a kind of experimental space where social conflicts may be expressed and social change simulated.[35] Romance may certainly include the representation of injustice and cruelty, and it may allow its readers to picture new forms of personal relation, but *Yonec*, in its moments of mysterious obscurity, goes beyond social representation to reflect on the logic of possibility, on how a character may undertake to imagine possibility, and why it matters. Generally, when we think of an alternate world, the world of fairy for example, or Muldumarec's realm, we understand it to be a *metaphysical* possible world. That is, we believe that only our own world actually exists, but we imagine the other as a possible world. That is, we imagine what it would be like to live in a world governed by a coherent set of laws different than the laws that structure our own world. The shape-shifting hawk/lover and his beautiful city would therefore be regarded as counterfactual, as fully available to wish fulfilment as to philosophical reflection.

An *epistemic* possible world, however, would be quite different. In this case, for the lady in her tower, the mysterious lover and his magical city might actually exist, as far as she knows. That is, rather than travelling to a metaphysically alien place, the lady travels to a place that really exists, though previously unknown to her. Its status is thus a function of her knowledge, not of its actuality. There is a moment in the narrative when the lady is frightened and confused about which of these two worlds has suddenly entered her chamber. If the hawk/knight is some kind of fairy-demon, then he is certainly from a world that is metaphysically alien to her own. But when he voluntarily receives the host, and recites his credo, shared Christianity appears to the lady to preclude essential difference and renders Muldumarec something more like a mysterious discovery about her own Christian world.

If he is a part of her world, heretofore unknown to her, then where does he exist? As the scholarly impasse discussed above suggests, Marie veils the location of Muldumarec's kingdom in obscurity. The insubstantiality of the knight's presence, neither clearly here nor clearly there, recalls Augustine's famous description of the present as an infinitesimally brief moment, as the future continually rushes into the past.[36] Consider how the lady actually frames the wish that brings her lover into her life:

"*Mut ai sovent oï cunter*
Que l'em suleit jadis trover
Aventures en cest païs
Ki rehaitouent les pensis.
Chevalier trovoent puceles
A lur talent, gentes e beles,
E dames truvoent amanz
Beaus e curteis, pruz e vaillanz,
Si que blasmees n'en esteient
Ne nul fors eles nes veeient.
Si ceo peot estrë e ceo fu,
Se unc a nul est avenu,
Deus, ki de tut ad poësté,
Il en face ma volenté!" (91–104)

I've often heard
that one could once find
adventures in this land
that brought relief to the unhappy.
Knights might find young girls
to their desire, noble and lovely;
and ladies find lovers
so handsome, courtly, brave, and valiant
that they could not be blamed,
and no one else would see them.
If that might be or ever was,
if that has ever happened to anyone,
God, who has power over everything,
grant me my wish in this.

The lady is not asking to escape into a counterfactual world of fantasy, a *metaphysical* possible world. Her *aventure* would be to an *epistemic* possible world, a world she has heard about in stories, not a strange and alien place, but the (Celtic) past of her own world, where, as far as she knows, women once found the love she so sorely lacks. The past is over, of course, and she could return to it only in her imagination, but the significance of the past is not its wishful comfort, but its unsettling logic: if the life of a young woman was ever different, then it is possible for the life of a young woman to be different. And so the crux of her prayer: "If that might be or ever was." Thinking about a past that might have happened, the lady is already imagining a possible future. Perhaps Marie is indeed hinting that suppressed Celtic law and custom allowing greater freedom to women lies behind the old Breton stories that are her source, but historical allegory or not, the story she tells is a story about time. Our argument that *aventure* opens to unknowable future possibility differs from that of Howard Bloch, who also sees futurity in the very term *aventure*, but in a highly constrained, teleological sense: "Within such a future-oriented semantic range, an 'aventure' contains its own genealogy, its own expectation for a meaning that is prescribed, predetermined, predestined. It is the equivalent of destiny."[37] The tale Marie tells (about a lady inspired by old stories) took place in an earlier time, and was heard "long after," by those who first composed a *lai* about it. Now she translates it into French and writes it down, but at every stage the future is folded into the past: from those who composed a *lai* in order to remember a story to Marie, who would make the story available in French to a future audience. That audience might then feel empathy for a young woman, imprisoned by her husband, who looked back to the same Breton stories to experience, just briefly, a different future for herself, a future perhaps less fanciful to the audiences Marie had vowed to reach at the very outset of the *Lais*. *Yonec* is a brief story, but in its elegant unfolding of a possible future out of the past, the speculative fiction of Marie achieves the very essence of romance.

Chapter Two

Perception and Possible Worlds in *Sir Orfeo*

What is love?
This drove him quite insane. Now he must knit
Time with apperception, bit by tiny bit.

Delmore Schwartz, "Concerning the Synthetic Unity of Apperception"

The Middle English poem called *Sir Orfeo*, most likely written in the early fourteenth century, expresses a multiply layered past, in its classical matter, its Celtic otherworld, its romance sensibility, and its appropriation of the Breton *lai* as passed to England through the Old French of Marie de France. But the English *Orfeo* looks forward as well as back, in details waiting to become the seeds of new tellings. In *Black Orpheus*, the 1959 film by Marcel Camus, the ancient past of the Orpheus legend is initially figured by a black-and-white still image of a classical stone frieze behind the opening titles. This serene image is immediately followed by a burst of vivid colour and music as the residents of a *favela* in Rio de Janeiro prepare for carnival. The chaotic presence of filmic realism is momentarily shocking to an audience that has just been shown the formal perfection of ancient imagemaking. The cool distance of the film's representation of ancient art is a construction of modernity, however, and its juxtaposition with the apparent chaos of the present emphasizes the mixture of strangeness and familiarity we feel whenever we encounter an old story told under new conditions or by new means. The visual storytelling of film was unthinkable in centuries past, though a Breton *lai* might be said to have had a soundtrack, as it was spoken to music. However altered the telling, though, *Black Orpheus* was already part of the future of every previous version of the myth, including that of the medieval *Sir Orfeo*. Our aim in this chapter is to think about what happens when time seems to be folded in such a way that past and future meet as an old story is retold in a new time, a new place, a new artistic language. The Orpheus legend is itself a reflection on aesthetic power, and we want to look in some detail at how a now anonymous early-fourteenth-century poet, writing in English after French and Latin models, made it part of the history of medieval romance.

Even in recent decades there have been too many retellings of the Orpheus story for us to catalogue here. By way of counterpoint, though, we must mention one other modern version. Salman Rushdie's 1999 novel, *The Ground beneath Her Feet*, is a long, complex saga of world-historical change, as well as a story of individual love and loss. In the terms of medieval rhetoric, it represents *amplificatio*, especially when set against the lyrical simplicity of either *Black Orpheus* or *Sir Orfeo*. If the theme music of the film quickly became an international hit and remains a jazz standard, Rushdie's novel is all about music in the late twentieth century, as it presents a history of rock and roll through the rise to superstardom of two lovers possessed of miraculous musical power. The Apollonian ability of the young streetcar operator in *Black Orpheus* to charm through the simple melodies of his acoustic guitar in the late 1950s becomes a Dionysian frenzy twenty-five years later in the elaborately produced stadium concerts of the novel, so loud the hero must perform in a glass box to protect his damaged hearing. In the film, when Orpheus is stoned by jealous women and falls to his death, he dies unknown, except for a little boy who picks up his guitar and begins to carry on the music. But Rushdie's novel is about celebrity, and when Vina, rock idol and figure of Eurydice, is swallowed by an earthquake in Mexico while on a concert tour, she lives on in the capitalist afterlife of the famous: Vina imitators, fan magazine fantasy, conspiracy theorists, and endless kitsch objects to buy.

The medieval *Sir Orfeo* is erected on already many-faceted references, Greco-Roman and Celtic, some claiming Orpheus's historical existence, some regarding him as mythic or legendary.[1] One tradition claims him as the founder of a religious system, in another, he represents the power of artistic creation. In all Orphic tales, the hero loses his dearly-loved wife and penetrates an alien realm to rescue her through the power of his music, but how the episodes of this skeletal account are related causally and what they mean ethically vary from pre-Homeric times to late antiquity as the story passes through many hands for many purposes. Although Orpheus is a familiar figure in the ancient world, his parentage, his self-imposed exile, and even whether the rescue of Eurydice was successful are not consistent from one teller to another.[2] Christian appropriations of the story from Boethius onward find Orpheus either heroic (even Christ-like) or sinfully bound to earthly matters. In addition, *Sir Orfeo* clearly marks its infusion of distinctly Celtic features – the "taking" of Heurodis from under a tree at noonday, Orfeo's subsisting on forest roots in a Merlinesque style of mourning, and the fairy hunting party[3] – into an already tangled, multi-valenced narrative.

The *Orfeo*-poet manages an ingenious folding of previous accounts and colourings into a specifically medieval English horizon of understanding. To start with, the poem is introduced as an "auentour" out of which "Bretouns maked her layes" (13, 15), and Thrace, his homeland for most of the ancients, is renamed Winchester: "Þis king soiournd in Traciens, / Þat was a cité of noble defens / (For Winchester was cleped þo / Traciens, wiþ-outen no)" (47–50). Like Marie, who was equally aware of the ancient world, and who adopted the Breton *lai* to distance her reflections on the Anglo-Norman world of her own time, the *Orfeo*-poet frames his poem as a Breton *lai* in order to defamiliarize the ancient story and prefigure a future of companionate marriage much like that of Dorigen and Arveragus in Chaucer's *Franklin's Tale*.[4] The *Orfeo*-poet replaces the more naturalistic account of Eurydice's death by a snake bite as she was either dancing in the grass or escaping from a potential suitor (the latter stressed by Virgil particularly) by an unexplained vanishing that leaves Orfeo's shield-wall ("scheltrom," 187) aghast. Eurydice's Hades is peopled by familiar figures like Cerberus, Ixion, and Tantalus, who do not appear in the upper world, while Heurodis rides past Orfeo's lair with a mysterious fairy troop in a hunting party that takes no game. Both the details of the hunt and the way Orfeo talks his way into the fairy kingdom as minstrels might have done in medieval England balance the otherworldliness of the "taking." The opulent castle of the Fairy King with its gruesome fore-court also seems an appeal to medieval sensibilities (the temples in Chaucer's *Knight's Tale* come to mind). The poet has brought the spine of the story inherited from the Greeks and Romans[5] into intimate contact with images from the everyday life of his own time with a Celtic twist, folding antiquity into medieval imaginative constructs.

The Times of the Poem

Sir Orfeo represents one moment in the long timeline of the Orpheus legend, a line reaching back to its first mention in the sixth century

B.C.E. and forward to the late twentieth century. Appropriating the classical version of Ovid's *Georgics*, the *Orfeo*-poet looked to a medieval past as well, but chose to write a Breton *lai*, in a tradition begun by Marie de France over a hundred years earlier. A timeline is generally imagined as straight, but any account of the Orpheus story is more like Bruno Latour's spiral of history, continually moving on to a place that is familiar and yet displaced, never a simple return. As a late medieval romance based on a richly layered textual past, *Sir Orfeo* is itself structured by time, when time is understood in a Leibnizian sense as the set of mutual relations among successive events.[6] The poem is also a profound reflection on its own received notions, as those notions are represented through the conceptual language of romance *aventure*.

Felicity Riddy has offered the most detailed discussion of time as a structuring principle in *Sir Orfeo*. She sees the time scheme of the poem as dividing the action into "a day and a morrow," followed by a period of ten years, and then another day and a morrow. Within this scheme, she points to moments when past and present are contrasted, usually in a mode of nostalgia, especially in the first half of the poem. Nostalgia foregrounds a concern with time and change, and underlies what is in her view the poem's central theme: the restoration of the past. She further argues that the poem is "profoundly Christian" and finally concludes that the past has not simply been restored in the return of Orfeo and Heurodis to the joy of their former life, but that the past has been "redeemed."[7] While we agree that the contrast of past and present is crucial to the narrative structure of *Sir Orfeo*, we will suggest a more complex time scheme within which the past is not restored, but strangely folded into Orfeo's present, where it is the occasion for a new level of consciousness. The poem begins at the still point of romance convention, an initial moment we might designate as T1, the time before anything has happened. Orfeo and Heurodis are king and queen, and hero and heroine of the tale we are about to hear. We know this because they look the part: Orfeo is "A stalworþ man & hardi bo; / Large & curteis he was al-so" (41–2), while his wife's being is equally customary in romance:

Þe king hadde a quen of priis
Þat was y-cleped Dame Heurodis,
Þe fairest leuedi, for þe nones,
Þat miȝt gon on bodi & bones,
Ful of loue & of godenisse;
Ac no man may telle hir fairnise. (51–6)

The accidents of appearance had become increasingly important to the identity of Orpheus in the Middle Ages, as the developing conventions of romance emphasized the hero's handsome appearance and strength. John Block Friedman points to a lyric from Augsburg found in a manuscript of Gregory's *Moralia*, in which the physical attributes of Orpheus are central to his identity: "His attractive qualities, moreover, are no longer mere descriptive tags, but provide motivation for the narrative. Eurydice loves Orpheus *because* of his looks, voice, and eloquence, much in the same way that a lady of romance might come to love, from a distance, the fine qualities of a knight."[8] Friedman goes on to show that the convention continues into the late Middle Ages, when Robert Henryson's Eurydice, as a rich queen, sends for Orpheus to come to Thrace and marry her only because she has heard about his fine qualities. There is no sign in *Sir Orfeo*, of course, that Heurodis and Orfeo love each other only for their physical appearances, but that convention is surely part of the expectation of audience and poet alike at the beginning of the fourteenth century, and we believe the poem is in part a serious reflection on the insubstantial nature of the convention with which it introduces its own hero and heroine.[9]

The happy couple, known by outward signs of personal beauty and royal finery, express a stable world, and yet audiences know (because of the familiarity of the tale) that the future is already folded into this present, and will emerge, bringing with it shocking change. When the queen and her ladies walk out to enjoy fields of flowers and blossoming trees on a warm spring day, Heurodis unwisely chooses to nap at noontime under a tree in the orchard, traditionally an uncanny and dangerous intersection of time and space. In doing so, she invites the intervention of fairy into her world, a disruption of her initial state entirely to be expected by listeners and readers at the end of the thirteenth century.

When Heurodis awakens, her perception of the familiar world is utterly changed:

> Sche crid, & loþli bere gan make:
> Sche froted hir honden & hir fet,
> & crached her visage – it bled wete;
> Hir riche robe hye al to-rett,
> & was reueyd out of hir witt. (78–82)

Her ladies, believing her to have gone mad, summon knights who convey her back to the palace, where she is brought to her bed and there held fast. In her frenzy, she turns on that very aspect of her self that had signalled her identity as a romance heroine, scratching her beautiful face until it was wet with blood, and tearing her fine clothes to pieces. In doing so, she initiates T2, a new time in which she will no longer be defined by the accidents of bodily appearance and royal garments. When Orfeo rushes to her chamber, what he perceives is precisely her bodily state, as it is now, but always as linked to what it was. Her voice that was so soft is now shrill, her body, formerly so white, is now torn by her nails, her face, that was so red is now wan, as if she were dead, her small fingers are now red with blood. Orfeo, about to endure ten long years of privation and loss, cannot yet see the future, and he perceives the present of Heurodis only by reference to images from past time.

When Heurodis screamed and tore her clothes and body with her own nails, she had perceived her plight and acted out of sheer emotion. In Leibniz's terms, she had perceived, but without apperception, without complete consciousness. But by the time she is finally able to speak to Orfeo, she has achieved a fully conscious understanding of her situation and, even more significantly, a self-consciousness that many critics have assumed could not be represented by medieval narrative art:

"Allas, mi lord Sir Orfeo!
Seþþen we first to-gider were
Ones wroþ neuer we nere,
Bot euer ich haue y-loued þe
As mi liif, & so þou me;
Ac now we mot delen ato
– Do þi best, for y mot go." (120–6)

Heurodis is able to express intimacy in powerful though simple language, but her self-understanding is enabled by memory. The apperception of her present situation is laden with the past of her life with Orfeo, as well as by the future she sees so clearly. The poet's representation of this complex fabric in which past, present, and future touch expresses a structure of felt knowledge that exceeds all concept, and which constitutes an aesthetic moment in the Kantian sense.

Orfeo's reply, echoing Ruth's vow to Naomi, promises that he will go with her wherever she is taken, but because he cannot yet imagine a world governed by laws so alien to those of his own, his promise is the kind of rash vow so often found in romance:

"Allas!" quaþ he, "For-lorn icham!
Whider wiltow go, & to wham?
Whider þou gost ichil wiþ þe,
& whider y go þou schalt wiþ me." (127–30)

Heurodis has seen further into the future, however, and tells Orfeo that it cannot be, saying that she will tell him "al hou it is." Regardless of her account of the Fairy King's threats, Orfeo and his knights take up arms to protect her, but fail, as she is mysteriously stolen away from their very midst. Orfeo's response mirrors the initial reaction of Heurodis upon awaking under the ympe tree. In a sudden gesture, Orfeo surrenders the kingdom to his steward and vows to enter the wilderness and live among the wild beasts. Like Heurodis, he rejects his kingly finery and takes only a pilgrim's cloak and his harp, as he goes off to the forest alone. He does not rend his flesh with his own nails, as his wife had done, but he accomplishes the same end of defacing his hero's visage in subjecting himself to years of abjection by assuming the traditional role of Wildman of the Woods.

At this point, the poem's narrative employs a formal device that configures time in a striking way. When Heurodis had earlier described her encounter with the Fairy King, she told how he had taken her to his own land, and there "schewed me castels & tours, / Riuers, forestes, friþ wiþ flours" (159–60). Later, when Orfeo has renounced his kingly identity and entered the wilderness, the poet repeatedly joins past and present in his narrative: he who was once served by valiant knights and lovely ladies is now surrounded by serpents; he who had once had plenty of meat and drink and his choice of dainties, now must dig for roots. And here the precise language that earlier described the fairy kingdom reappears:

He that hadde had castels & tours,
Riuer, forest, friþ wiþ flours
– Now, þei it comenci to snewe & frees,
Þis king mot make his bed in mese. (245–8)

Possible Worlds

Heurodis has been carried away to another possible world. For Alan J. Fletcher, the world of fairy is defined by the gallery of the taken that Orfeo witnesses as he enters the court. The gallery's horrors are part of a "baffling universe that obviates prediction or explanation," and the text of the poem offers no reasons that might make this world understandable "within known schemes of things."[10] But this is precisely what another possible world is: our familiar logic, our "known schemes," no longer hold. While the presence of those abducted by the Fairy King is indeed baffling, it would be no less incomprehensible for a man to stand before his lost wife and see her exactly as she had been ten years earlier. If such an experience is unsettling, it is also exhilarating, like the great pyramid of rooms in Leibniz's fable of the possible lives of Sextus, extending through differently imagined worlds to infinity. For Leibniz, those other worlds exist only because they can be conceived, in the restricted sense of conceived in the mind of God. Alternative worlds within fictions are also mental constructions, but the alternatives they posit may exist either as metaphysically counterfactual to the one actual world, or as epistemically possible – that is, as believed to be actual now or in some future time. Companionate marriage like that represented in *Sir Orfeo* could be no more than a way the world might be (i.e., an epistemic possibility) for the characters who people the *lais* of Marie.

When Orfeo journeys to the realm of fairy, however, he enters a world that is metaphysically other, a time/space counterfactual to the poem's only actual world. Momentarily enabled to look back at the actual world from this counterfactual perspective, but as true figures of romance allowed to return from their *aventure*, they do so having confirmed that their status as king and queen was mere accident, while the properties of artistry, loyal love, and mortal humanity constitute an essential identity persisting across worlds.

As a conventional fantasy of Celtic romance, the fairy realm resembles in many ways the courtly world in which the poem began. When Orfeo later goes to the Fairy King's realm, it even appears to be the "proude court of Paradis" (376), but it is Other, not because it displays more gold and more precious stones, but because it is differently premised with regard to time and causality. When the lines describing fairyland are repeated in the context of Orfeo's human world, they present the blooming flowers as part of a continuing succession of the seasons, bringing Orfeo to freezing rain and a bed on the ground. Time is lived as change for Orfeo, carrying him through privation and aging to a time increasingly distant from the two earlier moments of the narrative, the T1 of his lost life with Heurodis, and even the T2 of their parting. When Sir Orfeo returns to his own kingdom at the end of the poem, he is like a gnarled old tree, unrecognizable to his former subjects.

The otherness of the world of fairy is witnessed by Sir Orfeo during his years in the wilderness, when he occasionally sees the Fairy King and his men riding through the forest with all the outward trappings of the hunt, or accompanied by a mighty host of knights with banners flying and swords drawn. But the hunters never take any prey, and the armed knights never seem bound for any battle, however awesome their display. It is at such a moment of unearthly encounter in the woods that the poet suddenly violates the dream-like boundaries of the earlier visions and opens for just a moment a fissure between two worlds, a kind of portal between the time frames of mortal and fairy. When sixty ladies ride into view, their falcons are no illusion but kill their prey in the actual world. Among the ladies is Heurodis, and when she and Orfeo suddenly find themselves together, the poet draws a tiny detail out of the broader spectacle – what Leibniz would call a "*petite perception*," part of an infinity of unconscious sensation that may become distinct within consciousness, and so form the basis for a higher level of understanding. Gazing at Orfeo's face, Heurodis beholds in the same glance both his past greatness and present abjection, and tears fall from her eye:

> Ac noiþer to oþer a word no speke,
> For messais þat sche on him sieȝe.
> Þat had ben so riche & so heiȝe.
> Þe teres fel out of her eiȝe. (324–7)

Seeing this, the other ladies make her ride away because once taken to the realm of fairy, she has no future, and her present must no longer be laden with the past. The tear, however, is nothing like her frenzied emotion under the ympe tree, but rather signals a newly self-reflective understanding of what it means to live in time. Contrasting *King Horn*'s dramatized action with the lyrical mode of *Sir Orfeo*, Mary Hynes-Berry notes the aesthetic power of the poem's simplicity. She argues that the poem exhibits "a shorter and more 'organic' story, with far more complicated and abstract psychological and thematic implications."[11] The tear may thus be seen as a kind of microcosm, a tiny detail that nevertheless makes visible an inwardness of strong emotion, personal memory, and anticipation of the future, as well as a higher understanding of time as essentially relational.

Orfeo responds to the brief encounter with his wife by lamenting that he cannot simply die after such a sight, and the emotion he expresses is explicitly grounded in his experience of time as duration: "Allas! To long last mi liif" (335). But the representation of inner life is remarkably sophisticated in this passage, as Orfeo's perception of how painful it would be to face a future anything like his recent past leads him to wish for death, only to yield immediately to the contrary resolution to follow the ladies, wherever it might take him:

> "Parfay!" quaþ he, "Tide wat bitide,
> Whider-so þis leuedis ride,
> The selue way ichil streche
> – O liif no deþ me no reche." (339–42)

A moment earlier, to say he cares not about life or death while wishing to die would have signalled despair, but now it follows the very different "Tide wat bitide" (let happen what will happen), repeating his initial vow to follow Heurodis wherever she might go, but now with a deeper understanding of the dangers his pursuit will entail. This reorientation marks a crucial narrative turn in the poem, initiating Orfeo's rescue of Heurodis when he actively chooses to enter the alien realm of the Fairy King. But it is also a telling moment for continuing critical discussion about the extent to which the *Orfeo* poet shows his characters to possess self-understanding that could allow them to experience psychic growth and change. Dominiques Battle has recently argued that Orfeo does not learn during his time in the wilderness, that his exile "does not correlate with character development."[12] Others see the poem as an account of profound change in Orfeo (and, we would argue, in Heurodis as well). One argument of this sort is that the Fairy King is testing Orfeo, that Orfeo needs to learn that the outward trappings of kingship do not matter, that "the greatness of Orfeo's kingdom rests not in appearances, but in the human spirit."[13] While we are very much in sympathy with the notion that conventional features of costume and bearing, whether those of royal position or romance narrative, are not to be equated with the identity of a subject, we employ a set of terms which do not carry the allegorical sense of earthly appearance versus spiritual reality.

In philosophical discussion of possible worlds, the question of whether or not an individual may exist in more than one world is a crucial matter of debate. For Leibniz, who held that God had chosen only one world to exist (the best of all possible worlds), a man like Sextus may exist only in that actual world, however many other lives we might imagine for him: "Besides, if, in the life of any person and even in the whole universe anything went differently from what it has, nothing could prevent us from saying that it was another person or another possible universe which God had chosen. It would then be indeed another individual."[14] In more recent discussion a similar conclusion has been reached by holding that all properties of an object are essential, in which case the object in another possible world, with just one property changed, would no longer be the same object. Others, however, have argued that "objects have only some of their properties essentially," and so might indeed exist across multiple worlds if only contingent properties of their identities differ.[15] Alvin Plantinga, a proponent of the latter view, finds "the earliest explicit recognition of individual essences" in the writings of Boethius.[16]

The properties of being a romance hero, or a king, are contingent to Orfeo, and do not constitute the essence, or "thisness" which is his true identity.[17] Through this lens, a dominant literary convention of romance genre may be displaced by the representation of characters who, through a process of perception gradually raised to the level of broader self-understanding, come to accept the insubstantiality of conventional predication: the hero's mighty arm, the heroine's bright eye. The tear that Heurodis sheds is not a feature of her noble status, but rather a sign of inward growth, that now she fully understands why she had rent her royal gown and attacked her own fair skin. That *Sir Orfeo* represents a gradual divergence between the inwardness of self-identity and the accidents of personal and social appearance is noted by Morgan Dickson in the contrast with which disguise appears in Orfeo's exile and in the French romances which preceded it.[18] The earlier heroes need only don the cloak of a peasant, while retaining their personal beauty, to be unrecognized by a community that equates identity with social status. But Orfeo's visage is ravaged by time and hardship when he returns to his court, a sign, for Dickson, that Orfeo's inner and outer being no longer coincide.

The poet is not much interested in the brief journey that follows the encounter in the forest, but when Orfeo emerges into the fairy kingdom we are given an initial description that suggests Orfeo's own kingdom (or that of any conventional romance), but which is grander, brighter, more colourful, and decorated with so much more gold and so many jewels that it seemed to be the proud court of Paradise. Appearance only masks the horrors of the hall, of course, where all those who have been stolen remain exactly as they had been when taken, whether wounded in arms, drowned, burnt by fire, or lying in childbed, dead or maddened ("awedde," 400). When Orfeo sees Heurodis, she is miraculously back at what we have called T1, the time when she lay, bright of complexion ("bri3t on ble" 455), unchanged and asleep under the ympe tree before her first encounter with the Fairy King. Orfeo confirms by her clothes (not yet torn to shreds by her own hands) that she is indeed his wife, a sign that in the Hades of fairy identity is still defined by the accidents of conventional clothing and beauty. The Fairy King might be said to exist at Time Zero, a state without change, where the succession of seasons never fades the flowers, and where the present is never laden with the past or pregnant with the future. In contrast to classical versions such as that of Virgil, where those in the underworld are shades (or mere representations) of their whole former selves (only Deiphobus is mutilated), the "taken" in *Sir Orfeo* retain whatever material reality they possessed when they were taken, whether wounded, in childbed, or asleep under a tree.[19] That is, rather than representing simulacra of who they once were, like old photographs in an album, they continue to exist, but always at the Time Zero of their taking. Robert M. Longworth calls this state of the fairy world, when time suddenly stops in mid-event, "arrested motion."[20] And yet the experience Orfeo has in his encounter with an alternate world is far more complex and mysterious than any freeze-frame could possibly be.

When the taken are in fact allowed to move about the world, as Heurodis is when she rides with the hunt, they do so within an alternate reality in which movement through space no longer corresponds to change over time. So radical a disruption as this is of the normal lived experience of time/space grounds the shock of mutual perception which issues in Heurodis's tear and Orfeo's new resolution: "Tide wat betide." When Orfeo subsequently enters the Fairy King's court, habitual expectations about the relation between time and space are further distorted as time seems to fold in such a way that Orfeo's past (in the young Heurodis), and her future (in the aging Orfeo) are both present within the same space, as if time had folded back upon itself:

> A sori couple of ȝou it were,
> For þou art lene, rowe & blac,
> & sche is louesum, wiþ-outen lac. (458–60)

Orfeo is indeed lean and rough after his decade in the wild, but Heurodis is without lack only within the magic space in which she is imprisoned after her abduction. When Orfeo's two promises to follow his wife bring him to this realm governed by entirely different laws, two incompossible worlds are allowed to overlap briefly, and yet when the Fairy King makes a vow to Orfeo, he is as bound to honour it as Orfeo would be in the human world. In a sense, the laws of the human world have intruded into the realm of fairy, completing the *aventure* begun when the Fairy King had miraculously appeared to Heurodis.

Orfeo returns to Winchester in disguise, successfully tests the loyalty of his steward, and finally allows himself to be recognized through his harping. This conclusion has been described as a "wholly artificial convenience" by Neil Cartlidge.[21] He contends that the artificiality of the ending provides the reader with a kind of aesthetic escape from the troubling impact of an Otherworld represented as "paradoxical and so uncontainably beyond expression" that it may be felt as "existential confusion." Although he acknowledges that the Otherworld of Sir Orfeo is "disturbingly refractive," he does not share what he sees as a tendency in recent criticism to understand the boundary between human and fairy worlds as a kind of "event horizon" beyond which our familiar systems of sense making no longer apply. Critics who hold such a view tend to celebrate the Otherworld's impenetrability by viewing it as a brilliant imaginative construction that should not be reduced to any set of explanatory concepts.[22]

Medieval romance is filled with "possible worlds," as Leibniz called such imagined entities, internally non-contradictory themselves, but incompatible with the laws of our world. That is, the realm of the Fairy King is, in John Block Friedman's words, a "counter world" rather than any extension of our world, such as an afterworld or an underworld would be.[23] We would insist that such a world may be not only an object of dread and anxiety, but one of fascination and desire as well, inevitably raising curiosity about what it would be like to go there. Consider the narrative trajectory of *Sir Orfeo*. If the poem concludes with an artifice of traditional folk-tale motifs such as the rash promise and the test of loyalty, it opens with a concept that is equally formulaic within the context of romance. Hero and heroine alike are identified by a set of thoroughly conventional terms: stalwart, hardy, large, courteous, fairest, full of love and goodness. The reader expects that those attributes will be sorely tested as the tale unfolds, but that, in the end, they will be confirmed. If the poem were to do no more than represent the concept of handsome knight and fair lady, it might be highly agreeable, but in the Kantian sense, it would not convey the power of aesthetic experience any more than would a fine dinner or a pleasant melody. Similarly, if *Sir Orfeo* could be explained as an allegory of ethical value,[24] the poem would be seen to contribute to the good, but its force would not be experienced as aesthetic. For Kant, the aesthetic object must exhibit purposiveness of design without yielding to the closure of concept.

Although most criticism of *Sir Orfeo* has focused on the scene in the Fairy King's court as the locus of inexplicable otherness in the poem, the earlier moment when Heurodis awakens under the ympe tree, attacks her own beautiful face, and tears her fine gown constitutes an irruption of violence into the world of the poem more shocking than the expected horrors of the Fairy underworld. When, shortly afterward, Orfeo has left his kingly robes behind to enter the forest as a wild man, the conventional order of the poem's opening has been undermined through narrative details that far exceed the fainting and laments of conventional grief. The encounters with the world of fairy are then less about the variety of horrors on display in the king's hall than about the mystery of time: how Heurodis could sleep unchanged under the ympe tree; how she could appear on horseback as she must have looked before her dangerous nap, and yet see Orfeo in what to her was the future, and shed a tear; and how Orfeo could witness his own past in Heurodis, as well as in all those victims locked out of time entirely. An intrusion of the Otherworld provides the occasion, but the narrative of *Sir Orfeo* is driven by human perception. The trajectory begins when Heurodis and Orfeo destroy their received identities in two spontaneous, unreflective acts. When they meet again, a moment of mutual perception issues in a new level of self-awareness for both. The tiny detail of a tear signals that Heurodis understands what it would mean to remain outside of time as her husband ages into a future she could not share. For Orfeo, the ability to articulate his acceptance of change ("Tide wat bitide") empowers him to simply follow her, even if it means his death. Later, having witnessed past and future in the uncanny timelessness of the Otherworld, Orfeo and Heurodis return to their own court, where Orfeo acknowledges that the Steward will succeed him in time, and after a celebration of music they are simply said to live out the rest of their lives. Though filled with ideas that many scholars have discussed at length, the aesthetic power of this *lai*, which readers have always felt, cannot be reduced to a single conceptual idea. A shared glance may be full of meaning, but its meaning is as mysterious and uncontainable as any imagined land of fairy.

The Beauty of *Sir Orfeo*

Thus, mystery and conceptual uncontainability underlie our claim that *Sir Orfeo* is beautiful, that our pleasure in reading or hearing it quickens both imagination and understanding. We hope to have shown that the many sources and potential implications folded into the poem are held in a kind of teaming suspension. This very restlessness, though, raises the question of how a simple *lai* of just over 600 lines can contain all these energies and still express a unifying aesthetic idea, an aura of purposiveness. Medieval and Kantian aesthetic standards agree that a beautiful object is singular (itself and not a class of things), and shaped by a distinctive aesthetic idea, what Aquinas calls *integritas*. Examining the shape of the poem to see how the long and varied past with which it is pregnant is brought to new life will serve to demonstrate both its presence as a unique object and its economy of means.[25] A striking aspect of its compressed implication is its self-reflexivity: "Gode is þe lay, swete is the note" is among the last lines of a song about the world-historical maker of songs. *Sir Orfeo* is a poem likely to have been sung to a stringed instrument, and its hero is *the* singer/harper of the Western tradition. As Rilke writes, "Once and for all / it's Orpheus when there's singing."[26]

Another feature of its coherence is *Sir Orfeo*'s fusion of its ancient, Celtic, and medieval English life-worlds into an apparently seamless arc. The poem nonetheless provides surprising turns: Orpheus's being allowed into the Otherworld as a poor minstrel, the lie to his steward that he found the harp and corpse of the king, and the series of "if" clauses that tell the story of his absence aslant. And of course there are the vivid descriptions (*energeia*), especially that of the fairy palace with its paradisiacal façade and horrifying interior. This plotting and imagery powerfully activate imagination and yet beg to be understood. The sudden shift in the setting from subsistence in the wild forest to the even more alien world of the fairy court blocks any immediate explanation we might bring to the task of rendering the intelligibility of the world of the poem.

Formal coherence is often investigated through genre,[27] by noting differences among members of a generically similar set. From the outset, *Sir Orfeo* is a self-identified "Breton lay" (13 and 597), which places it among a small number of surviving poems. Most Breton *lais* are traced to Marie de France, but there must once have been many of them, since they are often referred to in the Middle Ages. Now they are usually described as brief, sung romances. "Romance" is itself, of course, a blurred category that, in spite of its familiar associations with the Middle Ages, reaches back to myth, legend, and folklore and forward to some of the "speculative fiction" currently being written. Since early in the Common Era (the Greek romances), it has suggested tales of adventure touched by magic in which "the rules of nature are slightly suspended," as Northrop Frye puts it in *The Anatomy of Criticism*. These *aventures* also involve love affairs and intimate examinations of personal subjectivity. *Sir Orfeo* may be said to be *structured* by the romance form, in the Gadamerian sense that art brings play "to its true consummation" by being transformed into structure.[28] Such a transformation of the many energies of the poem into a bounded aesthetic object is another step towards elucidating its beauty.

Amenable as it is to the form of medieval romance, *Sir Orfeo* also marks its distinctiveness. It veers closer to tragic contemplation than romance usually does: Orfeo flees to the forest in despair rather than in quest of his lost beloved, and he briefly wishes for death ("To long last mi liif," 335) before he follows her to the Otherworld. It specifies time more precisely than romances usually do, especially in its six mentions of "vndrentide" (mid-day) as threatening danger to humans from otherworldly powers,[29] but also in Orfeo's ten years of exile and his time-marked body and hair. Romances in general challenge commonsensical causalities, but *Sir Orfeo* outdoes them all in failing to resolve them.[30] The step is easily taken from the rather familiar, if idealized, Thrace/Winchester to the privations of Orfeo's subsistence life in nature (the familiar wild man), but the Otherworld is truly baffling. It is neither the inherited Hades in which Eurydice has her "place," nor Christian hell, nor yet the Celtic land of the dead, but echoes all three. Yet in that strange world, the plot takes another sudden turn when the king yields to Orfeo's demand for promise keeping, a demand that resonates with his well-ordered court in T1. The logic of the poem's world is elusive, but the narrative that presents it is brisk. This sharp narrative outline is achieved through the exclusion of well-known features of the Virgilian and Ovidian accounts he relies on, most notably the second loss of Heurodis.

The more difficult it is to explain an impressively serious tale in terms of fictional realism, the more tempting it is to allegorize it. While allegory proper is a mode rather than a genre, narratives of all kinds can be submitted to allegoresis, interpreted as patterns of ideas rather than literal actions, asking what the story *means*, what its actions *stand for*.[31] This hermeneutic from Augustine's *On Christian Doctrine* became one of his most important gifts to the Middle Ages, both in developing non-literal readings of scripture and in authorizing the use of pre-Christian intellectual insight, allowing medieval culture to account for its attention to pagan stories at all, and providing a way of reading them. Greek and Roman myth is *Sir Orfeo*'s ultimate source, and myths by nature surround narratives with religious, ethical, and/or philosophical implications. But, although they are read and retold for "what they mean," each new social formation adapts both the events and their meanings to its own purposes. Although a long history of allegorizing the myth of Orpheus was inherited by medieval Europe, Christianizing it required still more vigorous interpretive means.[32]

When the disguised Orfeo confronts his faithful steward, he calls himself "a harpour of heþenisse" (513), and in a sense the *Orfeo*-poet is too, in that he brings to medieval Christian hearers a *lai* based on ancient and Celtic pagan sources. The poet may have seen the old story glossed for Christian consumption, but he is unlikely to have known how deeply and in what ways some Orphic ideas had been entwined with those of early Christians: Orpheus appears as the Good Shepherd often in early Christian iconography, and even as crucified in a third or fourth-century amulet.[33] Guthrie argues convincingly that not only are Orphic ideas and imagery close to some Christian precepts, but that early Christians found Orpheus a convenient "cover" for a church that "did not seek notoriety."[34] The appropriateness of the crucifixion amulet lies in the fact that Orphic cults regarded Dionysius as their central god, who had twice been killed and resurrected. Yet Orpheus, by the early centuries of the Christian Era was the opposite of a Bacchic figure: rational and ascetic rather than frenzied. A theogony (myth of origin of the world) was based on "his" songs, apparently aimed at reforming Bacchic dogma. But in Greek thinking his singing to the lyre connected him with Apollo as well, and it has been argued that Orphism was the conduit through which Platonism reached Saint Paul.[35] His musical genius resembles that of the Old Testament King David, and his bringing peace to the lion and lamb to Christ. The "heþenisse" of the ancient story was therefore assimilable into even a "profoundly Christian" poem like *Sir Orfeo*, although probably not because the poet was guided by this history. It is later generations who can see these folds in time.

The *Orfeo*-poet is likely to have known at least Boethius's *Consolation of Philosophy* as well as one of the two boldest interpretations of the old story: Pierre Bersuire's *Reductorium Morale* (1325–37) and the anonymous *Ovide Moralisé* (1291–1328?). Boethius's authority throughout the

Middle Ages no doubt influenced the later moralizations in identifying Orpheus with both laudable power over nature and the underworld and lamentable weakness in looking back. But Boethius also defends Orpheus's lapse: "Who shall set a law for lovers? Love is a greater law unto itself" (book 3, metrum 12), a reminder of his earlier "Love binds with pure affection the sacred tie of wedlock ... O happy race of mortals, if your hearts are ruled as is the universe, by Love" (book 2, metrum 8). One might say that Boethius's Orpheus is a tragic figure who suffers from his greatness. Bersuire gives two allegorical readings: (1) Orpheus is Christ seeking Eurydice, that is, mankind's soul, in the bowels of hell and (2) Orpheus lost Eurydice through sin (the bite of the snake), sought her through enlightened repentance, but lapsed like a dog returning to its vomit. The *Moralisé* attempts to allegorize everything: morally Orpheus is understanding, Eurydice sensuality, the harp divine inspiration, the looking back his inability to resist his senses; "historically," the Thracian women kill him because, having lost Eurydice, he has scorned the love of women for that of young men; allegorically (another way) Orpheus is a figure of Christ who successfully frees Eurydice, but she, having been bitten by the devilish snake returns, like all daughters of Eve, to her captivity. In this last reading, misogyny dwarfs even the homosexuality condemned earlier: young men who "offer their hearts, bodies, and desires to do what God desires, them he loves, in them he takes pleasure."

Sir Orfeo's telling of the Orpheus *aventure* cannot be read in any of these ways. By excluding the backward glance that returns Heurodis to the Otherworld, a major episode for Virgil and Ovid, the poem evades the moralized conclusion about Orfeo's failed aspirations to higher, less human desire. Yet old associations hover about the poem: Orfeo's descent risks death to seek his human lover, calling up the energies of Dionysus, but his powerful art and his effects on the natural world suggest Apollonian civilization. The exclusion of the second loss of Eurydice also allows a different ending for Orfeo himself and evades the charge that in his grief he initiates a cult of homosexuality.

On the other hand, Orfeo does not appear as a type of Christ either. The allegory that would insist that he has cleansed Hades/Hell as Christ did in the Gospel of Nicodemus cannot be sustained in that he brings back only Heurodis. He seems instead a human lover willing to pursue any *aventure* no matter how risky (Tide wat Bitide) in order to be reunited with his wife, whose desire to rejoin him is signalled by her tear. Contemporary tales that stress the value and life-long commitment of individual, rather than dynastic love (Lancelot, Tristan) often also exhibit a secrecy and adultery subversive to medieval Christian mores and condemned by the church. But the same insistence on the value of mutual love for a fellow creature appears in *Sir Orfeo* without that taint. It would perhaps be overreaching to argue that the reconciliation of earthly love and "divine" striving glancingly suggest the companionate love ethic of later generations, but this lovely poem does set a precedent for the genre romance and its legacy to novels and filmed fictions. *Sir Orfeo* as we might see it now folds its ancient sources, the Orpheus of Apollo and Dionysius, into a medieval-English poem of remarkable power and unresolved mystery.

After-images

While the mid-twentieth-century film *Black Orpheus* and early-fourteenth-century poem are utterly different in many ways, they share a great deal with the ancient sources. The English Orfeo charms birds and animals during his sojourn in the wilderness, while Orpheus in Rio lives in a shanty filled with all manner of creatures, evidently charmed as well. Eurydice's only adornment is a scarf that Orpheus notices because it is decorated with animals, before she explains that they represent houses in the sky (the signs of the zodiac). But poem and film also share three details not found in any of the ancient sources of the legend. In the film, Eurydice arrives in the city already terrified by a premonitory visit of the figure of death, just as Heurodis is when she awakes from her dream visitation by the King of Fairy. Still more telling of the power of romance to suggest the inner lives of its characters is a tiny detail in the poem, when Heurodis looks at Orpheus, and sheds a tear as she understands the arc of their story. This moment is mirrored in the film by a close-up of Eurydice, a tear running down her cheek, as she exchanges a long glance with Orpheus, soon after they have met. Finally, and equally striking, is the moving sentiment from the *Book of Ruth*, spoken by Orfeo to Heurodis before she has been taken, and echoed by Orpheus in the film as he carries the dead Eurydice back up the mountain: "I know you will take me where I must go."

Modern film and medieval poem are both laden with the past, and nowhere is this more visible than in the inexplicable intrusion of mystery into ordinary life. In *Sir Orfeo*, the classical story has been clothed in the fabric of the Christian Middle Ages, only to suffer the disruptive threat of a pagan Celtic past less remote from common memory and cultural practice than ancient Greece, and so potentially more dangerous. Fairy mounds and the pre-Celtic passage graves of Brittany underlie the uncanny timelessness of the King of Fairy's palace, which challenges the very ground of medieval power and knowledge. Similarly, when the hero of *Black Orpheus* approaches the land of the dead in search of Eurydice, he crosses a dark street where several small mounds on the sidewalk are illuminated by candles. These ritual offerings signal the encounter Orpheus is about to have with Candomblé, the syncretist Brazilian merging of Catholic, Amerindian, and African religious beliefs and practices. In the ritual he witnesses, led by a priest with hatchet and bow, a cigar-smoking woman in white enters a frenzied trance that allows Orpheus to speak with the dead Eurydice. Like the multilayered history of pagan and Christian England, the entry to the otherworld in *Black Orpheus* is inscribed with its own past, in this case that of European colonialism and the Atlantic slave trade.

Orpheus and Eurydice in Brazil are not king and queen. Orpheus drives a tram and lives from paycheque to paycheque in a capitalist world visually symbolized by starkly modernist skyscrapers, government offices, and police posted on every street to contain the movement of carnival goers. The Fairy King's forecourt of the taken is, in the film, a city morgue of metal tables and cold fluorescent lighting. When he sets out to recover Eurydice's body, Orpheus is sent to the Office of Missing Persons, where he finds empty rooms full of stacks of paper and one old man sweeping up. All romance is subversive in its contrast between wish and local realities, and in *Black Orpheus* the sterile oppressiveness of modernity is clear, while its wealth is impossibly far away down the mountain from Babylonia, the *favela* where most of the action takes place. While the dialogue offers little support to any concept of social oppression, the film's striking visuality of rich and poor, like the subversiveness of romance, haunts the film even as it eludes conceptual closure. Orpheus dresses as Apollo in a gold, vaguely Greek, costume and carries a huge golden disk of the sun to the carnival, and two little boys think it might be true that the sun comes up only when he plays his guitar. Carnival is a unique moment, Dionysian in its exhilarating possibility (including the jealousy and violence of the maenads who kill him at the end), but Apollonian as well, in its celebration of the power of art. Though Heurodis is recovered and Eurydice is lost, music and dance end both works.

Salman Rushdie's *The Ground beneath Her Feet* reduplicates and disperses the themes of the Orpheus legend into the lives of multiple characters and situations.[36] The first third of the book is set in Bombay, beginning in the 1950s, and the city itself is the novel's first lost object of love. Several characters have helped to build the city and now want to see it live on in a kind of unchanged, eternal present. But Bombay is about to become Mumbai as the inexorable sweep of global culture and capitalist development literally demolish the seaside promenades and lush gardens of its colonized past to erect the severe apartment blocks of international modernism. The narrator nods to Marx (and probably to Marshall Berman's great book on cities) as he thinks, "All that is solid melts into air."[37] The nostalgic desire to restore the past is there, to be sure, but most telling is the narrator's final words before leaving India, which are the words of a lover to his lost love:

> It may be that I am not worthy of you, for I have been imperfect, I confess. I may not comprehend what you are becoming, what perhaps you already are, but I am old enough to say that this new self of yours is an entity I no longer want, or need, to understand.
>
> India, fount of my imagination, source of my savagery, breaker of my heart.
>
> Goodbye.

The remainder of the novel takes place in the London of the 1960s, and later in New York, where Ormus and his beloved Vina become Orpheus and Eurydice in a very much more ancient, Dionysian mode than that of the Christianized Orfeo of the Middle Ages. Rock and roll is ecstatic, irrational, summoning great frenzied crowds, and celebrity worship in which passionate love may become murderous at any moment. The artistry of Ormus and Vina is Dionysian not only in its ecstatic excess, but in its inevitable destruction of the artist. Unlike Orfeo and Heurodis, who seem destined to settle back into a wiser kind of marital bliss, Ormus and Vina are doomed – *poètes maudits* whose lives reflect darkly on the fate of art at the end of the twentieth century.

The underworld of *Black Orpheus* was allegorical, the cold and alienating morgue of bureaucratic modernity, while the eruption of Celtic fairyland into the peaceful realm of *Sir Orfeo* remained mysterious, unexplainable. Rushdie's other world is more like that of the medieval poem in its magical aura, but it is also a Leibnizian exercise in imagining possible worlds (Rushdie actually mentions Leibniz late in the book, and has one character wonder, with some irony, whether this is "the best of all possible worlds"). The other world comes to Ormus in the form of a kind of demon lover from a parallel universe that he learns to see into, as if through a rent in the fabric of reality. For *Sir Orfeo*, it is precisely at that moment of intense perception, when multiple timelines intersect with timelessness in the Fairy King's hall that Orfeo understands and accepts the human reality of Augustinian time: to live in a vanishing present, laden with the past and always already filled with the future. A remarkable passage in *The Ground beneath Her Feet* seems to comment on this crucial moment. When a second visitor from the other world comes to Ormus/Orpheus, she tries to explain what he has seen by resorting to the metaphor of a mysterious video store, where walls of videos from other realities are playing:

> You haven't noticed, how could you, but when we visit we don't age, okay? Like if you watch a video a hundred years can pass in the story, but for you it's a hundred minutes, and you can skip about also. Fast-forward, freeze-frame, reverse, whatever you like. Your time is not like that of the people on the tape. (507)

Seven hundred years earlier, the story had already been told: the perfect beauty of romance hero and heroine (like the celebrity of rock stars) is accident, not essence. But that is a difficult insight to attain in a world where accident is so richly rewarded. Only by entering a world incompatible with our own, whether through the what-if of philosophical logic or the counterfactual inventions of art, may the infinite details of perception be gathered to new understanding.

In the next chapter, we consider another fourteenth-century poem about legendary lovers, *Troilus and Criseyde*. Chaucer also appropriates and "medievalizes" material from antiquity, but Troilus does not achieve apperception in a metaphysically other terrain. The unchanging "Time Zero" in his tale is a Christianized "eighth sphere," an epistemically possible vantage point opened to him only after his death.

Chapter Three

Capturing Beauty: Chaucer's *Troilus and Criseyde*

Beauty is "a plank amid the waves of the sea."

Augustine, *De Musica*

The story of the Trojan War was old when Chaucer took it up, but not the tale he told of the double sorrow of Troilus, prince of Troy, who suffered initially for love and eventually for its loss. The alternative world that intrudes upon Troilus and Criseyde is not a metaphysically possible world like the fairy kingdom in *Sir Orfeo,* but one epistemically possible, a world that might be, for all we know, the actual world of the fiction. Homer's *Iliad* was little known to Chaucer's England, but the "Matter of Troy" so familiarized the doom awaiting the city and the names of the major characters (except Criseyde) that Chaucer could assume an understanding of his more intimate tale against that background. There would seem to have been, however, little in the grim epic to suggest the use of this material for the romance tradition's close attention to subjectivity or recourse to alternative worlds.[1] Inspiration of that sort stems from medieval rather than ancient sources: Benoît de Sainte-Maure's *Le Roman de Troie* (1160), Guido de Colonne's Latin prose *Historia Trojana* (1287), and more immediately Boccaccio's *Filostrato* (1330s), though Chaucer's narrator defers to a Latin writer named Lollius, actually non-existent though lore had it otherwise.[2] Moreover, according to legend, Brutus, grandson of Aeneas, had founded Britain just as his grandfather had Rome, so the prestige of Troy was high in "Troynovant," Chaucer's London. The philosophical colouring of the poem, in both its directly quoted passages and its causal structurations, owes much to Boethius's *Consolation of Philosophy,* which Chaucer was translating as *Boece* while he was writing *Troilus and Criseyde.*[3]

Chaucer's long narrative poem provides an instance of time folded so that three old narrative shapes – the ancient war, the medieval lover's tale, and the Boethian allegory – come together in the artistic language of a Continental romance open to appropriation in the future.

Beauty

The subject of this chapter is the manner in which *Troilus and Criseyde* interlaces its intimate account of human experience with the typological predisposition of medieval art. Beauty, both Criseyde's beauty and the beauty of the poem, are caught up in the subtle twists of that interlace. At one end of the critical spectrum, the explicitly rendered perspective Troilus achieves from the eighth sphere at the end of the poem is said to transcend the seriousness of the lover's tragedy by framing it within the timeless realm of metaphysical reflection. At the other, the epilogue is simply a pious gesture akin to the *Retractions* at the end of the *Canterbury Tales.* We take neither position. Instead, we will treat the allegorical perspective of the epilogue as an epistemically possible world, one that might be true for all we know. Unlike Orfeo's journey into a metaphysically "other" *world,* incompossible with his own, Troilus among the spheres comes to see the Trojan world of his love and suffering as little and worthy of scorn, as "blind lust, the which that may nat last" (5.1824). Chaucer's early audiences would be accustomed to the idea (whether or not soberly convinced of it) that the next world will turn out to be the real one, and the material one just a testing ground. The Kantian vocabulary for this interpretive crux is that the fusion of the sensible, grasped through imagination, vies for prominence with the intelligible, cognized through reflection. The question is, in what sense is Criseyde's beauty (and that of the poem) captured – in terms of fictional realism, like a portrait or photograph energized by tiny detail, or like an overarching philosophical system that makes her into an emblem and the poem into a cautionary tale.

Criticism emphasizing the creaturely lives of Criseyde, Troilus, and Pandarus has often been represented as antithetical to the impulse to pursue the ethical/philosophical implications of their story. Chaucer's narrative ends up refusing to resolve the tension it has introduced between the intelligible fable fully commensurate with received Christian doctrine announced in the "epilogue" and the exciting love *aventure* presented as the tale unfolds. Theodor Adorno characterizes textual modernity (in his view, writing since *Don Quixote*) as "realistic in aesthetic terms" because the individual subject has been emancipated from medieval typology by the autonomy of art.[4] We are claiming that Chaucer's treatment of subjective experience can – indeed must – be discussed in terms of emancipated individuality (the mode of fictional realism), but will stress as well the burden of the past in non-ironic religious themes and imagery (available through allegory). The *energeia* of the poem arises from the tension between them.

The beauty of the poem and the woman at its centre is interpreted in contending, almost contradictory, ways, both within the text and among readers. Criseyde herself is described by the narrator as appearing "like a thing immortal … hevenyssh" sent down "in scornynge of nature," yet her beauty is "natif" to her (1.100–1). The fact that she is and is not "natif" – produced by nature in the usual manner – is what "astoned" Troilus in the temple; she seems to have appeared suddenly from afar rather than from within Troy (1.274–315). Sometimes modern readers also find the fictional image of Criseyde unusually attractive: E. Talbot Donaldson famously remarked that he and most men are in love with her, David Aers is moved by her "intelligence and generosity," and Carolyn Dinshaw's argument underlines why feminist critics of various stripes have admired her selfless and realistic assessment of her role in the fate of Troy.[5] An opposing school of thought associated with D.W. Robertson holds that the poem is beautiful, worthy of attention, "a great Christian tragedy" precisely when we come to see Criseyde herself as unworthy of being called beautiful.[6] Is Donaldson seduced by the image of Criseyde and the pleasure of the text, polluting the disinterestedness of both moral and aesthetic thought with "positively valorized sensual experience," as Paul de Man might have argued?[7] Is Robertson insulated from that seduction only to be so indebted to the patristic legacy that he is unable to engage imaginatively with the subjectivity of these fictional characters? Kant's *Third Critique* can help us understand why both camps (and virtually everyone else) find Troilus and Criseyde a beautiful poem.

The relatively simple tale of Troilus's winning Criseyde's love and her exile to the Greek encampment where she finds a new lover, is told with great nuance in remarkably formal verse: five books, four of which begin with "prohemes," and rhyme royal stanzas consisting of seven lines of rhymed iambic pentameter. Few critics have disagreed with Stephen Barney's assessment of the poem as the "most important English writing" between Beowulf and *The Faerie Queene* and the "most accomplished English narrative in design, ambition, and poetic craft" before *Paradise Lost*.[8] Aesthetic design, according to Kant, brings imagination and understanding into simultaneous activity through the distinctive form taken by its aesthetic idea. A Kantian perspective on the poem would find the positions that stress the pleasure of contemplating a well-presented love affair between attractive people merely gratifying rather than beautiful, while those who stress the moral lesson of the poem are judging its goodness, which is commensurate with a concept, rather than its beauty, which is not.[9] Beauty is claimed when the aesthetic design of an object "pleases through its form," locating form in a work's "shape [*Gestalt*] or play [*Spiel*]," both of which involve an immanent lawfulness unique to the particular text (*CPJ*, 110). It is important not to regard Kant's position in the *Third Critique* as the rule-bound "formalism" (in the pejorative sense) with which it is sometimes associated, since a rule for the shape of an achieved work of art cannot be deduced: "The purposiveness in its form must still seem to be as free from all constraint by arbitrary rules as if it were a product of nature."[10] Rather than pitting form against content (matter, substance), we regard the shape of a fiction not as the shape of something that existed previously and is merely being represented, but something created by and within the fiction itself.[11] To put it as Gadamer does, form results from the transformation of *energeia* into structure.[12] But what is that form?

Competing Perspectives: Tragic Romance or Divine Comedy

Leibniz writes that perspective is all-important.[13] Perspective requires vantage points, and two of the vantage points from which literary works are often explicated are those of genre and mode. The epilogue of *Troilus and Criseyde* (5.1786–1869) suggests the literary mode of allegory, and generic types are mentioned explicitly throughout the poem. Criseyde and Pandarus refer to their reading as romance, and the narrator mentions canticus, littera, geste, storie, tragedy, and comedy. Scholarly comment has added many more. Monica McAlpine's *The Genre of* Troilus and Criseyde raised the question in detail in 1978, and Barry Windeatt summarized the entwined generic possibilities as epic, romance, history, tragedy, drama, lyric, fabliau, and allegory in 1992.[14] Matthew Giancarlo, construing generic structures as accounts of causation, claims that the poem exhibits not one but "a sheer multitude" of genres from "astral determinism and divine intervention" to "agent causality" and many more.[15] This is not arcane overthinking, but the deployment of a critical tool for wrestling the details of the poem into coherence and determining the logic of its textual world. The poem is atypical (although not alone) among romance fictions for its sharply causal logic and explicitness about time and space, but for our purposes its generic shape, its family of resemblances in the Wittgensteinian sense, may be best examined in terms of tragic romance, an *aventure*, much of which is centred on subjectivities and intruded upon by an alternative world. Both the narrator, as early as the proheme to book 1, and the characters explicitly refer to a narrative *aventure*.[16] Tragic seriousness claimed early (the dedication to the Fury Tesiphone in the first stanza of book 1) and late ("Go, litel bok, go, litel myn tragedye" [5.1786]). While the controversy over the nature of *Troilus and Criseyde*'s beauty is largely a debate over its mode, an analysis of its genre contributes to the seriousness of the imaginative investment it requires as fictional realism.

The tragic form inherent in *Troilus and Criseyde* is an important aspect of its distinctive beauty. Chaucer's aesthetic idea here differs markedly from the definition of Boccaccio's *De casibus virorum illustrium*, offered by the Monk in the *Canterbury Tales* as "a certeyn storie … Of hym that stood in greet prosperitee / And is yfallen out of heigh degree / Into myserie, and endeth wrecchedly" told in hexameters or prose (7.1973–7). H.A. Kelly's exhaustive account of the use of the term "tragedy" before Chaucer uncovers a surprising lack of familiarity with it as designating a specific narrative shape in anything like the story arcs (broadly Aristotelian) that run from Sophocles to Shakespeare and beyond. Since Aristotle's observations in the *Poetics* were not available to him, Chaucer could not have planned his "bok" intending to follow them as rules.[17] Seen from this perspective, the tragedy of the lovers' story is congruent with that of the fall of Troy: the Trojan Antenor, a war prisoner of the Greeks, is welcomed back at the price of Criseyde's exile, only to become Troy's betrayer later.[18] The prolepsis involved in "For after he was traitour to the town" (4.204) exhibits a fold in the carefully delineated time scheme of the poem, an instance of the tragic irony embodied in the trajectory of its aesthetic idea.[19]

What the lovers do is enact the destruction of their most cherished hopes through actions the consequences of which are beyond their ken. The universe in which they do so may be coherent, but its coherence is not available to the human apperception of the characters while they live. After the parliament's decision to trade Criseyde for Antenor, Troilus considers both begging Priam to renege and abducting his lady from Troy. His deliberations point up his loyalty to Troy and respect for his father's rule, together with his unwillingness to "don so gret unright" as Paris did (4.547–67). Rather than error or sin, these thoughts reflect a selfless commitment to Troy itself. Even more important is Troilus's reluctance to do anything without Criseyde's consent: he would protect her honour at the cost of his life (4.567), and he would die rather than carry her off without her consent, despite Pandarus's assurances that she would get over her anger (4.637). These avowals of his protection of Criseyde and the mutuality of their love reprise Troilus's behaviour through the earlier books – his tentativeness in books 1, 2, and early in 3, and his overwhelming, grateful happiness when Criseyde confesses her love for him. For him to agree to abduct her in this crisis or connive politically would lessen the intensity of his story; this tragedy is what happens to *just such a person* as Troilus. A similar gesture of patriotism is offered by Criseyde: God forbid that you should act for the sake of a woman, she says, when "Troie hath now swich nede" (4.1556–8). The Criseyde of book 4 is fearful of public action, quick to protect *his* name, and eager to find a consoling remedy. There is even a Boethian twist to her attempt to outface Fortune through patient suffering and make a "vertu of necessite" (4.1584–9). Nor is this inconsistent with her earlier self: in book 2, she laments this world's loss of "feyth" and calls it "this false world" (410, 420), and in book 3, she shows her grasp of the instability of happiness (813–40).[20] We can no more say what the lovers should have thought or how they should have acted in book 4 than we can say whether and how Hamlet should have fenced with Laertes in act 5 of his tragedy. Tragic gravity eludes conceptualization, something beyond *our* ken that dooms human actors to destroy their happiness and/or compromise their integrity.

Troilus's integrity while he lived is largely intact, but Criseyde makes deep concessions to Fortune in book 5, in spite of her similarity to Troilus in book 4, when they both made principled decisions and deeply sworn promises. Once in the Greek camp, Criseyde finds herself without the resources she bravely promised – to outsmart her father and evade capture as she slips back into Troy – and time, which is so scrupulously noted by Troilus, slips though her hands "knotteles" (5.769), making her seem numbed and ethically "slydynge of corage" (5.825). Moreover, she knows it:

> On Tyme ypassed wel remembred me
> And present tyme ek koud ich wel ise,
> But future tyme, er I was in the snare
> Koude I nat sen; that causeth now my care. (5.746–9)

Her promises of fidelity were not deceitful or careless, but failures to imagine the "snare" that lay in wait for her.[21] Examined in the mode of fictional realism, her failure of resolve, albeit under very trying circumstances, does compromise her integrity, and her giving in to Diomede contrasts with Troilus's steadfastness. External forces can cause suffering, but in Boethian terms only the degradation of the soul is actually tragic.[22] Differently played out from Troilus's as her experience was, both of the lovers lose what book 3 has presented as a precious human good. Tragic art celebrates the value of individual human happiness – its sensible aspect reclaiming their rights to desire, presiding "at the festival of the moment," as Daniel Poirion puts it[23] – as well as the suffering involved in its loss. In the world of the text this loss is the final word, producing what Aristotle called fear and pity, rephrased by H.D. Kitto as "awe and understanding," bringing us closer to Kant's play of imagination and understanding.[24] Yet even so strong a tragic trajectory does not disqualify *Troilus and Criseyde* from consideration as romance. What it does is make Chaucer the first medieval English poet to construct his narrative house by combining the durable resources of romance with his deeply intuited grasp of tragic irony – a remarkable feat of generic engineering. In addition to its unflinching focus on an *aventure* subjectively rendered (as Marie's often were), the self-consistent logic of its creaturely world is colonized by an alternative world familiar to medieval culture.

With the epilogue, though, the tragedy of Troilus's earthly fall is represented as his elevation to the other world of the eighth sphere.[25] It is controversy over the mode of the poem, not its generic fusion of romance with tragedy, which has divided critical assessments of the beauty of *Troilus and Criseyde*. The term "mode" in literary analysis distinguishes between fictions that provide hypothetical worlds of historical and/or emotional impact – attention is on *what will happen* – and allegories in which characters and events obtain significance as ideas – *what it all means*. Romances take place, like all fictions, in a real world (though not the actual one we live in) with a self-consistent logic, but they are distinctive among fictional forms in that an otherworld may appear inside them. Instead of a metaphysically other fairy realm turning up in Winchester as it does in *Sir Orfeo*, the literary mode of *Troilus and Criseyde* moves from its fictionally realistic plot to an epistemically possible account of the same events.[26]

For Leibniz, non-actual possible worlds are real in that they exist in the mind of God to be discovered by poets; for moderns, they are, as

Lobomír Doležel puts it, "*coherent cosmologies* derived from some axioms or presuppositions."[27] Each possible world is subject to the law of non-contradiction within its precincts, and the fuller its details the more inviting it is to the imagination. No fiction, of course, can offer a *complete* account of itself any more than any specific account of the actual world can. Marie-Laure Ryan argues that possible worlds can be arranged in terms of their "accessibility" – greater congruence with the actual world produces, for example, "realistic historical fiction," which may have been the way *Troilus and Criseyde* was received by its first audiences. For us it may seem closer to "historical fabulation," since the historicity of the Trojan War faded towards legend with advancing modernity.[28] Allegory does not appear on Ryan's chart of "accessibility relations" because she regards it as a thematic rather than a fully fictional mode: the characters are abstract, she writes, and cannot be expected to create "human density," since the focus is on the play of concepts.[29] The epilogue (as well as many subtler clues) place *Troilus and Criseyde* modally as an allegory of salvation history, a "divine comedy." Gadamerian recursiveness is involved in reading or hearing any long text, but this poem requires surprising shifts in levels of abstraction.[30] We will call the mode of the poem "fictional realism" when it is experienced as following Troilus and Criseyde's fortunes from moment to moment; but allegory when its seductive linear plot is dissolved by its emergence into the "realm of stillness and silence … of eternal ideas and the universe of discourse of classical logic."[31]

Fictional Realism as Possible World: "The Immense Subtlety of Things"

As congruent as the plot of *Troilus and Criseyde* might seem to the familiar medieval patterns of betrayal by false felicity, any complete intellectual capture of it is bound to feel like a starved version of the poem. In the first place, a formal allegory is identified by the difficulty of reading it as reference to human experience; it ought to display notable incoherences on the narrative level. Romance narrative like Chrétien's *Lancelot, Sir Orfeo,* and *Sir Gawain and the Green Knight* invite allegorical readings by their intrusions of magical or mythical elements. But *Troilus and Criseyde* establishes a world with events and characters familiar to Chaucer's original audiences and to us through the Troy story tradition, and keeps their religious aura, for the most part, clear of anachronism until the very end. Since much historical and practical discourse was presented in poetic form in the Middle Ages, *Troilus and Criseyde* may have seemed to some in its early audiences to be a partial chronicle of events in the Trojan War. Moreover, Chaucer represents his characters from the ancient world in the likeness of fourteenth-century aristocrats in the manner of a palimpsest: his telling involves both the distance due his Trojan setting and an intimacy with his own readers' culture. No need to seek allegorical significance when one is "learning about" the history of Troy in an idiom one can recognize.

Still more important, Chaucer maintains a delicate, but firm, causal chain readable in terms of human designs and everyday contingency throughout. In book 1, Troilus may be extreme in throwing himself around his room before he has even spoken to Criseyde, but his outburst is perfectly readable as the excessiveness required by medieval love-lore, and Criseyde's wary response to Pandarus's meddling-helpful streak in book 2 is altogether convincing in a more quotidian style. The timing of Antenor's exchange with Calkas's belated summons of Criseyde and the parliament's finding it a good bargain fall within bounds of "what may happen," as Aristotle would say. In terms of both the arc of the characters' desires and in the external events they suffer, the narrative line is thick with probability. No assumption of allegory need be called on to explain it. Moreover, the plot line is itself so highly coloured and engrossing that, as Jill Mann puts it, the narrator's early warning of an unhappy ending "fades from the reader's consciousness in the moment-by-moment excitements of the love affair."[32] The excitements result from the *energeia* of "vivid, sensuous" word-pictures addressed to imagination, bringing the scene to seem like life itself. If allegory is capture by the lure of sequential thought, perhaps fictional realism is capture by the lure of virtual experience.

Writing about medieval vernacular texts, often romances, Daniel Poirion defends the "rights" of the senses to enjoy the "pleasure of forms": "The senses, reclaiming their rights to desire, preside at the festival of the moment, at the rehabilitation of the beautiful, at the realization in which, within the confines of a single life or of human history, what defines mortal man is the affirmation of the value of the apparent, ephemeral, even imaginary things."[33]

"Even imaginary things!" Hamlet wonders how the First Player can weep for Hecuba, a mere "fiction" (2.2.529), but he answers his own question by designing the mousetrap, arousing both his own senses and Claudius's. Poirion's striking claim on behalf of the senses (and the sensible) is all the stronger because his project is to see allegorical significance in medieval narrative. He does so, however, without finding that significance to be stable or theologically determined, in spite of theology's ubiquity in medieval culture. Modal logic could see this as "centred" perception – I am here, smelling the flowers – every tiny detail contributing to the apperception of the whole.[34]

In fact, it might be claimed that the lovers' story is so richly detailed that it occludes any underlying argument that threatens to explain it. This is particularly true in book 2, which rehearses every movement, glance, sigh, and blush, as Pandarus tells Criseyde of Troilus's regard. This long sequence (from line 78 to 1302) is nearly all presented dramatically, with only the barest intrusion by the narrator.[35] Although in general medieval vocabularies for representing subjectivity are somewhat different from our own,[36] in this case the difference is scarcely noticeable; Criseyde's emotional life especially is keenly felt. Robert Solomon describes emotions as *"subjective engagements in the world,"* sometimes manifesting physiological results like blushing and fainting, but involved as well with underlying cognitive dimensions – perceptions, memories, and judgments (although not necessarily articulate or self-conscious ones). Emotion is a complex of judgments "*grappling* with the world" (italics in original).[37] Reading Criseyde's inner life from Solomon's standpoint allows us to claim access to the subtlety of her characterization as the story unfolds. We are as close to what is going on in Criseyde's mind as fictions can bring us.

The remarkable closeness to "real time" in book 2 is matched by Troilus's inner debate over predestination in book 4, which again is so detailed and explicit that readers are compelled to follow Troilus's emotionally heated intellectual struggles as he rehearses them. His penchant for seeking "distant, final, absolute causes," as Stephen Barney puts it,[38] complicates his characterization, which in book 1 seemed almost monolithically rash, impatient, and easily led by Pandarus – he matured as a result of his committed love. His dogged work on the contradiction between free will and determinism invites admiration for and empathy with him. The fact that he cannot "solve" the problem is a reminder he, being a pagan, cannot satisfy his quest with the Christian stoicism which medieval thought had attributed to Boethius's *Consolation*. (For modern readers, uncertain about how thoroughly Christianized Boethius's classical line of thought actually is, this dilemma is further enabled by the implication that a serious Trojan thinker might intuit it.) Criseyde is also an aspiring Boethian, properly suspicious of Fortune throughout the poem. The allegorical counters echoing

Boece appear *within* the narrative of the lovers' consideration of their life-world and its uncertainties. Both of them are "grappling with the world" intellectually as well as emotionally.

This complex style of characterization may be seen to prevent their capture as signs, like truth for Troilus and falsehood for Criseyde. Both are victims of a particularly precipitous turn of Fortune's wheel, each bringing different resources to the crisis. Her actions in book 5 are of course seriously blameworthy with respect to love-loyalty, especially in giving Diomede the brooch, but her reluctance to elope can be seen as acknowledgment of her duties to Troy, in keeping one of its warrior prince's engaged in the war, as Carolyn Dinshaw has argued.[39] And Troilus's much-praised integrity and courtliness are sullied by his offer to procure his sisters for Pandarus "to han for thyn" (3.413), a passage that marks an ugly contrast with Hector's "We usen here no wommen for to selle" (4.182). As a result, the poetry is so managed as to ask the reader for complex and sometimes conflicted responses. Even when Troilus has ascended (the reward for his integrity as is often claimed)[40] and repudiated the excitements and reversals of the world below, the poem cannot extinguish the afterglow of the lovers' conflicts and ecstasies, and their bewilderment in the face of their loss.

Poetry is especially well suited to producing the allusiveness and nuance that Leibniz implies by his looking-into-the-pond metaphor. Narrative sweep and complex characterizations contribute to the way the poem eludes the stasis of an allegorical concept, and the formal coherence of its figures and rhythms are just as complex and just as demanding of reflection. The capture imagery that gestures towards didactic propositions (to be discussed in later sections) is invested with varying degrees of depth and irony, more conducive to wariness than certainty. Under the surface of the pond innumerable details (images, phrasings, word choices) may be seen in relation to each other and to the whole, undergirding larger apperceptions without arresting the flow of meaning in a concept.[41] When the poem is seen as moving from human perceptions, at first confused but gradually taking on clarity – rather than developments in a choreography laid out by Providence – time and event are seen to be folded in this complex way.

Chaucer's poem gestures towards the foldedness of insensible perceptions in reporting that Criseyde "plited she ful ofte in many a fold" the details of Pandarus's disclosure (2.697), perhaps signalling the importance of tiny perceptions, even single words, for readers. The word "devise" is an example among many. In "wher hastow woned / That art so feyr and goodly to devise?" (1.276–7), Troilus seems to mean just "how come I haven't noticed such a good-looking woman before," but his glance soon seems to involve a "devising" closer to a sense of "formulating a plan about." Devise is often used to mean write (2.1063), recount (3.235, 1677, and 1689), or conjecture (3.435), but sometimes suggests active arranging (3.336). The parliamentary debate over the exchange is heard by Troilus's "spradde" ears as "this thing devysen to and fro" (4.1423) and later Criseyde considers eloping "as ye devyse" (4.1529).[42] These instances in book 4 stress manoeuvring over plain looking.

"Queynte" with its three-way pun, "quenched," "clever," and "cunt" is an obvious source of enjoyable wit in the *Canterbury Tales,* but it turns up at moments of painful reflection in this poem: Troilus's love song when he examines his tormented longing as "O swete harm so queynte" (4.1629), when Criseyde thinks she can outbid her father's "queynte pley" and when Troilus sees Criseyde's empty palace as a "lanterne of which queynt is the light" (5.543). The first two of these examples seem to foreground "intricate cleverness" with just a whiff of the sexy, and the third, denotatively "quenched," carries an erotic charge as well, though hardly the crude one Robertson claims.[43] The sheer volume and complexity of such tiny detail is one of Chaucer's gifts to the literary tradition, and to English culture generally. Attention to poetry with a structure of feeling like that imaged in *Troilus and Criseyde* arises from and nourishes a nuanced style of inwardness combining feeling and understanding usually before it is acknowledged socially.[44] For Leibniz these tiny details are not noticed separately, but taken in like the sound of an individual wave before it joins with others to become the roaring surf.

Concepts are clearly important to this poem, especially those concerned with time and causality; the issue is one of perspective – what such concepts are *seen as*. Criseyde's mood is sobered by her reading of the siege of Thebes and frightened by what her betrayal will mean to the world in the future. Calkas and Cassandra apparently read the future, and Troilus ponders the relation between human time and timelessness. These may be seen as the worries of fictionally situated persons. The same could be said of those instances when the narrator's voice raises philosophical issues, often in terms very close to those Chaucer had used in his *Boece*. Chaucer's poem depicts realistically conceived characters who think seriously (Shakespeare and Dostoyevsky, among many other writers, do this too), so the mere fact of the prominence of their ideas does not necessarily tilt the poem towards allegory. We argue that it deepens our interest in their human dilemmas.

The case for fictional realism, then, is based on the poem's plausible accounts of time and space, its anchors in the matter of Troy, told through medieval narrative conventions, the density of its details, and the resonance of the lovers' grapplings with reality. All of this produces so much *energeia* for the unfolding plot that no further layering of significance seems necessary. Regarded as fictional realism, *Troilus and Criseyde* demands serious attention for its intricate web of personal motives and historical turns, which ends up involving the lovers' own actions in the destruction of what they value most. The poem seen from this perspective is a fully realized tragedy. Yet even that description does not capture the emotional and intellectual intensity the poem elicits. A better account would recognize the oscillation of its realistic mode with a hovering, and at the end an explicit, tendency towards allegory that also contributes to its aesthetic effects.[45]

Allegory: Immense Subtlety Captured by Concept

Regarding the epilogue (5.1786–1869) as the conclusive authorial word serves retrospectively to make the poem available as something like a narrativized argument – an allegory. Criseyde becomes a figure for the idea of ephemeral earthly beauty; Troilus ascended sees his struggles to win and protect his lover as "blynde lust" (5.1824) attached to this "wrecched world" (5.1817). His sorrows are admonitory and addressed to "yonge fresshe folkes" (5.1835) in all eras. This move is not unprepared for: many features of the poem point to the looming allegory that threatens to catch the characters in its strong toils: Criseyde the faithless, Troilus the True, and Pandarus, well ... However subtle and extended the details, in this light they settle into a coherent allegorical pattern. There is, of course, such a thing as a beautiful argument, but it is a different thing from a beautiful poem or a beautiful heroine. The alternative world of *Troilus and Criseyde* is not a Greek or Celtic otherworld, but an alternative reading of what is at stake: the time-bound world of human affairs or the world of changeless ideas. C.S. Lewis and Northrop Frye offer very broad accounts of allegory, connecting it with reflection in general.[46] Appealing as these positions are, Gordon Teskey's analysis in *Allegory and Violence*[47] provides a more sharply focused lens for examining *Troilus and Criseyde.*

In *Allegory and Violence*, Teskey defines allegory as an analogy between two things, both complex, but one weightier than the other (*AV*, 2). If we regard *Troilus and Criseyde* as an allegory, the story of the lovers, intricate as it is, points to a larger truth for which the lovers serve as an instance. They become signs, indeed signposts, for "yonge fresshe folkes" towards the "pleyn felicite / That is in hevene above" (5.1818–19), Criseyde a sign for the temptations of this unstable world, Troilus a sign for sought-after integrity entangled in a misaligned loyalty. Regarded thus, Criseyde's appealing beauty, modesty, and vulnerability stand for *this* world of deceptive (especially ethically deceptive) appearances, which are ultimately traps for an aspirant to the *other*, eternal world. Teskey points out that fully allegorical forms contain instructions for interpreting them (*AV*, 3), and both Criseyde's prediction that her name will be "rolled … on many a tonge" (5.1061) and the epilogue set in the eighth sphere can justifiably be thought of as that kind of instruction.[48] Such "true allegory" may be distinguished from what Maureen Quilligan calls allegoresis: interpretation that moves literal narrative to a more abstract plane.[49] The Middle Ages committed allegoresis all the time, especially in reading the ancients (e.g., *Ovid Moralisé* and all its kin), and we think we ought to do it on their behalf, an unwarranted "presumptive historicism" as Maura Nolan puts it.[50]

Teskey's most apposite instance of a full allegory in Chaucer's intellectual milieu is his discussion of Francesca di Rimini as presented in canto 5 of Dante's *Inferno*. Francesca is "captured in order to act as a sign"; her story and its meaning managed to point to a "single, invisible truth" (*AV*, 6). It is a violent capture of the complexity and disorder of a real, though fictionalized, life by a system of ideas – an interruption of "the natural desire of things for their homes" (*AV*, 9). Generations of readers have struggled to find a reliable ground (formal shape, authorial intention, references to previous tellings, medieval moral imperatives) for the conflicting sympathy and censure around Francesca's image, but Teskey argues that Dante *reveals* his modus operandi: the violence of his move in displaying so delicate a love as a figure for blameworthy lust, thereby inviting the hermeneutic discomfort canto 5 has elicited over the centuries. Throughout the *Commedia*, Dante both deliberately blurred personal subjectivity, reducing the disordered complexity of narrative "to the violence of controllable thought," and called attention to what he was up to (*AV*, 24). Dante is clearly working in an allegorical mode, to which Chaucer's approach can be compared and from which it can be distinguished. More to the point is that Boethius gave away his modus operandi in that the author himself is allegorized as Lady Philosophy, who in turn ventriloquizes Fortune, using the philosophical and rhetorical resources that can be marshalled in narrative to control the debate.[51]

Medieval allegorical practice has a gendered aura about it, as Teskey writes: "Matter must be ravished by Form before being converted and returned to the Father" (*AV*, 18–19). Matter is female, of course, the raw material of the physical and biological world that must be impregnated by male organizing Reason (Form) in order to belong to the fully human domain.[52] Francesca's womanhood thus makes her a doubly apt figure for the "Matter" thus tamed (and note the aggressiveness of Teskey's term "ravished"). Allegory like Dante's presents an extreme case in which understanding – mental ordering – appears to reconcile the waywardness of detailed narrative. In Teskey's formulation, structures of meaning – he calls them "illusions of order" (*AV*, 19) – give pleasure by reducing complexity to familiar ideas (*AV*, 17), but narrative itself resists by creating "a background of resonant noise" (*AV*, 23). Such allegories, he argues, allow their oscillation "between a project of reference (which we have called fictional realism) and a project of capture" to reveal itself (*AV*, 8).

Chaucer's poem, of course, treats the lovers' situation in much greater detail than canto 5 of the *Inferno*, which allows greater scope for the complications of "resonant noise." Further, his tale belongs to both Troilus and Criseyde, who embark on their affair in different states of mind. The protagonists are shown puzzling over epistemological and ethical problems both in dialogue and in their private thoughts. Troilus speaks a more obviously Boethian language in book 4, but Criseyde shows considerable depth of thought especially in her analysis of time and prediction in book 5, which can be seen as a counterpoint to Troilus on predestination.[53] Haunting both passages is book 11 of Augustine's *Confessions*. The very fact that both hero and heroine, while involved in creaturely desire, try to understand their larger duties marks a difference from Dante's telling. Nonetheless, it is easy to see a clear parallel between Dante's handling of Francesca's story and Chaucer's handling of Criseyde's. Chaucer's narrator can be seen as the counterpart to the pilgrim Dante, both of them troubled by the harsh aftermath of passion. Dante faints, and Chaucer's narrator refuses to say ("men say, I not") that Criseyde gave Diomede her heart – both are reluctant to impugn the romance genre.[54]

Teskey claims that Dante *reveals* his allegorical strategy in canto 5, and a similar claim might be made for *Troilus and Criseyde*: Chaucer invites the reader's shocked disbelief that he is turning his back on the pathos and dignity of his story by making his characters into signs. These last lines of the poem (5.1821–69) may thereby reveal the violence of taming experience – even intricately wrought imaginative experience – by means of philosophy. Our claim is that the fascination of the poem lies in just this narrative design, which has inspired both aesthetic wonder and hermeneutic zeal. The experience of the poem entwines the vivid thoughts and actions of the lovers with conceptions addressed to understanding a world larger than theirs. The Troy of the realistic historical fiction contains – or is it contained by? – the timeless possible world of allegory.

The end of book 5 completes and announces the capture of the figure of Criseyde as seductive, unstable earthly joy (ironically, the very instability she had predicted and feared). The tragic, time-bound shape of the "litel bok" is followed by the comic shape of serene philosophical changelessness, stillness, and silence. Generations of critics have seen a convincing allegory that features Criseyde as Lady Fortune, as Dame Nature, or as Eve. Such readings show the "capture" of Criseyde, Troilus ("the True"), and Pandarus (priest of Satan), by a "will-to-power that subjects *physis* or growth to a knowledge it already has" (*AV*, 17). Any narrative resists this will-to-power by involving readers in its hypothetical world, making that world look authentic in some way; in romances the authenticity is often emotional, but even *exempla* add elements hard to tuck neatly into the lesson they purport to teach.[55] The turn towards allegory in *Troilus and Criseyde* marks the intrusion of a world in harsh tension with the realism of its slowly evolving love story; only from the eighth sphere could the tale look like Troilus's seduction by a mere illusion of happiness. A single sequence of events, therefore, tells two very different stories, as Chaucer handles the bare bones of his inherited plot (coyly called Lollius's work) by introducing details that complicate it at every turn, creating what Teskey calls "a background of resonant noise" (*AV*, 23), and Marie, a *surplus de sen*.

The Capture Imagery

Capture, the very heart of the allegorical project, appears directly in *Troilus and Criseyde* as both a thematic strand of the plot (the capture of Antenor, Criseyde, and for that matter Helen) and a series of striking metaphors. The level of imagery, then, is marked by a self-reflectiveness hard to ignore. The concentration of images of capture throughout the poem points to its importance as a lens that focuses the action, tempting instructions for reading a Boethian allegory as the structural principle of the poem. Yet these pervasive images of capture do not coalesce – or not without wrenching – into a stabilizing hierarchy of value within the poem or show which of the characters deserve approbation or how we are to regard the coerciveness of creaturely love as the narrative develops. They function to allow reflection on the very problem of how this narrative is to be read. The tone of this imagery is varied from one instance to the next, and often hard to pinpoint within a given passage. Those concerning Troilus and Criseyde themselves are playful, even funny, yet also entirely serious – serious in that they mitigate any willful hedonism we might feel towards the lovers' affair (and do feel at times in Boccaccio's *Il Filostrato*) and gesture towards the irresistibility of love as a cosmic, but always situated, force.

In book 1, the God of Love himself demonstrates his potency to punish Troilus's "surquidrie" [pride] by forcing the king's son down the chain of being to the state of Bayard caught in the trays (218–24). This metaphor folds together a mix too rich for conceptual summary; it is simultaneously a humorous comeuppance, a reminder that we are considering a pre-Christian tale, and a somewhat distorted echo of Chaucer's brilliant translation of the power of love in *Boece* 2, metrum 8 (love that constrains the sea "greedy to flowen" and prevents a general chaos). This last, even glancingly registered, suggests that a pattern of thought – an *allegory* of love, positively inflected – might be in the offing. The liming of his feathers (now he's a hunted bird, where earlier he was a peacock) further underlines his lack of agency in an even homelier tone. Book 1 is focused on Troilus's capture by love, imaged as natural, inevitable, disorienting, but ultimately protective of life. Stephen Barney has examined Troilus's constraints throughout the poem in his "Troilus Bound," emphasizing the range of Chaucer's contributions to his sources.[56]

Book 2 shifts the scene to Criseyde and associates the capture imagery with her rather than Fortune or Nature. Pandarus congratulates Criseyde on her successful catch "withouten net" (583, 328). These metaphors display Pandarus's rhetorical powers, since he is wielding a net to catch *her* imagination. As descriptions of Criseyde's motives, they work as pure irony, in that she has had no plan to catch Troilus and no knowledge of his having seen her. Yet there is a connection between this and the chilling passage in the Ancrene Reule in which women are always to blame for male desire, based on a passage from Deuteronomy in which the digger of a pit is liable for injury to any animal that falls in. The fact that it is a medieval commonplace (stressed in 328) that women trap "gilteles" men into their snares underlines Pandarus's shallow proverb-wielding style. So again, funny and clever as Pandarus's metaphor is, there is just a whiff of a contemplative sense in it that medieval readers might have seen more readily than we do now.

Book 3, though, shows Troilus, after his comical fainting spell when he is brought to Criseyde's presence, being figured as a sparrow hawk catching a lark, though it hardly describes his bedroom behaviour to refer to his lady as "caught" (1191–1207). In fact, at this point both lovers seem to have been captured by Pandarus. Criseyde must reassure him even at this point, which has been read alternatively as her "knowingness" or as her generous "pity" in medieval tradition of love lore. Troilus certainly has not been the predatory male, but later in the bedroom scene he imagines himself caught, bound, by Criseyde's eyes, which are figured as "humble nettes" (1355), perhaps humble in reference to the modesty of her glance in the temple when he first saw her. Later still, Troilus finds himself so bound in Criseyde's "net" that he cannot and does not wish to free himself (1730–6). These passages seem tender and positive, suggesting a value different from Pandarus's coarse banter in book 2, although he is still leading both lovers "by the lappe" (59, 742), which stresses his manipulation of the scene by depicting him taking hold of the young people's clothes.

The humorous irony of these images does not entirely occlude the questions of causation, determining conditions, and agency among the characters, not to mention cosmic forces, and therefore leads directly to Troilus's anguished musings on predestination in book 4. Troilus's return to the temple to ponder these question in the abstract is, therefore, no mere digression for the rhetorical purpose of *amplificatio*, but follows from his "estate royal" as a rational, contemplative thinker driven to consider felt problems in terms of abstract principles. He sees his experience as part of a larger picture, although (like the rest of us) he cannot reconcile his freedom with it.[57] Late in book 4, Criseyde plans to capture Calkas "withouten net" for her escape from the Greek camp (1373), exactly repeating Pandarus's phrase in book 2 and, as it happens, overestimating her powers. The fishing-net image recurs yet again in Diomede's plot to catch Criseyde, "To fisshen her he leyde out hook and lyne" (5.777), this time more chilling than amusing. Here the constraint that had been figured as a cosmic force is repeated in a more ominous tone, suggesting that what feels like a spontaneous giving of one's heart (5.1050) is the result of a planned campaign by a predatory human. This sequence produces an important semantic "fold" internal to the poem. The immediate contrast is between Troilus's figure as a hawk catching Criseyde in his talons, and Diomede literally clutching the reigns of her horse. In book 5, Criseyde is literally captured, both by her internment in the Greek camp and by her own inability to see the "snare" futurity had set (5.746), and Pandarus's fishing metaphors in book 2 are reversed. She is the "fished for," but the irony by this time has a bitter and ominous taste.

What we are arguing here is that the rhythm of this strand of imagery in *Troilus and Criseyde* has two kinds of effects. It both involves readers as imaginers of a specific, heightened fictional world, attractive and scary, and sets in motion a desire for contemplative grasp of weightier stakes concerning the relation between the desires of individual agents and the governance of the cosmos (in this poem sometimes figured as Olympic deities like Eros shooting Troilus or Apollo revealing the fall of the city to Calkas, but shaded by Christian thought too). Here several characters voice this dilemma openly, particularly Troilus in book 4 and Criseyde in book 5. It would be an easy leap to organize these images of capture along the lines laid out by Teskey. From the beginning Criseyde has been imaged (often ironically) as a captor, a seducer of guiltless men, and therefore a figure for the enticements of the sublunary world. Allegorical capture of the enchanting heroine as a type of Eve aligns her story with "a knowledge it [the medieval world] already has" (*AV*, 17). In the end she is literally a prisoner of war, unable to return to her doomed native city, and her capture by her father and then Diomede gestures towards the chaos of the coming apocalypse for Troy, completing the fable.

Such a judgment sweeps up the investment readers' imaginations have made in the "real lives" of the characters. No doubt allegories can be beautiful, but that is not what we first ask of them: we first want them to be *right*, to offer a moral imperative conclusively, to provide, as Teskey writes, "the satisfying pleasure [of] observing the subjection of the uncontrollable to the violence of controllable thought" (*AV*, 24). This form of pleasure is exactly what Robertson argues for in the *Preface to Chaucer*, from his study of the Fathers of the Church. Some medieval allegories *are* right. The Pardoner's allegory of the three rioters and their search for a wight named Death answers this description perfectly, and his fable is peopled with protagonists mistaken about the literal. Its "resonant noise" is intriguing, but not disruptive of the principle that *radix malorum est cupiditas.* There is a similar clarity in

Gottfried's handling of the story of the two "shifts" Brangane tells the woodsmen in his version of *Tristan.* Isolde has instructed them to kill her, but Brangane's allegory serves the purpose of saving her life by hiding one of its meanings from the woodsmen, but revealing it to Isolde. This instance is particularly close to Augustine's account of scriptural figures, for which alert interpretive work is requisite, and there are "insiders" and "outsiders."[58] But the scale of these instances is small; the more extended the narrative, the harder it becomes to counterbalance the noise with figures that exactly match their "weightier" implications. Even Angus Fletcher's magisterial *Allegory: Theory of a Symbolic Mode* stresses that allegory never quite fulfills its grand design.[59]

The Folds Forward: Criseyde's Future

In *Troilus and Criseyde* the characters themselves, especially Criseyde, think about time. Trapped in the Greek camp, she regrets her inability to accurately imagine the future: "future tyme, er I was in the snare / Koude I nat sen" (5.748–9).

Her word "future" in this passage is its first recorded occurrence in English, and we will use it in order to examine the future of Chaucer's narrative. It is hardly a new idea that Chaucer's work as a whole influenced the course of English writing in matters like semantics, syntax, and versification, and nudged causal plotting towards novelistic forms. *Troilus and Criseyde* has been read that way as early as G.L. Kittredge, who called it our "first novel" and Albert Baugh, who wrote that "the term psychological novel is both justified and illuminating."[60] More recently, Winthrop Wetherbee has asserted that we know the characters of the poem "as well as literary characters can be known," making Chaucer's presentation of inner life look similar to Proust's.[61] The poem's strong causal structure, attention to subjectivities, and Janus-faced imagery may be seen as a hinge between medieval romance and the pre-emergent novel, and the way its attention flits among the love story, its epic setting, and contemplative thought looks towards a realism more like Tolstoy's or Dostoyevsky's. The appropriations of its plot over the next two hundred years, however, do not replicate this move towards fictional realism. Nonetheless, placing Henryson and Shakespeare's retellings of the broad incidents of the tale beside Chaucer's version provides a "a relationship of mutual semantic illumination,"[62] pointing in particular to the features of Chaucer's text that propel it towards the literary future.

As the first sustained tragedy in the English vernacular, *Troilus and Criseyde* bequeathed the "instinctive" sense of tragic form to early modern dramatists,[63] as well as to later prose narratives like *Anna Karenina*. Chaucer's present seems in this way, as in many others, to be "pregnant with the future."[64] This Leibnizian phrasing implies that the welter of tiny imperceptibles that make up conscious perceptions register over time in reflective apperceptions, although not predictably. According to Raymond Williams, literature organizes scarcely recognizable social perceptions and names them, describing literary "emergence" in terms close to those of the philosophers' "novel emergent."[65] To take this view of *Troilus and Criseyde*, we must posit "modern" social inklings Chaucer could take advantage of, in spite of the formality of his poetic narrative. This is why we can expect to go on arguing about textual creatures like Anna and Criseyde, even though we are all reading the same texts – they are *present* to us, commanding attention in our own lived time. Other writers take up the story; they want to replicate an aesthetically felt presence.

In the next two centuries *Troilus and Criseyde* inspired new fictions, most notably Robert Henryson's poetic "continuation," *The Testament of Cresseid* (1492), and Shakespeare's *Troilus and Cressida* (1601–2). Henryson takes up the story of Criseyde (Cresseid) in the Greek camp when, oddly, Troilus could casually pass through Greek-held territory. Cresseid's characterization is drastically simplified as lustful and shallow.[66] When Diomede "had all his appetyt," he found another and "excludit [Cresseid] fra his company" / Than desolait sho walkit up and doun, / And, sum men sayis, into the court common" (352–3). She curses her patron Venus, and for this offence is punished with a leprous disfigurement of her lovely body. As he rides past a leper colony, Cresseid's image flits through Prince Troilus's mind, although he does not fully recognize her, and tosses alms in the form of gold and jewels into her skirt. The only empathy she is accorded after her betrayal turns up when she shares these alms with the others in her colony and faints when she learns it was Troilus who gave them. Henryson's poem reads like a cautionary parable, although not one about avoiding human love in favour of celestial calm; the "modernity" of Chaucer's telling is in all ways absent. He calls his poem a "tragedie," and it is close to Boccaccio's *de casibus* texts, but very far from Chaucer's tragic narrative.

The most famous fold forward is of course Shakespeare's *Troilus and Cressida*, which, though based on Chaucer's poem, changes it by including a stronger focus on the war and drastically altering its tone. When Shakespeare's Troilus expresses his anguished disbelief in his lady's assignation with Diomedes, he says, "This is and is not Cressid" (5.2.146).[67] Readers of both Chaucer's poem and Shakespeare's play might say the same thing: Cressida makes a vow and breaks it, just as Criseyde did, but the character herself is so thoroughly transformed in the play that it is difficult to see a full-blooded kinship between Criseyde's "slyding corage" and Cressida's canny flirtatiousness.

Troilus and Criseyde is clearly the major source of Shakespeare's plot, though Henryson's poem was probably known as well, since it was included in Thynne's edition of Chaucer's works (1542).[68] Shakespeare devotes a scene or two to each book of *Troilus and Criseyde*, and the poem apparently influenced his language as well, in that the dialogue of the play is "more explicitly philosophical than is usual" for him, as Anthony B. Dawson puts it.[69] Yet the play takes place in a completely different world with its own internal logic. The play has been considered under various generic labels from the first: it appears as a history in the Stationers' Register of 1609, an accompanying epistle refers to it as a comedy, and the Folio at first set it among the tragedies and later between the histories and tragedies, calling it "The Tragedy of Troilus and Cressida"; the current Norton edition includes it in the comedies volume. It fits into none of these generic categories comfortably, but it is particularly ill suited as either romance or tragedy. Linda Charnes called it "arguably the most 'neurotic'" of Shakespeare's plays; Heather James "a totality menaced by its parts."[70]

The dignity of Chaucer's lovers is enhanced by the widespread medieval elevation of the matter of Troy, but the sordidness of *Troilus and Cressida*'s imagined world undercuts that elevation, perhaps speaking to social understandings in seventeenth-century England (as Williams might argue). Its "philosophical" dialogue is often arcane or belied by events as soon as stated. Even Ulysses's seemingly Boethian speech on order is reduced to conniving (though ringing) political rhetoric. Many of the play's other named characters appear in both Homer and Chaucer, but none of them match their literary ancestors very closely. Hector is killed in a way that undercuts the idealism attributed to him in earlier versions of the story. And of course Thersites, the ever-present commentator, is new to the cast of characters. The early-seventeenth-century English penchant for satiric treatments of formerly sacred cows (like Nashe's scathing "Madame Troynovant") offers, according to Heather James, a topical explanation for the general debunking that "strips the Troy legend of its authority."[71] Whatever reasons might be given, the play empties out both empathy for the characters that romance normally calls up and metaphysical angst that accompanies the tragic loss of a genuine good.

The contrast between play and poem may be framed in terms of modal logic's take on intertextuality – "mutual semantic illumination" – by allowing each text to comment on others that share significant features.[72] Troilus's idealization of Cressida and imagined transcendence of time and experience (3.2.138–50) resemble that of his Chaucerian counterpart, although his adoration is given less weight in the play because it is immediately gratified, but Cressida shares far less with Criseyde. One of the most obvious features of Criseyde's characterization is its depth of inner life. But *Troilus and Cressida* is less attuned to inner lives than most of Shakespeare's plays – especially those masterpieces of inwardness *Hamlet* and *Othello.* Clearly, Shakespeare devotes more of his play to the war and less to the lovers than does his source: the lines and scenes in which the principals appear is only 33 per cent of the play. Moreover, the war is related to the lovers' inner lives largely by analogy (both are sullied), rather than being causally connected, as with Criseyde's fear and vulnerability (she was the "fearfulest wight" alive [2.450]). Criseyde is hard to win, rather than hard to seem won like Cressida (3.2.97), and close to suicide when the parliament traded her to the Greeks. When Ulysses remarks that Cressida's "wanton spirits look out / At every joint and motive of her body," and places her among the "daughters of the game" (4.5.56–7, 64), he seems justified by her participation in the "kissing game." This banter and her almost desperate appeal to Diomedes in 5.2 are far closer to Henryson's report that it is said she walked in "the court common" after Diomede spurned her than it is to the nervous distraction of Criseyde, who let time slip through her hands "knottles" (5.759). No sympathetic narrator explains Cressida's emotional distress; Thersites accounts for everyone in his insistence on the "botchy core" of everything. We see little of Cressida's grappling with the world, and Criseyde's patriotic regard for Troy's fortunes never enters the picture.

One particularly Chaucerian verbal echo in the play is the lovers' solemn oath witnessed by Pandarus. The prophecy echoes Criseyde's fear that she will be rolled on many a tongue throughout the world (5.1061). Cressida's promise is phrased in an "if I be false" form that will echo in history: "When time is old and hath forgot itself / When waterdrops have worn the stones of Troy … Let them say 'False as Cressid'" (3.2.185–6, 196). The stakes are very high: Pandarus summarizes the "bargain" with "Let all constant men be Troiluses, all false women Cressids, and all brokers-between panders!" (3.2.200–4). But two centuries separate the fictions. By the 1590s "pander" had been established usage for that dubious trade for some time. The complications that result from solemn vows are often crucial in romances, as the Fairy King's vow is in *Sir Orfeo*, but in this scene the vow is emptied of significance even as it is uttered. All three major characters are counterparts of Chaucer's in that they maintain their roles in the inherited love plot, but they do so with an almost mechanical alacrity, a strong contrast to Chaucer's unhurried development of their changing moods in response to events. They seem over-engineered to look like the typological entities implied by the epilogue to *Troilus and Criseyde*. James calls them characters "often weary with their status as tropes."[73]

Kant asserts that aesthetic response both denies the usefulness of the object for either practical or ideological ends and prevents us from finding a conceptual scheme that can account for it. Tragic fictions in particular preclude the more obvious satisfactions of wish fulfilment, frustrating both agreeable identification with the central characters and superiority to them through a moralized account of their story. The comparison of *Troilus and Criseyde* with Shakespeare's play highlights Chaucer's poem's wealth of tiny details that invite imagination of a living woman, complicated and fearful in book 2, in book 3 self-possessed and loving, despairing and then overconfident of her abilities in book 4, and finally drained and resigned, having fulfilled her own prophecy of being "rolled on many a tongue" (5.1061). She is herself, her "own woman," as she tells Pandarus, yet caught in the mysterious way humans sometimes are in the toils of tragic irony; nonetheless, she is also the Lady Fortune of a Boethian allegory. The beauty of the poem lies in its simultaneous particularity, especially about inner life, and the tension it maintains between that particularity and the intelligible schemes philosophy has devised to explain it, a restless vacillation between a general proposition about divine versus sexual love and a particular love story. Yet that restlessness may be – we claim *is* – experienced as rhythm rather than simply chaos. Much of the imagery of the poem, especially the capture images – Bayard between the trays, Criseyde's imputed fishing net, Troilus as sparrow hawk in the bedroom – displays such a rhythm, equally readable as warning against Fortune or entrance into the real world of *aventure*, replicating in little the poem's overarching shape. Its parts, even small ones, impel the action and echo it. The distinctive shape of *Troilus and Criseyde* gives the rule to nature, in Kantian terms,[74] and unveils the possibility of tragic romance for subsequent literary history. Stanley Cavell's description of tragedy stresses both the revelation and the wonder of aesthetic involvement: "wrapped in meaning, but the meaning has not come to us, and so is wrapped in mystery."[75] Something of this evocation of revelation and wonder, though differently presented, appears as well in *Melusine*, the subject of the next chapter.

Chapter Four

Melusine's *Aventure* among the Humans

"Lord, we know what we are, but know not what we may be."

Ophelia in *Hamlet*

Jean d'Arras's *Melusine: or, The Noble History of Lusignan*, takes us from a Middle English to a Middle French romance, acknowledging the multilingual nature of late medieval English culture.[1] *Melusine* was brought to completion (*parfaicte* is Jean's word)[2] on Thursday, 7 August 1393, some years after Chaucer's completion of *Boece* and *Troilus and Criseyde*, and while he was working on the *Canterbury Tales*. This long prose narrative resembles *Troilus and Criseyde* in its focus on the vicissitudes of lovers and its investments in alternative worlds, but it is related to Chaucer's work in more than just temporal and thematic ways, in that both writers demonstrate that romance is an inherently philosophical affair, and not just on account of their allusions to Boethius or Aristotle. In chapter 5, we will argue that, in the tales told by the Wife of Bath, the Franklin, the Clerk, and the Canon's Yeoman, Chaucer takes up many of the same plot threads, entanglements with alternative worlds, and ethical conundrums that are writ so large in *Melusine*.

Chaucer's Criseyde is so beautiful that she is thought to have come from somewhere else by both the narrator – "aungelik," she was sent down "in scorning of nature" (1.102–5) – and Troilus – "where hastow woned" (1.276). At their first meeting Melusine seems to Raymondin, her future husband, a marvel, "the likes of which he had never before beheld" (*M*, 32). Criseyde, of course, has not come from a supernatural realm "in scorning of nature," but from a tier of Trojan society fully represented in the text, her father a major player in the city's struggle with the Greeks. Melusine, by contrast, *is* from another world, the fairy world of Avalon. Her father, Elinas, is the human king of Scotland, and her mother, Presine, a powerful fairy.[3] Criseyde may be viewed allegorically in terms of another world, one that was epistemically possible for Chaucer's audiences (and is for some modern readers). Christian allegory depends on the belief that two worlds, divine and human, may be reconciled, that a proper viewpoint reveals the divinely created essence of the human world, however obscured by human sin and error. Troilus's enlightenment in the eighth sphere is an only slightly (and briefly) disguised image of Christian salvation not only possible, but necessary for believers. Although the two are abruptly distinguished in the poem, the world revealed in the eighth sphere is not incompossible with that in which Troilus had lived his mortal life, but the distinction is blurred in Jean's account of Melusine's marriage to a human, Raymondin, where sharply incompossible worlds exist together. The subjective *aventure* for both pairs of lovers is something that happened to them, but for Melusine it is also a quest undertaken. Melusine's journey to the human world is her deliberate attempt to attain in life the state that Troilus, as a pagan, can only see after death. The metaphysical otherness of Melusine's origin is more troubling to narrative coherence than the epistemic reconciliation of human and divine revealed to Troilus at the end of Chaucer's poem.

Like *Troilus and Criseyde,* the genre of *Melusine* is complex and tangled, starting with its title: *Melusine: or, The Noble History of Lusignan.* Long stretches of the narrative, especially those concerned with the warlike careers of Melusine's sons, many of them compressed versions of the historical record, are accessible as fictional realism. As the founder of that dynasty, Melusine figures somehow in those episodes as well, but the framing story of her origins as a half-fairy and her quest to live solely in her husband's human world impel it towards folklore.[4] Whereas in *Troilus and Criseyde* the other world is presented as a (slightly secularized) Christian eternal alternative superimposed on ancient history, Jean invokes an alternative world from legend and traces its effects on a (partly) authentic, although greatly foreshortened, historical past.[5] This gathering of tales about a *fée* familiar in folklore interlaced with a "historical" account of Lusignan's far-flung conquests provides a full, dense, and crowded narrative "now" (in Carolyn Dinshaw's terms).[6] For Melusine, as for Criseyde, it is a tragic romance, although a triumph for the dynasty to which she gives her name. This chapter will investigate the practical and aesthetic effects produced by Jean's generic engineering. To make the case that its incompossible worlds can be swept into a coherent aesthetic idea, we will argue that: (1) As a commissioned tale, it must fold the temporal record, presenting distant events as contemporaneous, and invoke diverse kinds of evidence; (2) Its narrative arc and deeply imagined scenes cause it to overflow and outlive its practical purpose, largely through Melusine's enigmatic identification as a trans-world traveller; (3) Jean's telling renders the whole tale ripe for allegoresis; and (4) Its rich afterlife (translations, versions, and remediations) testify to a continuing fascination with its aesthetic idea.

The Commission: Romance and the Actual World

Jean, Duke de Berry, needed to buttress his dynastic claim to the fortress of Lusignan, and he commissioned Jean d'Arras to write an account that would prove his case. The duke, brother to Charles V, was one of Europe's most influential patrons; the fortress was real and imposing. Built in the tenth century by Hugh II of Lusignan and not razed until the sixteenth, it had reverted to the French crown in 1308, been restored to Jean and his line in 1356, and held by the English from 1360 until the duke recaptured it in 1374. Jean d'Arras's tale was to have been a rejoinder to Jean Froissart's English-leaning *Chroniques*, and the third appendix to *Melusine* speaks directly to the Englishman Cresswell's recent possession of the fortress.[7] The duke no doubt also wanted to reinforce the reputation of a crusading Lusignanian lineage that established "a European Christian bulwark against Islamic expansion" due to its campaigns in the twelfth century.[8] Both Melusine's folkloric establishment of the fortress and chronicle-like accounts of the Lusignan holdings in the next generation serve the objectives of Jean d'Arras's commission, but they must be based on different kinds of evidence. Eager to authenticate his account, Jean also writes that he followed "les vrayes croniquez" given him by his patron and the duke of Salisbury and "plusieus livres" in Jean de Berry's library, including such ill-assorted authorities as Aristotle and Walter Map. The long middle section detailing the military manoeuvres and marriages of the sons who expand the dynasty were downplayed in popular retellings, but the real-world scenarios in which they are couched form part of the rich tapestry of the narrative and contribute to the author's gusto in fulfilling his commission.

Stressing its origin in a commission, Jane H.M. Taylor regards *Melusine* as "in essence a genealogy" employing textual strategies "characteristic of the genre in the late Middle Ages," while E. Jane Burns calls it an "illusion of Jean de Berry's lineal right of inheritance."[9] This true story, Jean begins, chronicles "how it came about that the powerful and noble fortress of Lusignan in Poitou was founded by a fairy … The noble lineage that issued therefrom … shall reign until the end of the world, just as it has been seen to reign until now" (*M*, 21). "Illusion" though it might be, *Melusine*'s genealogical project was not unique; the twelfth and thirteenth centuries saw a rash of such projects intended to secure geographic holdings. Even the idea of a historical line founded by superhuman forces was not unusual – Arthur's own conception resulted from an enchantment by Merlin – and was sometimes combined with founding myths involving saints or descendants of Troy.[10] In the early fourteenth century, Pierre Bersuire's *Reductorium morale* claimed that the Lusignan fortress was founded by a female fairy, although it does not call her Melusine.[11] Jean says in his *Prologue* that he consulted many time-honoured local legends about the Lusignan dynasty and drew on tales from Gervase of Tilbury's *Otia Imperialis* (early thirteenth century), one of which is quite close to the outline of his story (*M*, 21), as well as eyewitnesses who claim to have seen physical evidence: Melusine's footprint in the stone casement from which she leapt to fly over the village (*M*, 194, 196). He concludes his account by claiming to have presented the true story tracing "the noble and powerful line descended from its illustrious founders; may God keep their souls in His saintly eternal paradise." Only coarser minds, he notes, are unwilling to believe these higher truths (*M*, 227).

Melusine: or, The Noble History of Lusignan evokes two temporal and causative worlds by its very title as well as its unfolding story. From the beginning in Avalon, the inviolable promise is linked with the irreversible curse. Herself the offspring of the beautiful fairy Presine with the human King Elinas, Melusine is cursed by her mother for imprisoning her father, who had broken his vow not to visit her mother in childbed and thereby prevented Presine and her daughters from eventually achieving full humanity through the paternal line. Melusine herself will appear as a serpent from the waist down on Saturdays and can become fully mortal only by marrying a man who will vow not to try to see her then. In Raymondin she finds a man to make that vow and keep it for many years. She steadily advances his fortunes, building him a magnificent fortress in what had been uncultivated forest, helping him regain his dynastic holdings, and bearing him ten sons who extend his dynasty militarily into many parts of Europe and the Near

East. The faces of eight of those sons, though, are variously disfigured, bearing the "mother-marks" of Melusine's non-human inheritance.[12] The Melusine-Raymondin love story frames a long middle section – parts 6–10, about half the tale – that describes the military campaigns and marriages of the various sons in Cyprus, Armenia, Luxembourg, and Bohemia, and in defence of Christian interests against the Saracens. When the story returns to the couple, two events trigger its unhappy end. In the first, Raymondin, taunted by his brother, spies on Melusine in her bath, to see a thick serpentine tail below her navel. Rather than being shocked or disgusted, he is immediately remorseful at having broken his promise, and Melusine alone is aware of his intrusion. The second event is Raymondin's public accusation that his wife is a serpent when he hears that his son Geoffroy Big Tooth has burned the monastery in which his brother Fromont is enclosed. Again Raymondin immediately repents. Melusine readily forgives him, but the curse issued by her mother in the fairy world is binding. She leaps to the casement, leaving her footprint in the stone, and assumes the form of a fifteen-foot dragon that flies over the domain she had successfully ruled, shrieking piteous goodbyes to the court and the townspeople. Onlookers lament, describing Melusine and Raymondin as two faithful lovers ("deux loyaulx amans") parted by cruel Fortune ("Faulse Fortune"). The pope arranges for Raymondin's retirement to a hermitage at Montserrat to pray for Melusine until his death, leaving the governance of Lusignan to the now repentant Geoffroy.

The world of the son's political-military conquests is mapped onto known history, compressed into a single generation, and presented in considerable detail. When the tale ends, they rule eight kingdoms: Cyprus (Urian), Armenia (Guyon), Luxembourg (Antoine), Bohemia (Renaud), Marche (Eudes), Forez (Remonnet), Parthenay (Thierry), and Lusignan itself (Geoffroy). Fromont the monk has expired in the monastery fire and Horrible (too destructive to live, as Melusine had said just before flying away) has been lured into a cave, where he was burned to death. The historical record testifies that many of these lands did fall under Lusignan's control, but not all simultaneously. Moreover, the battles in which these territories are acquired are described in convincing detail that accords with what is known of medieval warfare. Specific campaigns are fought in named places with details of intimidatingly well-equipped forces, individual fierce battle prowess, and clever stratagems. In defending Alsace, for example, Geoffroy employs a squire fluent in German to help him penetrate a defended castle (*M*, 212) – not the sort of detail one often finds in romanticized epic accounts. A striking episode built on known historical events is the pivot that returns the story to the parents: the burning of Fromont by Geoffroy. In 1232 one Geoffroy, Viscount of Chatellerault, did in fact burn the abbey of Maillezais, although not out of resentment towards a brother's vocation. An extant letter records Geoffroy's contrition before Pope Gregory IX in 1233 and his willingness to pay restitution.[13]

Because the story line extends from the construction of the original fortress in the tenth century to its recapture by Jean de Berry's forces in 1374, it must be severely compressed in order to focus on the first generation of Melusine's progeny, eight of whom are alive at the end. The inevitable anachronisms turn up in both setting the tale against the historical record and in the folded timeline Jean provides within particular episodes. In a striking example of the latter, Geoffroy Big Tooth arrives in Northumberland to kill the giant Grimaut, who has menaced the people for 400 years, and still guards the cave in which Melusine's father is buried (*M*, 199), yet Raymondin is still alive during this episode. On the other hand, some instances make very specific references to time: five or six years after Melusine's flight from the tower, a tribute was left for an unknown collector *on the last day of August* (*M*, 219). Jean's text is well described by Michel Serres's "time that is gathered together" or Bruno Latour's "past that is not surpassed but revisited, repeated, surrounded, protected, recombined, reinterpreted and reshuffled."[14]

Jean seems keenly aware that the different causal regimes to which episodes in his "true" story belong might strain belief. He fiercely defends its accuracy in his prologue and again at the very end of his tale. First he identifies his sources as chronicles found in his patron's extensive library and regarded as authentic, and then launches a vigorous defence of unseen forces at work in history, including belief in fairies. This second bid for trust in his story asserts that ordinary historical scholarship is not capable of unlocking the marvels that God's unfathomable mind has produced in many places and in many forms throughout the world (*M*, 20). Both Aristotle (probably from *Metaphysics* 1.8) and St Paul (Romans 1.20), he writes, urge belief in invisible entities; since God created everything; it would be "oultrageuse presumption" (*FM*, 2) to withhold belief in marvels when so many have testified to their manifestations.[15] In the "Legacy" section with which *Melusine* ends, contemporaries who reported having seen the dragon are called to witness, and God is said to have provided such marvels in his secret plan for the created world. Whereas "coarser intellects" ("personne grossier" [*FM*, 311]) cannot believe, "those with more subtle intelligence and an innate grasp of science will more readily intuit that such things are possible, although no one can clearly know the secret workings of God" (*M*, 229).[16] Jean is striving to include the world in which Melusine becomes a snake from the navel downward and then a flying dragon within the actual world God created. He does not, like Paracelsus, accuse her kind ("melusines") of dealings with the devil or mention Satan in connection with her, and he invites readerly empathy for her throughout.

Melusine's story includes references to lore from the early Christian era and the Celtic oral tradition. Her chimerical side is close to Philostrato's (170/2–247/50 CE) account of Apollonius unmasking a lamia who had seduced one Menippus Lycius into living with her near Corinth and marrying her, but disappeared when outed. Philostrato's story is retold by Robert Burton in *The Anatomy of Melancholy*, which suggests that this "lamia" motif was not unknown to later generations, nor was it lost to John Keats, since Burton's account was printed with his famous 1819 poem "Lamia."[17] Closer to Jean is Celtic lore that is amply stocked with tales of fairies or enchantresses who appear as seductive women and mate with human lovers. Laurence Harf-Lancner's classic work on the subject notes that folklore, in spite of the difficulty posed by its oral transition, remains remarkably stable at the level of what she calls "*schémas*." The "Morganian fairy," like Lanval's unnamed benefactress in Marie's *lai*, whisks the hero into an unknown land from which he never returns, while the "Melusinian fairy" chooses to live with her lover in the human world.[18] The Melusinian arc moves from a meeting in a forest between a preoccupied knight and an omniscient fairy, their marriage conditioned by an interdict the man must obey, to the eventual transgression of the interdict and the disappearance or transformation of the wife.[19] She sees Jean's *Melusine* as the clearest and fullest instantiation of the "melusinian *schema*." The church extended "relative tolerance" towards the "merveilleux" of collective imagination, as this old and popular story type thrived in oral traditions and learned accounts of them alongside official doctrine.[20]

Three appendices to the tale in different ways embed the story in Jean de Berry's claims for the influence of Melusine and her family. In the first, Geoffroy, the heir of the Lusignan Fortress, discovers that the enormous hand that shakes the fortress has been a penance laid on Raymondin by the pope for betraying Melusine, yet another sign that her influence was not diabolical. The *aventure* of the Sparrow Hawk (from Mandeville) denies Melusine's sister Melior's love to a son of King Guyon of Armenia for the unmagical reason that he is her blood relation.[21] The third appendix describes a visit from Melusine as dragon to the Englishman Cresswell just before he yielded the fortress to Jean de Berry in 1374, supporting the duke's claim to be its true owner. This aggregation of history and folklore may have been convincing in its time and remains intriguing, but, as Kant argues, beauty inheres in the power of an aesthetic idea, somehow coherent without being reducible to a concept. Donald Maddox and Sara Sturm-Maddox, its modern English translators, call *Melusine* a "literary masterpiece of late medieval France," and Stephen Nichols notes that the image of its heroine "gripped the Western imagination for the last five hundred years."[22] We agree that Jean's long prose narrative is a remarkable accomplishment and will devote the next sections to showing how critical tools from possible-worlds theory can reveal its coherence as an aesthetic idea and its continuing fascination.

Melusine, Trans-World Traveller, at the Centre

For modern readers, it is difficult to keep *Melusine*'s two worlds equally before us as we encounter detailed battles and fires likely to have occurred, on the one hand, and enchanted transformations, on the other. The intuition of aesthetic power impels readers to look elsewhere when the surface of a text seems to deny coherence. This is a common critical strategy; as Peter Rabinowitz writes, some works contain "a surplus of information that we need somehow to tame, including details that seem to contradict one another and that we need to reconcile."[23] One way this has been done with *Melusine* is to marginalize the long middle section with its (relatively) authentic detail and concentrate on the love story between Melusine and Raymondin, finding there enough evocative detail of a different sort to excite the imagination and set the mind in search of understanding. Our tactic is to recognize both worlds without letting either swallow the other. Yet it is certainly true that the tale has been disseminated and remains current to the extent it does through its romance, rather than its epic, *aventures*. Another way to perceive its coherence is to regard the two kinds of causation that operate in the tale as its deliberate unifying principle: the intrusion of a force not recognized by sober histories, a kind of chthonic power, unaccounted for, but old – the stuff of myth and folklore, simultaneously female and androgynous. Behind this, the text harbours a suspicion that historical developments are not well accounted for by strictly rational propositions. Jean argued this directly in his recourse to Aristotle and Paul's letter to the Romans.

Melusine is, of course, central to this perspective. She enters not just a human world, but a man's world, and a militarized one that the activities of the sons stipulate in full detail. Yet she takes control as soon as Raymondin makes his vow, managing the wedding preparations, successfully winning over his family, and mustering apparently limitless material resources. The only thing she cannot produce is land, so she has to trick the powers that be in Poitiers out of it, which she does with Machiavellian élan. With those resources, she transforms a wild forest into an organized community with elegant and generous manners, fulfilling her promise to make her husband rich and respected. As a master builder, she works in exactly the way male engineers would, drawing up plans and hiring and supervising workers (see cover illustration). The striking abnormalities ("mothers' marks") of eight of the ten sons she bears to Raymondin, in accordance with her promise to raise the fortunes of his biological line, seem to be advantageous in battle, associating their victories with her influence. If we imagine the two metaphysically incompossible worlds of *Melusine* as a Venn diagram with two overlapping circles, Melusine will dominate the area the circles share. The events of her life continue to be constrained by the rules and powers of Avalon, in that she must leave Raymondin and assume the shape of a dragon when he breaks his vow, but she is equally subject to the rules of the fictional real world when she moves around France or erects buildings. Jean convinces us that she is the same being in both realms, that she is a genuine trans-world traveller.

Although there is some debate among possible-world philosophers on the issue of moving between worlds,[24] we will take the view that Melusine carries her essential self with her into the human world and thereby becomes the main focus of the overlap between worlds. The way the text evokes her inner life is a clue to her trans-world existence. Romances generally treat the action of fairies as inscrutable, revealing little of their inner lives.[25] The rules that govern the moods of *fées* and their resulting actions cannot be identical to those we assume for the actual human world; if they were, these figures would cease to be fairies. Melusine, though, may be an exception. Melusine's emotions are not as often or explicitly delineated as those of the men early in the fiction, but they are by no means opaque, and late in the tale they are fully rendered. Medieval discourse has at best a different way of signalling thoughts and feelings from our own, yet we may justifiably claim that we have some access to the inner lives of many of the characters we meet in literary texts. Except in the work of Chaucer and the *Gawain*-poet, where emotional shadings are often distinct and readable, Jeff Rider is right that we should assume neither a complete continuity between medieval methods of signification nor a total alterity that severs our connection with the sensibilities at play in the text.[26] What we can assume is that emotional life involves cognitive engagement with the world, and physiological results of emotion like fainting are signs that a person is "*grappling* with the world," as Robert Solomon puts it.[27] Such signs, as well as direct accounts of subjective states, are abundant for Troilus and Criseyde and many of the characters in the *Canterbury Tales*, and even for Raymondin in *Melusine*. They are less readable for Melusine herself, whose engagements must involve two worlds simultaneously.

Although Jean's vocabulary for emotional states may be limited,[28] he provides adequate authorial descriptions of and indirect clues to the subjective states of his characters. When he first encounters Melusine by the fountain, Raymondin's grief at having inadvertently killed his beloved uncle has plunged him into in a trance-like state. Wakened by Melusine's touch he explains that he was "lost in thought about a grievous affair" (*M*, 32; "pensoye moult fort," *FM*, 25). Later, Raymondin is apparently incapable of checking the wrath and suspicion [*M*, 181; "espris de yre et de la jalousie," *FM*, 241] his brother has provoked, and his wholehearted reaction to seeing Melusine's half-serpentine tail is immediate remorse rather than the shock or repulsion readers might expect; he says *to himself*, "my love, at the wrongful behest of my brother I have betrayed you, and broken the promise I made you!" He barely avoids killing his brother, calling him a traitor perpetrating a false rumour: "I have broken my promise to the being who, after the one who bore our Lord, is the best, most loyal lady ever born" (*M*, 182). At first the couple return to their conjugal life, neither husband nor wife mentioning the spying, but later, when he hears that Geoffroy Big Tooth has set his brother's monastery afire, he concludes that Melusine's malign genetic influence is behind Geoffroy's rash act, and accuses her before the court: "Ah! you deceitful serpent, by God, you and your deeds are nothing but phantoms, nor will any heir you have borne ever come to a good end!" (*M*, 190). Again, his immediate remorse is openly expressed. Although throughout he seems a brave fighter and loving husband, he nowhere appears as successfully reflective. When he is not guided by Melusine's detailed strategic plans, his every impulse flares into reckless action. The emotional lives of the sons are also clearly marked, but not with the complexity of Raymondin's.

Melusine's inner life is set in contrast to her husband's. Her actions exhibit self-control and patience, so much so that they may look like omniscience and an accompanying impassivity. Her gift of prophecy could mark her as from another world, perhaps one with a different order of time, like the Merlin of Arthurian tales, suggesting that she controls events rather than grappling with them. But Jean brings the worlds together on this point by including the prophecies of Count Aimery before Raymondin inadvertently kills him in a boar hunt. The much-loved Aimery, who knew more about astronomy than anyone since Aristotle and prayed ardently for insight from the "One True God," was able to predict the future by reading the stars (*M*, 29). He predicts the same future that Melusine describes to Raymondin when she offers to marry him, even mentioning Aimery's godly learning in astronomy, which she subtly aligns with her own (*M*, 33). The fact that Melusine's startling, seemingly supernatural, perhaps even malign, foresight is shared with a positive character in Raymondin's human family suggests an overlapping area, a shared world, within the fiction.

Melusine's gift for prophecy remains a key feature of the narrative long after Aimery has disappeared from the story. She exhibits specific knowledge of the trouble he faces before Raymondin tells her; she also knows how he can successfully extricate himself and marry her, a being unknown in his world. Again, Jean's telling mitigates her "otherness." The advice she gives him – to pretend he knows nothing of Aimery's death, to declare his love for a woman they don't know, saying as little as possible about her, and to invite his kin to a lavish wedding – does solve his problem. What diverts his family's suspicion in the long run, though, is her wealth. She must be an heiress from somewhere, since she treats the wedding guests to a resplendent feast and showers them with expensive gifts. The festivities are planned with sophistication and decorum, including a joust that Raymondin wins and then modestly denies winning. The marriage itself is a familiar Catholic ceremony, with a bishop blessing the marriage bed, where that very night Urian is conceived (*M*, 42–5). Such extensive attention to details suggests a heroine who knows how these matters are handled and how these stories of handsome knights and beautiful ladies are supposed to be played out. Her control looks impressive, but not superhuman.

The wealth itself may seem supernatural (although scarcely more than Portia's in *The Merchant of Venice*), but its uses are humanly shrewd. This episode, though, does not yield much insight into her mind and heart. Nor does the text record any emotional reaction (from either wife or husband) to the "mother's marks" with which the first eight sons were born. The pious advice she gives them when they set off on their careers as warriors is as traditional as the marriage arrangements.

When Geoffroy burns the monastery and kills his brother, though, Melusine's control of events spins away and the reader gets a much fuller sense of her vulnerable inner life. If the sangfroid she had shown earlier had held when one of her children murdered another, it would have been hard to credit her humanity. In fact, she grieves distractedly for three miserable days, thinking of how to comfort Raymondin, whose anguished disappointment and impulsive wrath she could readily imagine. She needs no powers beyond human reason to fear that this occasion will drive her husband to an outburst that would destroy their compact. Shaking off her own misery, she rejoins Raymondin to assuage his anger with an apparent calm that Jean d'Arras presents as deliberate, hard-earned self-control, expressed as Boethian stoicism. He recognizes her cool, rational argument that his ranting cannot bring back Fromont and the dead monks as the counsel of godly patience, but he denounces Melusine as a "deceitful serpent" anyway. In this scene, the strongest possible contrast is drawn between Melusine's measured attempt to avoid disaster and Raymondin's rashness. Once his public denunciation is uttered in violation of his promise, Presine's curse takes effect in the arbitrary logic of the fairy world. Melusine must leave him forever and relinquish her human form and her hope for a natural death. In the few minutes left to her, she gives orders for protecting Lusignan, mandates the destruction of Horrible to prevent further damage to the world she is about to leave, and predicts (correctly) Geoffroy's rehabilitation – in an impressive illustration of this action, she is seated calmly as if dictating her will.[29] Her leap from the windowsill leaves a footprint as evidence for Jean's account (as eyewitnesses have, he says, seen it), and her piercing lament as she flies away is in a woman's voice, though it issues from an airborne dragon. Her subjectivity includes goodwill towards her human compatriots, and without exception they recognize her feelings, even though she now looks like a dragon.

Unlike the epilogue to *Troilus and Criseyde*, *Melusine*'s appendices continue the story without insisting on it as moral allegory. It is difficult if not impossible to read the tale as a warning against marrying a fairy, or against being impressed by beauty, riches, loyalty, and wisdom. If Melusine's virtues are taken as illusory or diabolically controlled, the Lusignanian line is sullied and Jean d'Arras's project works against its announced objectives. Such a case would not, of course, be unheard of – not every fiction fulfils its avowed intentions. But we think it is a misreading to respond to the pathos of Melusine's final transformation without acknowledging its fully tragic irony: Melusine's motives become fully known as she admits in her parting scene that she desired Raymondin's beauty, his graceful body, his gracious manner, his handsome face (*M*, 191), and trusted his promise on their marriage, just like a mortal woman. The pope himself assigns Raymondin's penance for his intemperate promise breaking (in both the tale and the first appendix), and that, along with the admiration she has elicited from the court and townspeople and the durability of her building projects, places her firmly in the actual world of Lusignan, notwithstanding her imminent transformation into a dragon. The distinctive way Jean d'Arras has woven together a real-world history and ancient and medieval lore presents us with a genuine mystery featuring a protagonist who remains "resistant to our comprehension."[30] The intricate interlace of moving detail and philosophical reflection, full of concepts, but resting firmly on none of them, grounds the haunting beauty of *Melusine*.

Allegoresis in Several Keys

We have argued that for *Troilus and Criseyde* an allegory of salvation history, clearly announced in the epilogue, may be considered an epistemically possible world – *for all we know* the world of experience is really just the shadow of and precursor to a weightier reality. Although *Melusine* contains no similar announcement, modern criticism has found the tale ripe for allegoresis. Its narrative coherence may be enhanced by this interpretive move. The Melusine/Raymondin love story is particularly amenable to such readings, the sections concerned with the expansion of the dynasty by the couple's sons being replete with political and battlefield detail serving as a historically realistic contrast. Christian allegory depends on the belief that two worlds, divine and human, may be reconciled, that a proper viewpoint may reveal the divinely created essence of the human world, however obscured by human sin and error. Troilus's enlightened assessment of earthly concerns seen from the eighth sphere is not only possible, but necessary for believers. The world revealed in the eighth sphere is not, from the vantage point of at least some of Chaucer's readers, incompossible with that in which Troilus had lived his mortal life. The fairy Melusine's founding of a well-known historical dynasty creates a possible world in the epistemic sense, true for some in Jean's early audiences, illusory (but gratifyingly so) for others, with a clear resemblance to the claims of other aristocratic families who dignify their lineage with supernatural beings or saints.[31]

For modern readers, though, the intrusion of fairy powers into the historical world will make that intrusion metaphysical and require vigorous allegoresis to bridge the rift between incompossible worlds of causality. One interpretive strategy focuses on Melusine's gender. Her powers are awesome and they extend well into medieval (and to some degree modern) realms dominated almost exclusively by men: management of wealth, political effectiveness, building skills, freedom to travel, prophetic insight. In addition, she can bear children. This strand of allegoresis suggests deep chthonic female forces familiar in ancient and medieval myth and folklore, usually at odds with patriarchal ways of knowing and acting. Women who exercise such power and also love men and nurture children may be revealed as – or represented as – monsters. Whereas female beauty is commonly figured as the lure for male heroes into an ultimately illusory world of sensual and emotional delight, Melusine extricates Ramondin from his troubles and elevates his status.[32] Melusine bathing on Saturdays or flying above Lusignan registers this male point of view without impugning her moral stance or faith. The allegory is that she must *look* monstrous from a male perspective. In the next section, we will discuss how A.S. Byatt's *Possession* makes use of this reading.

Another avenue for allegory is suggested by the Sparrow Hawk appendix, and reflects on the consequences of unions like that of Melusine and Raymondin. Just as Chaucer's epilogue seems a provocation to the audience's sense of what they have just heard or read, the second epilogue to *Melusine* (originally from Mandeville) is a warning about lines that sexual unions must not cross. When a young king of the Lusignan dynasty succeeds in meeting the challenge of the Sparrow Hawk, he asks for the hand of Melior, the castle maiden, violating the one rule he has been given. She refuses his request for this reason: "Are you not descended from the line of King Guyon, who was my sister Melusine's son? I am your aunt, and you are such a close kin to me that even if I were to consent to have you, the Church would not allow it" (*M*, 225). This moment of potential incest at the very end thus stands in contrast to the tale's opening question of whether a fairy might enter the mortal world and marry a human. The stricture against lovers too closely related is the mirror image of impossible love between Raymondin and Melusine, who are too deeply different. Aunt and nephew, fairy and mortal human – both pairs violate boundaries. Dynastic marriage depends on the union of families, but the world and the Church define a closeness beyond which that union cannot be carnal. Alternatively, erotic desire may be seen as desire for the other, but perhaps not if the other is truly alien. This reading hints at a conceptual argument just beneath the events of the text. Yet when Melusine is obliged to leave her human family forever, the tale is surprisingly moving, precisely because Melusine's quest to become human has nearly succeeded, leaving the question of human/fairy liaisons tantalizingly unresolved.

Yet another strategy for unifying the obligatory alternate worlds – obligatory because of Jean's commission for the work – is even more self-reflexive: his *Melusine* itself as an allegory of the tangled impulses of truth telling through stories. Jean insists that he is presenting evidence for the duke's dynastic claims to the fortress, and entwines historical with folkloric accounts, claiming that they are all true. Moreover, he meshes his incompossible worlds within his frame story. Extreme as Melusine's transformation into a flying dragon may be, Raymondin immediately repents, publicly denouncing his wife, enters a hermit's life, and endures a penance imposed on him by the pope. The pope's interpretation of the denunciation suggests that in this text it is a sin to break faith with a fairy, or even that Raymondin has caused a soul who might have been saved to be lost. Melusine herself hopes for salvation at the Last Judgment, incorporating her fate in a Christian world as understood by humans. Jean's narrator, lightly hinting at his intentional production of this allegory, unites Aristotle's defence of the unseen world with St Paul's, regarding "pagan" thought to be convincing (the positive, Augustinian position, on the question of the value of pagan authorities). What is useful ethically and philosophically we profit from regardless of its origins.[33]

Reading *Melusine* as the tragic tale of a half-fairy's heroic *aventure* as she seeks inclusion in a human family and redemption into a Christian ethic and eschatology brings a sweeping historical allegorization into view. Melusine's "structure of desire" is erotic in that she falls in love with Raymondin (the text makes this clear in her lament that she had desired him from the first [*M*, 191]), but also religious in its embrace of the contingencies of human life and "natural death." Melusine not only wants to be human, she wants to be a good human, who urges her husband and sons to be just and generous to both rich and poor. Her life in the world of men is chaste, prudent, and nurturing, her advice to her sons pious and practical.[34] She becomes the chief agent in bringing civilization to a sparsely inhabited, mountainous, and deeply forested region of Poitou. In common medieval parlance, such forests are not likely to know God, as *Sir Gawain and the Green Knight* explicitly specifies (see chapter 6). No matter how impressive her accomplishments, Melusine's ultimate fate rests on her husband's keeping his vow. For most of the tale, he is a loyal, loving mate, who does not challenge Melusine's artful management of political and familial matters. He can see that she is right. His rashness, the rashness nearly synonymous with proud medieval patriarchs, eventually erupts, initially in response to his brother's incitements, perhaps especially in the thought that "everyone" knows there is something wrong with Melusine on Saturdays, and later when one son kills another out of (misaligned) familial pride. Dynastic "honour" is at stake, and it precipitates Melusine's tragedy, the failure of her benign human project. Raymondin, from this perspective, may be read as a figure for a destructive scepticism about the pagan world of occult knowledge.

Afterlife

Melusine the love story was not only popular in France and translated into many European tongues, it was retold over centuries. Jean's tale gathers time in an intricate way, creating wonder without explaining events with determinate concepts, but the immediate afterlife of his telling, Couldrette's *Mélusine or Le Roman de Parthenay* (1401), took no such risks. His work too was commissioned, this time by Guillaume de Parthenay, who also claimed descent from Melusine, but at one time had sympathized with the English claim to the fortress. The rhymed octo-syllabic *Roman* is often described as a poetic version of Jean's; Couldrette merely "set the prose version to rhyme," writes Matthew Morris in introducing his facing-pages French/English printing.[35] Actually, though, Jean's tantalizing invitations to activate imagination and understanding simultaneously in suggesting the poem's marvellous causality and ethics are much weakened by Couldrette's inference that Melusine is sent by God to save Raymondin's soul. Whereas Jean stresses the shock and anguish of Raymondin's accidental killing of his uncle, Couldrette refers to it as a murder and a "grave sin." Instead of the aspiring announcement of Jean's Melusine: "I am on God's side and believe anything a true Catholic must believe" (*M*, 33), Couldrette's Melusine declares: "I am an instrument of God" and proceeds to recite the whole Catholic creed (lines 19–35). Couldrette's text explains her prophetic powers and inexhaustible resources by claiming she is an agent of divine providence. Even her serpentine form is explicable as providential, in a particular adaptation of St Augustine's thought (Morris's introduction calls Couldrette's viewpoint in the poem Augustinist). Rather than Jean's ethically puzzling world, the *Roman* presents a single world riven by clearly defined forces of good and evil and lacks much of the tension that prevents a concept from stabilizing meaning. Couldrette's poem omits all three of Jean's appendices and ends with a paean to the "Glorious Trinity" in lines 7013 to 7145, submitting the poem "to the violence of controllable thought," as Gordon Teskey would put it.[36] The moral world of his poem works by familiar rules.

Other adaptations testify to varying interpretations of Jean's tale, often readable by the visual images with which they are illustrated. By 1500, thirty prose and verse manuscripts (nine with miniatures) and six illustrated prose versions had appeared. *Melusine* seems to have invited visual imaging more regularly than other medieval romances, and images of Melusine herself predominate. Even in Jean's text, only nine of the thirty-four illustrations concern the exploits of the sons, although they take up more than half his pages. Melusine's half-serpent body or her shape as a dragon are frequent subjects for illustration, but some fifteenth-century representations focus on her womanliness more than on the serpentine or bifurcated body. In particular those found by Tanya Colwell in the Upton House Bearsted Collection show courtly scenes with Melusine as a woman among other women, registering readable human emotions, although fairies are not usually presented in terms of their inner lives at all, as Colwell writes.[37] The Upton House images testify that Melusine's humanity was apparent to the late Middle Ages. Later visual depictions of half-serpentine Melusines pop up as all kinds of styles, from the early woodcuts to sinuously beautiful pre-Raphaelite paintings to an early logo for Starbucks coffee (or so it is said).

The trans-world affiliations of the heroine have dominated the recent narrative afterlife of *Melusine*. The Cahiers du Centre de Recherche sur le Surréalisme in Lausanne, Switzerland, entitles the annual journal it has published since 1981 *Mélusine*. Sarah Monette's fantasy novel of "decadent magic" is called *Mélusine*, the name of the city where most of it takes place.[38] Neither has any direct link with Jean d'Arras's tale, but refers instead to the general idea of an unfamiliar, disorienting presence in modernity, the former in terms of artistic style, the latter with the folklore aura of much fantasy writing. "The Story of Melusine" (Hind Suzanne Hedis, 2010) links Melusine's story, not much connected to the medieval one, with Dracula. Two operas have been based on her story. Aribert Reimann's *Melusine* was first performed in 1971 and recorded in 2010. Steven Jobe's "The Legend of the Fairy Melusine" had been presented as a work in progress before its full premiere in 2013. Jobe designed special instruments like sets of pitched glass bells and a drone he calls the Bosch Hurdy Gurdy to convey Melusine's otherworldliness.

Most of the modern instances might be called allusions to the medieval tale rather than attempts at recreating its energies under new circumstances, the way *Black Orpheus* recalls *Sir Orfeo*. A.S. Byatt's *Possession: A Romance* is a different matter.[39] Jean's Melusine is evoked both by including a poem that recasts Jean's plot (some episodes of which appear directly) and by suffusing a good deal of the rest of the novel with its imagery. *Possession* tells nested love stories: the largest frame concerns the twentieth-century English scholars Roland, a researcher into the major Victorian poet Randolph Ash, and Maud, whose subject is the "minor" poet Christabel LaMotte (both poets are fictional). Byatt includes a good deal of their poetry. Roland's chance discovery of Ash's unsent letter to Christabel impels him to confer with Maud and together they unearth more letters in the Bailey house, now owned by Christabel's descendent. They find that, after a long literary correspondence, the Victorian poets had briefly become lovers, but their story, like Melusine's, ends tragically. Meanwhile, their scholarly collaboration moves slowly towards committed love. All along, they read "tiny details," many of which concern Christabel's *The Fairy Melusina*, leading to their scholarly breakthrough, and readers of *Possession* can see connections to Jean's *Melusine* through such details, both direct and imagistic.[40]

Melusina is Christabel's most ambitious and best-known poem. From the description of it Roland hears from his colleague Fergus early in the novel, the story arc is close to Jean's version, as is the bifurcated subject matter, which "keeps changing focus. From very precise descriptions of the scaly tail to cosmic battles" (38–9). Fergus adds that feminists are "crazy about it," which brings us to the first of several ways in which Byatt's book is both an allusion to and an interpretation of Jean's. Christabel and Ash both know the story well (even Paracelsus's commentary on it), and both appreciate the duality of its characterization of the heroine: "Unnatural Monster – and a most proud and loving and handy woman."[41] To explain "handy" Christabel writes: "All she touched was well done – her palaces squarely built and the stone set on rightly, her fields full of wholesome corn."[42] She finds herself inhabiting Melusine's skin (191–2). Maud, in turn, has internalized Christabel and can quote *Melusina* by heart, which she does as a response to a particular slant of light in a Scottish cave (289–90). The whole of chapter 16 presents the proem (three parts of it direct allusions to Jean's telling and the fourth a lament for Medusa, Scylla, and the Sphinx, mythic women transformed into monsters) and book 1 of the poem itself. What we see of Christabel's version distinctly humanizes her Melusina while fully registering her "monstrousness," an appropriation of Jean's tale in defence of strong-willed women treated by male traditions as unnatural monsters who came from somewhere else. Her Melusina may be thought of as an androgynous figure – Montaigne had called her snaky tail a "sausage" – transformed by patriarchal cultures, medieval and nineteenth-century, into a demon exiled from full human identity. Maud, from her perch in the Women's Resource Centre at Lincoln University, appropriates *Melusine/Melusina* for a brand of feminist rejection of romantic heterosexuality. *Possession*'s valorization of strength and independence for women, including lesbian liaisons, takes up a strident strand of 1980s feminism ("Women need men like fish need bicycles"), but treats it with whimsical irony.[43]

Christabel's known biography – she lived with a female painter and never married – seems tailor-made to suit disdain for male domination and heterosexual love. Maud is initially inspired by this biography and has long since broken off an affair with Fergus. The received understanding of Christabel's nineteenth-century female household (whether maiden ladies committed to living together or actively sexual) makes the discovery of her love affair a major academic "find" for them, as well as for the Randolph Ash scholars, who also want the letters to fill out the biography of an important poet. But it also brings into focus the question of forbidden love at the centre of Jean's *Melusine*: the fairy/human unions of both Melusine and her mother end tragically (too alien?), but in the Sparrow Hawk appendix her sister Melior rejects her nephew on grounds of consanguinity (too close?). The revelation of the Victorian couple's intense affair, secret because both are "married" to others, mediates between medieval and modern estimations of which unions are allowable. The spiral of time brings these story arcs together.

Jean d'Arras was commissioned to legitimize a real-world dynasty and thereby buttress the Duke de Berry's claim to a real-world fortress.

To do so, he wrote a romance. *Melusine* fuses historical actualities with otherworldly fairy powers, incompossibles in our actual world, creating a figure who has continued to grip imaginations and puzzled understanding for centuries. *Possession* seizes on that blend of actual-world detail, in this case the academic world (Roland's experiences in the London Library are spot on), with an almost magical series of exciting discoveries. The real-world stakes of his work with Maud are considerable, including the literary reputations and biographical understandings of Ash and Christabel, the economic health of literary study, international scholarly standings, and Roland's own job opportunities.[44] At the very end, though, the clever Machiavellian moves of the academics are parodied in a rollicking car chase that ends in a gothic scene in a graveyard on a dark and stormy night. In this matter, too, Christabel's poem mediates between medieval and modern, for as Maud and Roland find, the aftermath of Christabel's liaison with Ash in some measure parallels Melusina's. While Christabel does not turn into a shrieking dragon, her resulting pregnancy and the suicide of her partner Blanche render her desperately unhappy and bitter. The discoveries Maud and Roland make about Christabel, in turn, wear away at the fierce self-protectiveness of Maud's demeanour, and Roland's patient tentativeness gradually builds towards confidence, even derring-do. Roland and Maud are pursuing academic analogues to Jean's ducal commission, and their investigation of a Victorian romance plot has effects in their fictionally realistic world.

Possession can evoke the *energeia* of *Melusina/Melusine* and vice versa and also deepen our sense of what romance can mean across the centuries. It records an *aventure* in three eras, folded together in mutually enlightening ways. For Gadamer the relation of all literary texts to their readers "has something unique and incomparable about it." "Nothing is so purely the trace of the mind as writing, but nothing is so dependent on the understanding mind either. In deciphering and interpreting it, a miracle takes place: the transformation of something alien and dead into total contemporaneity and familiarity" (*TM*, 163).

The vantage point of romance in particular is relevant to the history of thinking about time. Nathaniel Hawthorne's claim, quoted at the beginning of *Possession*, is that the key to romance is "the attempt to connect a bygone time with the very present that is flitting away from us." He sounds a bit like Augustine in book 11 of *The Confessions*.

The final voice of *Possession* comes from another temporal world, one that Roland and Maud could not discover. Ash *had* seen his daughter, as the reader finds from a postscript (552–5) written from a still more distanced point of view (the eighth sphere, perhaps?), a parting gesture that underlines the status of the novel as a romance.[45] *Possession* not only identifies itself as "A Romance," but takes on a meta-role, exploring what the term might come to mean under post-medieval conditions. Its liberal attention to medieval poetry impels thought about *Melusine,* in which, however earnest his intended purpose, Jean d'Arras's narrative clearly overflows the Duke de Berry's commission to justify his ancestral holdings. *Melusine*'s tale of a trans-world heroine has taken on a life of its own, probing the nature of romance writing and its entanglements with "real world" history: *Zweckmässigkeit ohne Zweck.*

Chapter Five

Romance by Other Means: The *Canterbury Tales*

"I will go so far as to say that Alchemists think in metaphors that are sometimes instructive." He shared a private look with Leibniz, and smiled. "Or perhaps we are all born with such habits of thought ingrained in our minds, and the Alchemists have simply fallen into the trap of making too much of them."

Neal Stephenson, *The Confusion*

The claim of the *Canterbury Tales* to aesthetic force is nicely described by Kant's useful but tricky precept that beautiful objects both call attention to their humanly organized designs and yet seem as spontaneous as nature itself, eschewing a mechanical rigidity.[1] Chapter 3 demonstrates the way Chaucer's "realism" in *Troilus and Criseyde*, his deployment of tiny details that conjure up lived realities, is intertwined with his evocation of an overarching aesthetic idea that binds details together through a law particular to that work and not amenable to conceptual statement. *Melusine* is a romance that contains something very like an epic. The long narrative at its centre begins with the construction of a castle fortress and then moves to nation (even empire) building on a grand scale indeed. All of this is initiated, however, by the intrusion of an immortal fairy into the realm of historical reality because she desires to marry a human man and become mortal herself. In the dialectic of its two competing genres, the poem tests the boundaries of romance, leaving a mysterious aesthetic appeal that continues to intrigue. The poem lives on as a powerfully moving story long after the real-world fortifications have fallen. In both *Troilus* and *Melusine*, the tendency of romance to portray desire as counterfactual is entangled with the real.

The *Canterbury Tales* exhibits a still larger and more complex array of details and more varied possibilities for ordering their coherence.

The many voices of the pilgrim narrators produce a dense verbal texture unrivalled in medieval writing. Romance *aventures* are recounted in some of the pilgrims' tales, so in this chapter we hope to further dispel the idea that Chaucer disdained the genre romance. Moreover, we will argue that in a number of his tales, Chaucer engaged in a profound reflection on romance, including the very human impulse to invent possible worlds. Our focus is on the performances of the Wife of Bath, the Clerk, the Franklin, and the Canon's Yeoman (although these are by no means the only possible choices), in part because they are deeply concerned with the desire to change the world, whether through transformation, translation, or alchemy. Though his chief mode is that of fictional realism, Chaucer's sympathetic understanding of why we seek recourse to alternative worlds, and his own deft skill in inventing them, is perceived by many readers less as a contradiction to be resolved than as a beautiful image of how men and women grapple with the reality of their lives.

In the *General Prologue*, Chaucer lays out a sizeable array of characters, each with a particular vantage point on the world of the late Middle Ages.[2] Their stories and reactions to each other take us further into their actual worlds and the worlds they can imagine. The social arena we see for the whole becomes kaleidoscopic, reminiscent of Leibniz's comment that "the same city viewed from different directions appears entirely different, as it were, multiplied perspectively."[3] Almost all of the tales seem crafted by a distinct person responding more or less spontaneously to the occasion. Many of the pilgrims seem purposive in offering their stories – some describe their aims directly – but in the telling itself often undermine the clarity they intend. Such slippage suggests a purpose in the design of the whole, but the sheer exuberance, complexity, and interconnectedness of the details thwarts any impulse to contain that purpose as a concept. Yet even if they could avoid the inevitable way narrativity itself undermines theses, the variety of tales and tellers would complicate any overall thesis for the whole fiction enormously. As with Leibniz's fishpond, the closer you look, the more you see. A *Lebensgefuhl*, a feeling of life, is evoked by the foldings within and among the plots of the tales and continually refreshed by the interaction of the pilgrim narrators (themselves composites) between tales. Nowhere is this complexity more evident than in what Kittredge called the "marriage group," to which three of the tales we will investigate in this chapter belong. The transformative impulse that takes place in romance *aventures* is treated differently in the tales of the Wife, the Clerk, and the Franklin, and satirized by the Canon's Yeoman's.

The *Wife of Bath's Tale*

Chaucer's Wife of Bath is clearly one of the most complexly and "realistically" conceived figures in medieval literature. Although she can be captured by pan-allegorical discourse to represent Eve, she can just as readily be seen as a proto-feminist, or an early entrepreneur.[4] Her tale, though, is cast as an Arthurian romance. The disjunction in both tone and plot between her irreverent *Prologue* and her graceful *Tale* has provoked much controversy, but few would deny that an analogy of some kind exists between them. Many see the Wife reaching for the authority of the Arthurian tradition and longing for the ethical high ground and suspension of the rules of nature that characterize romance. She succeeds in telling a tale that features a marvellous shape-shifting crone, a *fée*, not unlike Melusine in offering instruction to the everyday world of patriarchal arrogance. We will argue that, although the register is different, the structure of her *Tale*, as an expression of female desire, is not very far from that of her *Prologue*.

Once we appreciate the distinction in folklore types between the "morgan" and the "melusine," it is an easy step to see the crone in the *Wife's Tale* as a melusine. The *wyf* – "A fouler wight ther may no man devyse" (3.998–9) – is inexplicably left sitting at the edge of a forest where the knight, whose life will be spared if he can find out what women want most, has just glimpsed twenty-four or more ladies dancing, who vanish as he approaches.[5] The dancing, disappearing ladies are familiar to folklore as supernatural and connected by Alisoun of Bath to the "olde dayes of Kyng Arthour" when "The elf-queene, with her joly compaignye, / Danuced ful oft in many a grene mede" (3.860–1). The *wyf* seems to know what he is seeking and how she can help, as Melusine does when Raymondin rides into her ken deep in troubled thought. As different as her foul appearance is from Melusine's astonishing beauty, she is able to save him from his impending death sentence for rape, much as Melusine saved Raymondin from the charge of treason. Before she gives him the life-saving answer to his question, she asks him to plight his "trouthe" that he will obey her next request, which he does. Like Melusine, she is a prophet, in that she knows that Guinevere's court of ladies will accept her answer to Guinevere's question: sovereignty in love. The knight himself is convinced, addressing the assembly in a "manly voys, that al the court it herde" (3.1036). Point of view belongs to the knight, although we hear a good many of the crone's words, and he is the least knowledgeable character in both Arthur's world and in the world from which the crone has come (wherever that is). His is an *aventure* like Raymondin's, something that happens *to* him, rather than, as it may be for the crone, a quest deliberately undertaken.

The trajectory of the *Tale* is that a mysterious figure turns up in a plausible Arthurian court (historically distanced from the Wife/narrator, as she points out). The crone's origin is unspecified, but she convinces him of her goodwill so thoroughly that he swears to grant her next request, making the binding promise so familiar in romances. When she claims from him marriage and "love," takes her case to Guinevere's court, and wins, he cannot keep himself from registering his objection:

> "My love?" quod he, "nay my dampnacioun!
> Allas, that any of my nacioun
> Sholde evere so foule disparaged be!" (3.1067–9)

His kindred (nacioun), he concludes, would be lowered (disparaged) more by his marriage to a poor old woman than by his reputation as the rapist of a virgin. This passage is reminiscent of the importance of dynastic pride in Raymondin's marriage plans; his kin were suspicious of an unknown lady-love, but they are persuaded first by the earnestness of his love and later by Melusine's beauty, sophistication, and wealth, none of which are apparent in the *wyf*. The account of the lavish marriage celebration common in romances as pleasurable descriptions of food and array is absent in this case: "I seye ther nas no joye ne feeste at al" (3.1078). Nor was there the usual eager sexual consummation: the Knight's wallowing to avoid touching his wife is a comic moment, while the *wyf* "lay smylinge everemo," gently taunting him as unmanly.[6]

The crone does not have to defend herself as a Christian the way Melusine does when she tells Raymondin she believes everything believed by "good catholics," but her famous pillow lecture marks her voice as that of prudent Christian counsel, very much like the counsel with which Melusine sends her sons on military forays. His new *wyf* (which at this point in the plot means married woman rather than just old female) answers all three of the knight's objections to her suitability with extended reasoning and learned allusions. Her superior knowledge and self-possession (also like Melusine's) contrast with the rash unreflectiveness of her husband. Her patience could even be seen as otherworldly impassiveness. She defends willing poverty through both scripture and classical authority, and cites many authors who revere old age, but her analysis of *gentillesse* is her more extended and impressive focus. She touches on both ethics and history – gentle deeds rest on grace granted by Christ himself, and many virtuous men were born into "rude" ancestral lines – quoting Dante, Valerius, Seneca, and Boethius (3.1109–77) as she expands her argument. In the middle of this long disquisition, though, is a claim about "kinde" which uses fire as an example of essential nature. Fire will burn whether it is seen by twenty thousand or hidden in a remote house in the Caucasus; until extinguished, its "office naturel wol it holde" (3.1143). If gentility were "annexed to possessioun" (3.1146), dukes and earls would show it as consistently as fire shows its inherent nature, which is clearly not the case. Her reasoning is not only pious, but philosophically acute, and it raises the issue of essential-ness.

The turn from ethical argument back to situational humour is elegantly made: unattractiveness and old age are "grete wardeyns upon chastitee" (3.1216) – you are unlikely to become a cuckold, she tells him. The knight is then asked to make his most active decision since the rape: his wife may remain as she looks to him now and faithful or young and fair, in which case he must "take youre aventure" about her loyalty (3.1224). Unlike his ill-considered outburst when the court insists he keep his word, he "avyseth hym and sore siketh" (3.1228), which is to say that he takes time to reflect. Presumably, he reflects on his sorry prospects before he came upon the crone and on the (now ratified) answer that women want sovereignty in love. At any rate, he addresses her with a new respect and even affection:

> My lady and my love, and wyf so deere,
> I put me in youre wise governance;
> Cheseth yourself which may be mooste pleasance
> And moost honour to yow and me also. (3.1230–3)

Gone is the worry about the disparagement of his line, not to mention his own bodily recoil from his olde *wyf*. Although she is not (at this point) beautiful, he is able to love her for her wisdom, so much that he trusts her to provide pleasure and preserve honour for both of them.

Now the trajectory of the tale is melusine-like but with a happy ending: the man *does* trust the *fée* and follow her counsel. He is rewarded with a wife so young, fair, and true that "his herte bathed in a bath of blisse" and he goes on to live in "parfit joye" for his whole life (1250–8), having avoided the mistake that cost Raymondin his happiness. The clarity of the "lesson" the knight learns contrasts with the mysteriousness of what actually happens at the end. Possibly, the enlightened knight sees his foul old *wyf* as a benign and beautiful soul. Or possibly, his trust in her "wyse governance" releases her from a curse imposed by someone else, like Presine's curse on Melusine, or even a self-imposed vow to herself to educate him. Like most romance transformations (including Hermione's in *The Winter's Tale*), this one remains unexplained, mysterious.

The aesthetic thrill of the *Wife's Tale*, of course, results not only from the elegantly told Arthurian plot with its many ties to medieval folklore, but to its unexpected fit with the Wife's initially jarring *Prologue*, in which she does not much resemble the prophetic, patient crone. The Wife's autobiography presents her as learned in ways of the world and the words of the Bible,[7] but also as conniving, lustful, and loquacious, a victim to be sure of patriarchal control, but capable of harsh and tricky retaliation. With disarming candour, she tells the other pilgrims about her handling of four husbands from whom she benefited economically (the first three were old and rich) and sexually (the fourth was a reveller, but a pleasing lover). As a rich widow, she chooses (attracted by his great legs and feet) a poor clerk half her age for her next conquest and entices him by claiming he had enchanted her by "killing" her in bed in a sexually tinged, fabricated dream. He becomes her fifth. After the "greet solempnytee" with which they married (3.628), she finds that he continually reads from the book of wicked wives – just what she thought clerks were usually up to. Exasperated, she tears three leaves from his anti-feminist anthology and knocks him down, but not before she rehearses a neat overview of medieval misogyny based on his book (3.634–786). The surprise ending of the *Prologue* is that following a terrible fight in which she seems dead, he cedes not only the governance of the fortune she had given him, but of his tongue and hand as well. They burn the book and she, now having gained sovereignty, uses it to become "as kinde / As any wyf from Denmark unto Ynde, / And also trew, and so was he to me" (3.823–5). It should be noted that Alisoun uses *kinde*, as benevolent, to describe her behaviour, making use of the pun on *kinde*, as nature, in the crone's sermon (3.1149).

Considering the *Prologue* and *Tale* as a single performance by a Canterbury pilgrim (as prologue and tales are for most other pilgrims) presents a coherence problem not unlike the disjunction between the Raymondin/Melusine frame and the episodes devoted to the dynasty-building sons. But as in the case of *Melusine*, we see the two parts as reciprocally informing. Among the many interlocking pieces in the Wife's performance are the repeated word "*wyf*" and the issue of enchantment. As early as the *General Prologue*, where all the other pilgrims are specified by their work, the joke is that wife-hood is a profession for the Wife of Bath even though she is a successful weaver. The crone in her *Tale* is initially called *wyf* as a general title, like "madam," for an older woman whose name is not known, but in the course of the tale she becomes a *wyf* to the knight in its more restricted sense. The fabricated charge of enchantment in Alisoun's seductive account of her dream results in a genuine fulfilment of her desire for both autonomy and affection. In an odd sense, then, both *Prologue* and *Tale* are romances, in their "structures of desire" and in the strain they exert on probability in the actual social world. Both reply from an alternate world of valuation to a flawed actual world, much as Marie's *lais* did centuries earlier. The Wife of Bath turns to a legendary past in which a woman's discourse won the day by setting her tale in the "olde dayes of the Kyng Arthour," just as the lady in *Yonec* frames her love-longing in terms of a past era: "If that might be or ever was … grant me my wish" (*Yonec*, 101–4). Unlike Marie's women, locked in their towers, however, the Wife has begun to experience emerging modernity, a time when she can take her future into her own hands and act with at least some chance that she will succeed. In balancing the Wife's two kinds of storytelling (we might call them nonfiction and fiction), Chaucer respects the desire that yearns for an invented world as much as he credits her wish to act to change the real one.

The crone in the *Tale* looks like a melusine figure, in accompanying her husband into human society and in confronting, and deflating, the male arrogance that characterizes it (she uses the very word in 3.1112). But the teller is still the Wife of Bath, and the one feature of the *Tale* that approximates her tone is the story of Midas's wife, who told the secret of her husband's furry ears to the water in the marsh to show that women cannot keep secrets.[8] In this longish digression (3.951–78), though, Midas's wife does keep his secret from other people, just as Raymondin did after seeing Melusine's deformity. The digression concedes a point to misogyny – but a small one – keeping the Wife's frankness about women in play, in a tale with a remarkable and ultimately inscrutable heroine. The self-indicting tone of the Wife of Bath's own story makes it harder to see her as a figure like the crone. Her tactics are coarser, even to the point of physical aggression. Yet in the end

Jankin values her so much that he grants her the very sovereignty that answered the riddle in the *Tale.* His concluding words – "Myn owene trewe wyf / Do as thou lust the terme of al thy lyf" – sound as respectful as those of the knight in the tale. The Wife's role as the narrator inflects the story, just as Christabel's inflects her *Melusina* and Jean d'Arras's his *Melusine*; behind them are Chaucer, Byatt, and the commission issued by Jean de Berry. Plenty of purposiveness, but no finality of purpose, *Zweckmässigkeit ohne Zweck.*

The Clerk's Kaleidoscopic Tale

The most complicated instance of *Zweckmässigkeit ohne Zweck* must be the Oxford Clerk's tale of Griselda. The Wife's overt purpose in both her prologue and tale is to discredit clerical teaching about women and sex that comes from men whose service to Venus is not "worth his olde sho" (3.708), so the Clerk's turn at storytelling is expected to be a rejoinder. Of course the Wife's announced theme is quite different from the achieved effect of the *Prologue* and diametrically opposed to that of her *Tale.* The Clerk is not only a smart man who had spent a lot of time on the curriculum in logic (1.286), but an astute reader and subtle writer. His recourse to the authority of Petrarch and his highly formal style – rhyme royal stanzas divided into *pars* by Latin *incipits*[9] – initially masks his tale's subtle rapprochement with the Wife's commitment to respect for women's experience. Although he "benignely" agrees to avoid obscurity by telling a "murie thing of aventures" (one ultimately based on folk tales) and by speaking plainly, his formality seems to be saying "no mere folk tale, this." Yet our claim is that he too writes a romance, and that, seen as romance, possible-worlds theory, and even *Melusine* specifically, can help us see into it.

The Clerk's explicitness about the geography in which the story takes place locates it in a real region of Lombardy, naturally fertile and well governed. Parts 1–5 specify real-world possibilities: how a nobleman can victimize a peasant, a medieval husband a wife. Marquis Walter, pressed by his people to marry, chooses Griselda, the poorest of his subjects, taking her from her widowed father Janicula, then pretending to haul their daughter and then their son off to death, and finally banishing his wife from court in her shift and asking her to return to prepare the mansion for a new bride. All this she endures without complaint, keeping to the letter the vow she had made before the marriage (once again the inviolable promise). In the final section, he reinstates Griselda as marchioness, revealing that his lovely new "bride" is actually their daughter, raised by his sister, the Countess of Panico. Pathos, generally a populist appeal, is the tale's most prominent emotive effect, in contrast to Petrarch's more distanced register. Griselda's pain is fully and intimately rendered, and the Clerk, being poor and dependent himself, does not keep his distance from it. His involvement turns up in his many asides (4.456–62, 617–23, 696–707), and also in details of the plot. For example, Janicula had his suspicions that Walter never intended a dynastic marriage and (presumably) that Rome would abet his desertion of Griselda when he had satisfied his "corage," his sexual appetite (4.904–10).[10] The Clerk conveys her alienation from both her status as aristocrat and as maiden-peasant in a moving plot detail not found in Chaucer's sources: her father tries to cover her near-nakedness, but her rude old coat cannot accommodate Griselda's now womanly body (4.911–17). Such a homey detail presents a convincing fourteenth-century life-world that evokes pathos and gestures beyond the formality of the Clerk's rime royal.

The Clerk's first description of Walter as "gentilleste yborn of Lumbardye" (4.72) recalls the emphasis the *wyf* in the *Wife's Tale* had placed on *gentillesse* in her pillow lecture. The fact that Walter has inherited *gentillesse* in a list of positive qualities – good looks, youth, strength, honour, courtesy – provides another clue that the Clerk intends to answer the Wife in some way, but it turns out not to be the expected defence of lineage. Walter agrees to a request from his people that he marry, only reserving the right to choose his wife freely without restricting his choice to the "gentilleste" and "meest." "Bountee comth al of God, nat of the streen / Of which they been engendered and ybore" (4.157–8), he says, a virtual précis of the crone's lecture (3.1109–77). He then exacts an oath, to which they kneel and swear unanimously, to "neither grucche ne stryve" against his choice (4.170). His sober ("sad") choice fell on Griselda, who was only "fair ynogh to sighte" but as to virtue "faireste under sonne" (4.209–12). So far his position sounds like that of the crone in devaluing birth and physical beauty in favour of good deeds, in which Griselda is rich.

Until the wedding day, Walter wilfully refuses to disclose his choice, but (and this is another homely detail) has suitable clothing made for the bride by measuring a girl of her stature (4.257) and asks her father rather humbly for her hand. She too must vow not to grutch or to show displeasure with him by any sign, and she too solemnly takes this oath, going still further by promising that even her private thoughts will conform to his will. Griselda is not wed in her dirty peasant rags, though. Walter's women are directed to strip her, comb her hair, and dress her in such finery as to make her scarcely recognizable. She is "despoiled" of the markers of her class origin – untended hair and clothing distasteful to the ladies of Walter's court – and dressed in new garments, jewels, and a bridal crown. She rises to the occasion by becoming an excellent marchioness, managing the estate, settling disputes, and receiving foreign dignitaries. Both Griselda's appearance and her role have been "translated" (4.385). The extent of her translation is underlined by the fact that the people began to think she was not the daughter of Janicula but "another creature" altogether (4.406).

Moreover, after her marriage, she takes centre stage in the tale; no longer merely experiencing an *aventure*, she pursues one, the quest to fulfil her vow no matter what Walter might demand. Translated, she looks less like Raymondin and more like Melusine, whose body and social role take several forms in her story. Although readers of the tale do not know what she looked like as a fairy, Melusine looks like a surpassingly beautiful woman when Raymondin sees her by the fountain, in her Saturday baths like a woman with a snake's tail, and finally like a flying dragon. In another sense, Melusine was translated from being an unknown and therefore unsuitable bride for an aristocrat to being an honoured lady once she was seen in expensive clothes bestowing splendid gifts. Griselda's transformation was of course more earthbound, more "realistic." She stands with other young girls in the doorway of her hut, rather than beside a fountain in the forest (a frequent retreat for nymphs and fairies), and her gifts are those of humble labour and prudence rather than inexhaustible riches. Although Walter's choice is surprising in a patriarchal society, it does not greatly trouble the realistic surface the Clerk has conjured up.

Griselda's story suddenly turns gruesome when Walter distrusts her, in spite of her obvious virtues. His wilful curiosity cannot be satisfied by her daily conduct, but must be tested by extreme measures. Let's see what she is made of. Let's tear her babies from her arms and pretend to haul them off to death. Let's send her home to the ox's stall in nothing but a shift, and bring her back to clean the house for a new wife. Let's tell everybody the pope said OK. At this point, Griselda's quest/*aventure* turns dangerous. Melusine's is to become a human Christian and die a natural death, but the achievement of it depended on Raymondin's keeping his promise. Griselda, before and after her translation, wants to be a good Christian too, and her oath suggests that she considers obedience to her husband and feudal lord part of that commitment. Her fate presents her a cruel dilemma. She must know that it is wrong to kill or abet someone else in killing your children – unless of course the someone is God himself, as in Abraham's case. But she has made a solemn vow to Walter that she will not oppose him, not even in her private will: "But as ye wole yourself, right so wol I" (4.361). Being bound by an oath to be fulfilled in an unforeseeable future is the very stuff of romance, often the lynchpin of the narrative. Melusine's behaviour is judicious, but her form becomes monstrous; Griselda makes a choice that any actual-world ethical code finds monstrous. The interpretive problem of the *Clerk's Tale* is as difficult as assessing the part-serpentine heroine of *Melusine*. Here the "realistic" story solicits sympathy for and empathy with Griselda as she enacts a deeply flawed ethic of obedience to a depraved master.

A woman who would let her children be murdered without resistance is often tried for complicity these days. Decades of criticism have applied the word monstrous to Griselda, the Clerk, or the tale, but, as Allan Mitchell argues, its extreme and undecidable nature – the monstrousness of the tale itself – bestows on it the energy of an alternating force field, a phenomenon calling for ethical responsibility. The tale is haunting, he writes, because "no explanation is totally persuasive, no decision sufficiently justified, no response good enough."[11] Considered ethically, this interpretation of the issue is unanswerable and coincides with Kant's denial that a beautiful object can be fully captured in a concept, especially a moral concept. Melusine's character and role are at the centre of her story like those of Griselda in the *Clerk's Tale*, and both are monstrous, but in different ways. Both seem inscrutable for much of their stories. Although Griselda's words appear in the text, her inner life in the face of this extreme domestic tyranny is only to be guessed at, obliquely planting the suspicion that she is not human – indeed, she is a marvel, a wonder. It is the more fully characterized Clerk who remonstrates against Walter – he did not swear an oath not to.

Yet the narration treats Griselda's steadfastness as virtue. The Clerk lets her story gradually morph into a saint's legend rendered as a domestic exemplum. Saints' legends form one branch of medieval romance and hagiography's gift is to feminize the genre, as Geraldine Heng has argued.[12] These legends usually move from everyday reality to the marvellous (called miraculous in the legends) and elicit pathos for victims of cruelty, who are often women. When she is first introduced, Griselda's sanctity is suggested by her patient poverty, hard work, and loyalty to her father, and the biblical imagery of the well and ox's stall (4.206–30). Later it is underlined by the stanza in which she is favourably compared to Job (4.932–8). And of course in the end she is transformed again, arrayed in cloth of gold and crowned (4.1117–18). Although saints' lives may have been expected to inspire wonder (like other romances) rather than sober guidance for behaviour, Griselda *was* offered as a model for wives in the French translation of Petrarch's tale likely used by Chaucer, and in many of its later versions circulating all over Europe. On the Canterbury pilgrimage, the exemplary mode does kick in for at least the Host and Merchant, both of whom wish their wives were more like her (4.1213–14 and 1221–5). So long as Walter is an Italian marquis rather than God, the reading "Saint Griselda" would be a direct rebuttal of the *Wife's Tale.*

The whole story has unfolded – the reunion with her children, the years of accord with Walter, their prosperous reign, and the dynastic succession of their son – before the Clerk announces what his tale did *not* mean (4.1142–8). Rather than a wife who patiently endures suffering and humiliation, the figure of Griselda is once more translated, this time further up the ladder of abstraction, to allegorize the ideal Christian soul in its relation to God. This sudden return to Petrarch abruptly confuses the poem's generic logic. It may be seen as relieving some of the distress the tale has aroused by its apparent approval of passivity in the face of domestic tyranny – the narrator/Clerk himself seems worried about that even though he knows how the story will turn out. At the same time, it raises new problems, not only about Walter's standing in for God in the allegory after his obsessive curiosity had been questioned so openly, but also about the Clerk's literary relationship to his source. For Petrarch, this story may have been a stark allegory "seyd nat for that wyves sholde / Folwen Grisilde" in obedience towards their husbands (4.1142–3), but in the Clerk's telling it is painfully obvious what is happening in a realistically detailed domestic relationship. The image of Griselda turning over her kids without complaint (whether as saintly patience or a monstrous version of self-control) cannot be erased in favour of the cool allegorical/logical demonstration the Clerk announces in these lines. It is not merely a question of the Clerk/narrator introducing too much narrative noise; he lays bare the fact that allegorizing like Petrarch's violently captures experience (including the experience of reading) for service in the world of ideas, binding it "to a knowledge it imagines it already has," in this case that the soul must patiently endure God's slowly unfolding plan without complaint.[13]

The Clerk uses an interesting word to deny that he is offering Griselda as a model for wifely behaviour: it would be "inportable" for real-life wives to behave this way (today we would say criminal). Rather than the usual gloss for this word, "intolerable,"[14] we suggest that it be taken absolutely literally: not portable from one domain to another. What this does for the Clerk's about-face in translating his story from a domestic outrage to an allegory of the soul's proper obedience to God's inscrutable providence is to ironize his tale once again. Whenever the allegory is discussed, the likeness of Walter to God is the obvious stumbling block. The domestic realm in the tale is incompossible with the world of eternal verities, where God's will is unopposed. The logical Clerk could certainly see this himself, and save readers from the interference between competing interpretive impulses most readers experience while reading the tale. Had the Clerk distanced his narration, by eliciting less pathos, criticizing Walter less harshly, or emphasizing his motives towards Griselda as benign, he could have muffled the incompossiblity (as Petrarch's version does), although it cannot be effaced entirely.

The fact that he sharpened it instead allows another reading: that the allegorization of a story like this one is itself found wanting. Medieval sermons often made use of misogynistic old stories and then used allegoresis to turn them into pious fables. The *Gesta Romanorum*, a compendium of 181 tales from Roman history and also the East (even the *Arabian Nights*), was used all over Europe as source material for preachers, who allegorized these often entertaining stories. A good example is the tale of Paletinus's tree, from which three of his wives had hanged themselves. His friend tells him to stop lamenting and take cuttings to give to his neighbours; doing so, this tree became his most lucrative asset. The "application" is that the tree is Christ's cross, the wives are pride, lusts of the heart, and lusts of the eyes, and anyone who took a cutting is a good Christian.[15] The translator, Charles Swan, concedes that the pious moralizations that justify pulpit retellings often distort the implications of the tales themselves and that succeeding generations read the *Gesta* as simple entertainments. Because the Clerk's particular telling of the Griselda story fails to prepare for its allegorization so spectacularly, the Clerk undermines the glossing tradition he is expected to support and focuses instead on the suffering of real women at the hands of unjust class and gender systems. He is, ultimately, on the victim's side.[16] In this light, he is no longer the Wife's opponent, but her ally, although in a circuitous way that baffles several of the pilgrims and a good many readers since. He does praise a woman, and a sexually active one (unlike most protagonists in the saint's legends) and judge male arrogance harshly. As if that were not enough, the details of his telling critique the exegetical tradition that gave a pious sheen to ugly plots.

But even that is not where everything ends. The Clerk's discourse suddenly takes another turn. Since there are no more Griseldas in the actual world, he says, wives should imitate the Wife of Bath instead, and I will advise you by singing "a song to glade yow," leaving "ernestful matere" (4.1163–76). The final six stanzas attached to the tale in some manuscripts, called "Lenvoy de Chaucer" is a song, a double ballad in form: six-line stanzas with only three rhymes circulating through the whole. This form, intricate as it is, does not continue the Clerk's formal intricacy, nor does its tone match his voice in the tale itself. Although it seems to be the song promised in line 1174, it can also be read as a commentary by Chaucer the pilgrim, its form being one the author Chaucer had used in many of his short poems. There is considerable dispute about this; Helen Cooper, for example, takes it to be the Clerk's "mock encomium" to the Wife of Bath.[17] What it says is that Griselda and her patience are dead and "buryed in Ytaille" (4.1178). Moreover, no clerk should write of such a "mervaille" any longer. Instead, women are urged to dispute with the strength of camels or tigers, since no husband's armour can stand up against their "crabbed eloquence" (4.1203).

The allegorization of a tale of patience in the face of domestic abuse relies on polysemy – discourse that means other things than are said on the surface – but treating the tale with irony like that of "Lenvoy" negates both that surface and anything it implies figuratively. As Gordon Teskey writes, "Irony can disrupt everything, since there is nothing into which its disintegrating force cannot reach and nothing above which its scorn cannot rise." And yet "it is utterly weak before the brutality of power, whether the powers of history, of oppression, or of *physis* [growth] itself."[18] Whether Lenvoy is imagined as the Clerk's response to his tale or the pilgrim Chaucer's, it treats the tale with a withering irony as a realistic fiction, a saint's legend, and an allegory of the soul's duty to God. That is its power, but history has weakened its destructive force, certainly for Harry Bailly and the Merchant, who thought Griselda did the right thing and wish their wives were more like her, and for many subsequent readers who admire the allegory that relieves discomfort with the domestic tale. For Bailly and the Merchant the history is that of a familiar patriarchy and misogyny, for others the historically resilient theology surrounding an inscrutable Abrahamic God. This dizzying struggle between the polysemy of allegory and the antiphrasis of irony ends up producing beauty, precisely the beauty Kant defines in the *Third Critique*: a whole irreducible to concept yet full of conceptual claims, evocative of lifelike images that do not settle into mimesis. But another word among these last lines gestures towards the romance of possible worlds: "mervaille."

The Clerk meekly promises Harry Bailly "a murie thing of aventures" (4.15), which is not that unusual for a clerk because many romances were known to have clerical authors, but for a long time he does not seem to deliver either merriment or entertaining *aventure*. "Lenvoy," though, dissuades wives from letting clerks "write yow a storie of swich mervaille" (4.1186). The logic of romance is that there is another world, one in which Griselda is not just an Italian wife, nor yet a saint facing worldly persecution, but a creature translated from one reality to another. As a mervaille, she resembles Melusine; that is the meaning of Melusine's name. Until Melusine loses her son Fromont to violence within the family when his brother Geoffroy burned him in his monastery, her inner life is merely hinted at, which is also true of Griselda in parts 1–5 of the *Clerk's Tale*. Melusine, no seer in the matter of the fire, is informed of the crime by letter, just as Raymondin had been, and grieves for two days, wandering aimlessly "uttering bitter laments and heaving deep sighs" (190). Once her fully human inner life has been revealed, she is shown resuming her accustomed stoic (and strategic) calm, turning from her own grief and shock to comfort her husband: "Do you wish to challenge the will of the Maker of all things, who also unmakes them when it pleases Him?" She goes on to speculate that perhaps the monks were being punished, "for God's judgments are so secret that they pass human understanding" (190–1). We know that she loved her children and was horrified at Geoffroy's violence, but she behaved as Philosophy counselled Boethius, bowing before "what cannot now be changed" expressed as an effect of God's will. Griselda finally reveals her inner life when she recovers her children. She admits that for all these years her imagination had been at work on a horrible scene: "Youre woful mooder wende [believed] stedfastly / That crueel houndes or som foul vermyne / Hadde eten yow" (4.1094–6). She then faints, clasping the children so tightly that they had all they could do to extricate themselves. But before she falls, she credits God and "youre benyngne fader" for preserving them (4.1097). She forgives her husband as freely as Melusine does hers after his public denunciation, demonstrating the egalitarian definition of gentillesse Walter had described at the beginning of the tale. Griselda too is a mervaille.

Melusine is presented as both fully human and yet a marvel, and she brings the worlds of Lusignan's founding and the Avalon of her birth together in her person. The analogy is not exact, but there is something similar going on with Griselda. Like Melusine, she inhabits the space where the two circles of a Venn diagram overlap, at first in the actual medieval world when she is translated from the peasantry to the court (a big step in itself), and later from a person to the allegorical figure of patience. She is defined throughout by her uncomplaining adherence to her promise of obedience, both as a wife and as an allegory of the soul. "Lenvoy" undermines Griselda's story by comparing it with that of Chichevache, the starving cow who ate only patient wives. Do not be inspired by it, he tells wives, consigning it to fairy lore set in a world incompossible with that of medieval realities. Such irony can undermine the *Clerk's Tale* by calling it a fairy tale, but history testifies to the way fairy tales linger in cultural imagination to be reappropriated and reinterpreted across centuries despite all their elusive mysteriousness. As a marvel, like Melusine, Griselda occupies the centre of a beautiful enigma.

Promises, Promises: The *Franklin's Tale*

The third tale we will investigate also zeros in on *gentillesse*, dominance in marriage, authority and experience, and especially troth-plighting, but from yet another set of givens, linking the Franklin's tale with the Wife's and Clerk's in a three-way dialogue. The intertext that interrupts the Squire's unfinished tale consists of the Franklin's praise for the *gentillesse* of the young teller's wit and eloquence. The Franklin uses *gentillesse* to refer to refinement of ethical character: "Fie on possessioun, / But if a man be virtuous withal!" (5.626–7). His praise for the Squire's performance implies that storytelling may inspire virtue, which suggests didactic aims, again like the Wife and Clerk. His tale is attributed to "Thise olde gentil Britouns" (5.709), briefly reprising the beginning of *Sir Orfeo*, and implying that such oral and written tales model gentility. Unfolding implications for the future from these old Breton tales is a strategy Marie de France had pioneered. The issue of sovereignty in love relations is also explicit in early lines of the tale. The tale begins as Arveragus persuades Dorigen to marry him by swearing to serve her as her knight and exert no husbandly "maistrie" except to retain "soveraynetee" for the sake of appearances (5.748–51). In return, Dorigen, because of his "gentillesse," pledges her "trouthe" that she will be his "humble trewe wyf" (5.758–9). Arveragus will be "servant in love, and lord in marriage" and both will practise patience, which is always better than rigour (5.793, 772–5). The nature of the unusual promise that seals the marriage is reminiscent of the arrangement between Melusine and Raymondin, in that Raymondin will be the externally recognized patriarch, but strategic decisions and plans for erecting the buildings and extending the dynasty are managed by Melusine. Both of these private agreements lie outside the authority of the dominant discourse on marriage, and both plots test them against experience.

A gentle accord like that between Dorigen and Arveragus is more likely to be found at the end (as in the Wife's and Clerk's tales) than at the beginning of a romance *aventure.* The integrity and good sense of the married couple in the *Franklin's Tale* seems unlikely to produce a crisis, but of course it does. While Arveragus is away earning his stripes in England, Dorigen refuses the seductions of the lovelorn squire Aurelius, and then, as a kind of afterthought, says she will love him best when he removes the dangerous black rocks in the harbour to which her husband will return. Aurelius, after two years of pining, enlists for a huge sum the services of a clerk/tregetour (magician), who does produce a coastline apparently free of the offending rocks, but by that time Arveragus had already returned home and resumed his serene married life. Dorigen suddenly finds herself bound by two promises and sees her only way out as suicide, her mind turning to stories (mostly classical) she has encountered about pure maidens and faithful wives who kill themselves rather than submit to rape. When she confides in her husband, Arveragus tells her she must go to Aurelius as promised because "Trouthe is the hyeste thyng that man may kepe" (5.1479); using "man" to mean "human being," he recognizes a woman's promise as no less binding than a man's.[19] The tangle of authority is thereby brought to crisis: is the husband mastering the wife by ordering her to go, or is he respecting her selfhood as he had vowed he would.[20] Dorigen meets Aurelius in a formerly paradisiacal garden in tears, saying her husband sent her, Aurelius cannot bring himself to threaten such a couple by taking advantage of her oath, and the clerk/magician forgives Aurelius his considerable financial debt. Which of them, asks the Franklin, is the most "*fre*," most truly gentle?

The Franklin has evidently constructed his tale purposefully around three recurring terms: *gentillesse*, *trouthe*, and *fre*. He could even be taken to have fashioned a lovely parable, a secular exemplum focused on marriage, but sending ripples out towards broader societal trust. From the frame onward, *gentillesse* is defined in various circumstances, and the word itself knits up the tale. In the garden near the end of the tale, Aurelius looks into himself and sees his continued "lust" as "cherlyssh wrecchednesse / Agayns franchise and alle gentillesse" when compared with Arveragus's respect for his wife's trouthe (1520–4), bringing the three terms together. This insight breaks his will (another meaning of "lust") to sleep with her. He knows that in spite of the phrasing of her promise – then "wol I love yow best of any man" – she will not love but only submit to him, weeping as she does so. (The knight in the *Wife's Tale* could be forced to marry but not to love the crone – love is *fre*.) When Aurelius told Dorigen about the disappearance of the rocks, he specifically denied that he was entitled to her body by "right" (5.1324). Desperate as his love-longing has been, the "greet routhe" that now seizes him is not unprepared for. He is no crass predator. Inspired by Arveragus's gentillesse (5.1527), and Dorigen's truth (loyalty) – "the treweste and the beste wyf / That evere yet I knew in al my lyf (5.1539–40) – Aurelius relinquishes his power over her in crisply legal terms (serement, bond) to which he plights his *trouthe* (5.1534–7), hoping only to be remembered as a squire whose deed is as gentle as a knight's (5.1543–4). Nor, having sworn by his "trouthe" (5.1231) to pay the Orleans clerk a ruinous thousand pounds, does he ask his debt to be forgiven, just that half be paid later "of his [the clerk's] gentillesse" (5.1574). But once the clerk has heard the whole story, he is moved to release Aurelius from his bond, and does so decisively, that he might be counted among the "gentils" (5.1609–11).

Yet the beautiful, and somewhat baffling, effects of the tale are not reined in by the purposiveness of its earnest Franklin/narrator any more than the Clerk or Wife, both trickier types, were able to control theirs. *Trouthe* is inextricably bound up with *gentillesse*. It is the "highest thing," but also a trap and an enigma, as it often is in romance. Obligations incurred through a rash promise, especially important for a king, serve as lynchpins in the romance tradition. They render promisors helpless no matter how powerful they have been. The beginning of Chrétien's "Lancelot," in which Arthur promises to give Kay whatever he asks for if he will give up his plan to leave court, and Mark's turning Isolde over to Gandin in Gottfried's *Tristan* are prominent examples. Even a king of fairy cannot evade the consequences of a rash vow, as we saw in *Sir Orfeo*. A plot can pull apart the two medieval meanings of *trouthe* – loyalty, steadfastness versus veracity, accuracy[21] – and the *Franklin's Tale* certainly does that. Plighting *trouthe* is not simply a legal matter, it is a matter of honour – how will anyone, king included, maintain a respected identity after having broken a promise publicly made? But Dorigen's promise to Aurelius was a private matter; her intent, surely readable at the time, was actually a second refusal of her love, as far as she knew. Yet both she and her husband treat her words as binding, just as Gawain's words bind him to seek the Green Knight, as we shall see in the next chapter.

Of course "*fre*" and "franchise" have a social resonance that makes the men in the tale competitors for status and chimes with the narrator's name: Franklin, landed without feudal obligation, but not titled. *Fre* is used throughout the period to point to both high birth and the magnanimity that high birth makes possible, while a second related meaning, "unconstrained," is also implied. When the squire and clerk in the tale relinquish their claims, they expect their generosity to in some way raise them level with Arveragus's knighthood. The implications "gracious" and "unconstrained" overshadow the sense of *fre* as social standing at the end of the tale, entwining it with the independence of *trouthe* and *gentillesse* from "possessioun" (5.686). All three men can claim that they have unconstrainedly given up something valuable and thereby proved themselves gentle. Yet this, though a likely purpose for the Franklin, does not entirely untie the knot produced by the original vows Arveragus and Dorigen make when they marry. They abandon the prevailing legalistic definition of marriage in order to prevent their mutual love from dwindling into obligation; as the Franklin/narrator asserts, "Love is a thyng as any spirit free" (5.767). "Maistrye" will blight it for both women and men. This is, of course, a commonplace for romance plotting, readily seen in nearly all Marie's *lais.* Here, though, it creates a problem in ethical logic: Dorigen is free to meet Aurelius in order to keep her word, but not free because she has pledged her trouthe to Arveragus to be his "humble trew wife" (5.758). Arveragus's marriage pledge makes him unfree to order her to go to the garden, but his order is intended to stop her from killing herself and demonstrate his respect for her plighted word. Dorigen says that the promise about the rocks has become a "trappe" for her (5.1341) – it is also a trap for the impulse to make her tale an exemplum.

The Franklin identifies his tale specifically as a Breton *lai,* although scholars have not found a Breton *lai* with this plot. (Marie's may not all have been firmly based on such earlier tales either.) The identification, however, gives us reason to expect some magic or the intrusion of an alternate world, and indeed there is (potentially) an element of magic in the disappearance of the rocks. In this regard, the tale as a whole resembles Marie's earthly love triangle in *Eliduc* more closely than her *Yonec* with its shape-shifting hawk/prince. Eliduc's going off to establish his credentials as a knight errant is predictable, and so is the rescued maiden's love for her champion, a repeated pattern in the stories of Melusine's sons. Only the red flower Guildeluëc, Eliduc's wife, uses to bring Guilliadun, his lover, back from apparent death (Marie's text does not settle the issue of whether she was really dead or not) defies the normal rules of nature in this feudal world. Guildeluëc's generosity in taking the veil to allow Guilliadun's marriage is awe-inspiring, but not supernatural. The story of Dorigen and Arveragus's companionate marriage is ultimately based on a similar optimism about human potential. Its disruption by a particularly unofficial "promise" to Aurelius keeps the otherworldly at arm's length by making it seem commensurate with the historical world of the Canterbury pilgrimage, providing distance (as Marie did not) between himself and what the Franklin takes to be the givens of his source tale. The world of the "olde gentil Britouns," especially the magical illusions produced by the clerk of Orleans, seems to the Franklin an earlier causal domain, which brings us to the tale's investment in possible worlds.[22]

Breton *lais* traditionally allow intrusions by other worlds into the actual worlds of their texts, but the actuality of this textual world already consists of classical, Celtic, and medieval Christian settings, entwining the strands of our argument for foldings of time and possible worlds. "Thise olde gentil Britouns" supplied the plot line in which Aurelius prays to classical deities and Dorigen to a possibly classical Boethian God (no specifically Christian terms mark her prayer), while the Franklin disparages their era as heathen. Historical time is folded within the fable itself: in a reading that distances the world of the tale in the same way the *Wife's Tale* does, its setting seems to suggest a pre-Christian past presided over by the Apollo and Lucina Aurelius prays to and an "Eterne God" who may be seen as classical. But if Dorigen's Boethian address is read as Christian (as Chaucer and his era undoubtedly read the *Consolation*), the fable may be taken to signal a tension between Aurelius and Dorigen's beliefs, allowing her to appear as a fully Christian moral agent. Moreover, she and Arveragus will then appear to move towards the Franklin/narrator in providing a pattern of gentility and trust that harmonizes with medieval idealism about married love, but also exceeds it to predict a more egalitarian future dispensation. We agree with Steele Nowlin that the manner in which the tale is told "fashions a new world," regarding the characters to be "testing out cultural paradigms and struggling to conceive new alternatives in the face of precedent."[23]

The Franklin pointedly addresses the issue of magic, even "magyk natureel," in a strict Christian context, consigning the clerk's practices to those that "hethen folk useden in thilke [such] dayes." He himself rejects the magic through which the rocks "semed" for a week or two to be away (5.1293–6). He is very specific about the clerk's methods, employing technical terms for astrology at some length (5.1261–96), while interspersing his explanations with disapproving asides like "japes," "wrecchednesse" and "supersticious cursednesse" (5.1271–2). His description of the astrological tables and calculations ("roots") the clerk relies on, though, are not particularly dated. The detail in this section produces a curious familiarity with this "wrecchednesse," and tends to undermine the distinction between the Franklin's enlightened present and the deceptive "japes" of an earlier era. His telling requires his own dismissal of magic in order to preserve the realistic, orthodox Christian point of his story, while endorsing the reality of its effects for his characters. Against the grain of his characters' perceptions, he recognizes no genuinely alternative world invading his story's space, just chicanery. Yet his story cannot proceed unless those perceptions are credited within his narrative. The rocks are really missing *as far as they know*. Aurelius, having asked Apollo for a miracle earlier (5.1056), believes that one has taken place, thanks the Orleans clerk and Venus, and rushes to catch Dorigen in a temple (5.1299–1307). Miracles are marvels resulting from otherworldly intrusions, but Aurelius has appealed to the wrong deities, as the Franklin sees it. No possibility that would account for the disappearance of the rocks lies within Dorigen's understanding of the "proces of nature" (5.1343–5), identified earlier with a Boethian sense of the "certein governaunce" of "Eterne God" (5.865–6). For her an alternative world of process must have intruded.

Nature is a goddess who keeps secrets. Medieval culture was generally ambivalent about investigation into them, and laymen especially were warned not to speculate. The Miller in the *Canterbury Tales* puts this commonplace warning to humorous use in the prologue to his tale: "An housbonde shal nat been inquisitive / Of Goddes pryvetee, nor of his wyf" (1.3163–4). The long history of astrology and alchemy (of which more in the next section) often claimed (or threatened) both to uncover "Goddes pryvetee" and produce practical effects by doing so. The Miller's Nicholas was a clerk adept at various of these arts and used his sleights to fool his host the carpenter and bed his wife. The Franklin seems aware of the ambiguous reputation of such learning and eagerly distances himself from anything that could look magical. A small sign of his distrust comes through in his phrasing: Aurelius's brother remembers the clerk/magician as someone who seeks curious scientific learning "in every halke and every herne" (nook and cranny, 5.1121). "Herne" sounds especially scruffy; the *Canon's Yeoman's Prologue,* openly dismissive of the claims of alchemy, discredits the charlatan alchemist by revealing that he lives in a "herne."[24] Moreover, he makes use of the unusual term "apparences" four times. Its connection with magic is clear from the *Squire's Tale,* in which "apparence" is "ymaad by som magic / As jogelours pleyen at thise feestes grete (5.218).[25] In the first two instances in the tale, Aurelius's brother gleefully ponders the illusions he knows "subtile tregetours" can produce (5.1140–1 and 1157); in the third the tregetour refers to his own "apparence or jogelrye" (5.1265). In telling his tale, therefore, the Franklin uses "herne" and "apparence" to ratify a Christian sense of trust in a world order. These instances keep the Franklin's understanding of his tale in the actual world of late medieval enlightenment.

The fourth occurrence of "apparence," though, intensifies the energy the term exerts. When Aurelius tells the magician of Dorigen's distress, he relates how loathe she was to be an unfaithful wife, and how, in her innocence "She never erst hadde herde speak of apparence" (5.1599–1603). This melts the "philosopher's" heart too, as well it might, since he now sees his arts as aiding in the betrayal of a vulnerable Christian, who believed herself to be living in Boethius's stable world of nature under God's *purveiaunce*. What it tells us about Dorigen is that she believes in the orderliness of natural process and is unsuspicious of the perceived world. This is consistent with her characterization all along. When Dorigen contends with God over the appropriateness of the rocks that threaten his fair creation mankind, she does so in the spirit of Boethius's *Consolatione* (Chaucer's *Boece*): an intelligent, humble soul seeking to understand a seeming paradox. Troilus concludes his philosophical inquiry in book 4 of *Troilus and Criseyde* by deferring to clerks in much the same way Dorigen does. Although her complaint is motivated by the hope of Arveragus's return, she prays for an understanding of providential order, not, like Aurelius, a miracle.

Dorigen's inner life is not veiled, as are those of Griselda or Melusine. Allowing for the somewhat different vocabulary medieval authors had at their disposal for subjectivity, Dorigen is as knowable as a medieval character is likely to be. Her spoken words are more often directly quoted than those of others in the tale, and the narrator represents her inner life as uncomplicated by hypocrisy or self-delusion. Therefore, her case is unlike Criseyde's, she of the "slydyng corage," in that readers are not directed to look for hidden motivations or slippages. We see her thought at length in her contention with Providence over the black rocks and again when she rehearses the misogynous patristic tradition in the list of suicides. In both cases, she is presented, as Robert Solomon puts it, as grappling with the world, a matter of emotional intensity produced by and consisting of perceptions, memories, and judgments, although not necessarily articulate self-conscious ones.[26] Her unfortunate vow to love Aurelius when the rocks are gone is therefore based on her unfamiliarity with the world of "apparence" produced by the clerk of Orleans's arts.

Dorigen's predicament produces a deep situational irony in that she is among the most verbal of romance heroines and yet betrayed by her own words. Her subjectivity is bound up in the intricacies of possibility. She thinks she is decisively turning Aurelius down because the rules of nature are predictable, and he thinks so too – "'Madame,' quod he, 'this were an inpossible'" – and he may as well go away to die a horrible death (5.1009–10). "Inpossible" is a term in logic, but the world of marvels works by unknown rules. Aurelius was later introduced to the power of illusions. While he was actually sitting alone with his brother and the clerk, he was shown hunted animals and jousting knights: "al this sighte merveillous" (5.1206). Dorigen, of course, receives no such initiation. Suddenly faced with the seeming disappearance of the rocks, she reacts with shock and horror: "For wende I nevere by possibilitee / That swich a monster or merveille myghte be! / It is agayns the proces of nature" (5.1343–5). The marvellous that Aurelius thought of as a miracle is monstrous to her. This point in the tale swerves close to tragic irony: her concern for Arveragus's safety, her confidence in a Boethian order of nature, and her care for the integrity of her trouthe combine to impel her to consider suicide – and all because of her own words. An alternative world, whether or not a conjured one, is suddenly made epistemically present to Dorigen. *For all she knows*, the rocks may really be gone, a new causal order imposed on the familiar "process of nature" – and the attempts of critics to determine whether and how the clerk's magic "worked" are beside the point.

Dorigen might have set any kind of impossible test for Aurelius as a way to deny him her love ("bring me the head of a giant"), but while the counterfactual she does invent is a logical impossibility in the real world, at a deeper level it speaks to her desire to see her husband safely home again, a wish fulfilment as poignant as that of any romance heroine.

As he turns to Arveragus's painful decision, the Franklin calls attention to his own storytelling function, as the Wife does when she laments the current absence of fairies and as the Clerk does when he wonders what drives Walter's malign curiosity. He worries that the pilgrims (and many readers since, as it turns out) will think Arveragus a "lewed man" for putting his wife "in jupartie," and censure the teller for relating a story in which this action was presented as wise. His answer makes an internal use of time-folding: "Herkneth the tale er ye upon hire crie. / She may have bettre fortune than yow semeth; / And whan that ye han herd the tale, demeth" (5.1495–9). Unlike the readers who might censure him, he already knew the end of the affair, but this advice is the counsel of patience that he had commended in marriage agreements. Just wait, he says. And indeed, in time Arveragus not only gets his wife back unharmed, he fulfils his marriage promise and inspires other men to gentle deeds. The Franklin finds Arveragus so "weel apayed" that it was "inpossible" to write about his happiness (5.1548–9). Yet in this passage the narrator reveals the strain his plot has placed on the original marriage agreement: to save both her life and her *trouthe* Arveragus must order Dorigen to go to the garden at the cost of his husbandly pride and her suffering ("jupartie").[27]

The intrusion of an alternative possible world saves the knight's life in the *Wife's Tale* and teaches him some valuable lessons about gentillesse and the respect he owes authority when a woman wields it. Considering the rape that initiates the story and his reluctance to honour his *trouthe*, his enchanted *wyf* rewards him with more than his actions deserve. Lifting up the bed curtain he finds himself "bathed in a bath of blisse" and happily married ever afterward. In romances, another world often rescues the actual one, allowing escape from unrelenting misery and/or a new vantage point from which to see it. One might say that Arveragus too is bathed in bliss at the end, but in his case the apparently alternative world of the magician is the source of the wrenching decision which he had faced. Dorigen and Arveragus's private agreement of mutual trust is not based on the authority of institutional religion or patriarchal society, but it is ratified by the harrowing experience that tested it. What the *Franklin's Tale* has to say is that escape from the trap of binding vows and changing circumstances is an alternative world made visible through committed love, the sacrifice of pride, especially male possessiveness, unguaranteed trust in the future, and the contagiousness of gentle deeds. This aesthetic idea accords with Kant's assertion that beauty "directly brings with it a feeling of the promotion of life" (*CPJ*, 128; Meredith's translation has "furtherance of life"), and it opens through imaginative play into a future in which, in some places at least, such aspirations become the ideals of dominant discourse, rather than private bargains. The tale is laden with the past of the olde gentil Britouns and pregnant with a future in which (though with uneven progress) companionate love-marriage and respect for female *trouthe* can seem, not *lewed* but wise.

Although all three of the romances we have been looking at avoid potential disasters, the *Franklin's Tale* is the most untroubled by corrosive irony. We turn next to its polar opposite, a tale that takes Dorigen's momentary wish to move rocks more seriously, positing an alternative world in which matter and not persons are translated.

Coda: The *Canon's Yeoman's Tale*

Romance as a literary form invites us to imagine that the world we live in now could be different, somewhere else perhaps, or sometime in the distant past or future. Often romance posits a possible world alien to our own, a world of fairy where human visitors may be transformed forever (like Lanval), but where, more often, they return to the actual with new insight into the implications of their human mortality (as do Orfeo and Heurodis). Melusine makes the journey in the opposite direction, but loses the longed-for transformation from immortal fairy to mortal human wife she had all but achieved. The Wife's fictional knight encounters a fairy enchantress, but ends up exemplifying a new kind of marriage ethos. The momentary wish that causes so much grief for Dorigen is a wish to change the physical world in order to preserve her already happy marriage. Her wish is simpler and more fundamental than entering into the metaphysical otherness of the world of fairy, but it goes to the heart of Chaucer's understanding of romance, his respect for the desires that drive the counterfactual fantasies of his characters, but at the same time his belief that in the end they must live their lives within the actual world. In its refusal to accept the limitations of the actual, and in its radical hope, alchemy may be the medieval world's ultimate resort to romance. Rather than riding off into the forest to encounter an enchanted lady, the alchemist sets out to change reality itself, to construct a possible world by using the pots and jars in his own workshop. The *Canon's Yeoman's Tale* makes brilliant comic use of the resistance of things to such human endeavour, but it may also be seen as Chaucer's ultimate reflection on the fictions of possibility in the literature he had inherited.

The Canon and his Yeoman, latecomers to the company of pilgrims, are introduced in the Prologue by an exchange with the Host in which the Yeoman begins by praising his master's wisdom and discretion, but ends in bitter recrimination. In the course of the exchange, the Yeoman begins to reveal their alchemical work, but dwells mostly on their failures and the cost to his own body and fortune. In the first part of the tale, he offers a much fuller account of the Canon's "pryvetee," describing the materials and the apparatus of their work in astonishing detail, and culminating with a disastrous explosion in their primitive laboratory. In the second part, he turns to his actual tale, an ostensibly fictional account of an unscrupulous alchemist who bilks a gullible priest out of forty pounds. Like Nicholas in the *Miller's Tale,* the alchemist of the Yeoman's fiction is adept at using language to spin a narrative, contrive his props, and close the deal when his victim's emotions have eclipsed his reason. The long history of astrology and alchemy often claimed (or threatened) both to uncover "Goddes pryvetee" and produce practical effects. Although often outlawed by the church because in a Christian context the secrets are God's and people have no business prying into them, alchemy thrived and attracted clerical experimenters as distinguished as Albertus Magnus. The alchemical treatises of the Middle Ages were deeply concerned to make a distinction between those philosophers who work with matter in the hope of refining it until it finally reveals divine truth, and those charlatans who simply seek a technology capable of making them rich.[28]

When the Yeoman describes the work he and his Canon do in part 1, his account is heavy with the materiality of the process:

> Watres rubifiying, and boles galle,
> Arsenyk, sal armonyak, and brymstoon;
> And herbes koude I telle eek many oon,
> As egremoyne, valerian, and lunarie,
> And othere swiche, if that me liste tarie. (8.797–801)

But these raw materials of the natural world only reveal themselves through the mediation of human-fashioned things, which are equally abundant in the Yeoman's description:

And sondry vessels maad of erthe and glas,
Our urynales and oure descensories,
Violes, crosletz, and sublymatories,
Cucurbites, and alambikes eek,
And othere swiche, deere ynough a leek,
Nat nedeth it for to reherce hem alle. (8.792–6)

What emerges from all of this is an abundant richness of materiality, but also a richness of the technological language through which all these powders and herbs and essences and smoky fires are made visible, and so made knowable. That is, a kind of dialogue between humans and objects takes place, and out of that dialogue emerges knowledge, whether of technological mastery or divine insight.

The process of shaping matter in search of divine truth may be understood as metaphoric if Chaucer's tale is seen to be about the artistic process, and therefore as ultimately celebrating humanity. While the things of the world are regarded in a much more positive light in this formulation, they still exist primarily to point beyond themselves, though this time to a transcendent allegory of mortal human existence: "We may read the *prima pars* for its vision of the artist at work, casting for eternal truths among the solid and intransigent matter of the world."[29] Regardless of whether we privilege eternal truths or intransigent matter, the relation between art and work is always central, so let us return to the Yeoman's lengthy list of the elements and instruments of his craft. His list contains an additional category, hardly surprising, but deserving of our attention, namely, words that describe process: sublyming, amalgamyng, calcenyng, ascencioun, calcinacioun, albificacioun, coagulat, enbibyng, encorporyng, citrinacioun, cementyng, fermentacioun, mollificacioun, induracioun, fusible. These words all describe normal processes of change, and we could go on to the volatile aromas, the fires and smokes that blacken our poor Yeoman, and of course the occasional explosion. A nice contemporary medieval statement about all of this might be Geber and Arnald's advice that the Philosopher's Stone must "by way of sublimation be made volatile, and the volatile fixed; and the fixed, dissolved; and the dissolved again volatile, and the volatile again fixed, until it flow and alter."[30]

Desire in romance is always about translation. A fairy crone becomes a beautiful woman and a disgraced knight is redeemed through his encounter with such otherworldliness. A young peasant woman becomes a marchioness when combed hair and an elegant dress translate the semiotics of social identity. Working at a still more fundamental level, the Canon seeks to transform the very fabric of the world, but the "metals been of so greet violence" (8.908) that when his pot explodes the stuff pierces his wall and the rest remains "scattered al the floor aboute" (8.914). The Yeoman might well have repeated his earlier complaint, that "lost is al our labour and travaille" (8.781). What in fact he does, however, is shovel the debris onto a canvas, put it through a sieve, and return to the endless work of separating the elements, only to be able to combine them once again. When the Yeoman laments how much they have spent in their efforts to arrive at the philosopher's stone, he says it would have made them mad, "but that good hope crepeth in oure herte" (8.870), and earlier, relating to the Host their failure to multiply gold, he says that nevertheless they "han good hope / It for to doon, and after it we grope" (8.678–9). Hope is the counterfactual that underlies all their work, the faith that what is before our eyes may change, may become something different, something better.

As Chaucer's characters work to make things new, they find that they themselves are caught up in the dynamism of change. The physical changes the Yeoman undergoes in the course of his service are a slow and contrary version of the makeover experienced by Griselda at the hands of the ladies of Walter's court. His clothes are distressed, the work has bleared his eye, and his colour, which was formerly "both fressh and reed" is now like the basest of his raw materials "wan and of a leden hewe" (8.727–8). The Canon too has almost become the things of his profession. When he arrives sweating profusely, his very body has become an alchemical apparatus: "His forheed dropped as a stillatorie." And the narrator is captivated by this image of a human distillery: "But it was joye to seen hym swete!" (8.579). If alchemy seeks permanent change in the stuff on which it works its magic, the Yeoman warns that appearances can be deceiving, that "al thyng which that shineth as the gold / Nis nat gold" (8.962–3). His message might as well have been meant for Dorigen, who also trusts too much in the illusion of what she had initially hoped to see. But whether change in these tales is miraculously real, or merely the appearance of change, the potential for change remains. When the Yeoman tells the story of his master's transgressions, he blushes:

Evere whan that I speke of his falshede,
For shame of hym my chekes wexen rede.
Algates they bigynnen for to glowe,
For reednesse have I noon, right wel I knowe,
In my visage; for fumes diverse
Of metals, whiche ye han herd me reherce,
Consumed, and wasted han my reednesse. (8.1094–1100)

The blushing Yeoman's leaden cheeks turn red, and in recalling his long-ago lost redness, become a counterfactual sign of hope. The point of his most detailed account of alchemical practice, as the criminal deception of a poor gullible priest, is equally undercut by its own telling. Quite simply, the description of how the Canon of the *pars secunda* creates his illusions is vivid and delightful, displaying not only deft sleight-of-hand, but also expert knowledge of how to use the instruments and the materials of his craft. The silver only appears to appear, but the illusionist's trick has consequences, as it does for Dorigen. Like DVD extras on how the special effects were done, this part of the tale delights because insider knowledge is delightful.

The Yeoman's two moments of storytelling may be seen to cohere around two ideas: "I am an exploited labourer," and then "my master exemplifies the fraudulence of alchemy." Far removed from the inviolability of the romance vow, the master's promise to change base metal into gold in no way constrains him, as he betrays Yeoman and priest alike. But the details of the telling exceed the closure of his intention. The *Canon's Yeoman's Tale* does not show us lifeless, unchanging matter essentially alien to the human, but rather a picture of endless human endeavour to shape a world that is continuously emerging. The Canon and his Yeoman live in the liminal space of the suburbs, and when the tale ends, the Yeoman has left that space to begin a new life – or not – we cannot know. Describing a striking photograph of a drop of liquid just about to fall, the physicist Sidney R. Nagel writes that "photography provides a means of catching the shadows cast by the ephemeral objects of our world."[31] Like photography, the language of literary romance is also able to capture the fascinating and beautiful moment on the cusp: metal melting, a cheek turning red, a man resolving to change his life. But romance captures the longer rhythms of time as well, incorporating the memory of Breton storytelling but also the potentiality of fiction to resonate with readers yet unborn. Gold may be changeless, but alchemy never arrives at its still point, and the alchemists of Chaucer's tale certainly do not. The Canon and his Yeoman remain in a world of work, where change only occurs through the agency of human labour.

The gullible priest, eager to believe that one more experiment will reveal the miraculous, and the alchemist who seriously seeks to find the philosopher's stone both desire to transcend the real. But Chaucer's characters always return from their *aventures* to an unfinished world, and therefore to another kind of possibility, equally endless, always open, and so in a fully Kantian sense, always potentially beautiful. The Canon and his Yeoman pick themselves up after the explosion and begin to sort through the rubble; Griselda falls senseless to the floor when she is reunited with her children, but eventually she stands up and resumes her life; the Wife negotiates a happier marriage. To see the emergent possibility in things is to see beauty in the ephemeral. This is the perilous hope of the Canon and his Yeoman, but it is also the persistence of romance even in this most unrelentingly material of all of Chaucer's *Canterbury Tales*. The *Canon's Yeoman's Tale* depicts and deconstructs a long-held notion about the volatile nature of the physical world, but it also provides an "instructive" metaphor for other kinds of transmutation. It is only that, as Neal Stephenson's character Daniel Waterhouse says to his character Leibniz in the epigraph for this chapter, alchemists take the metaphor too literally.

Chapter Six

The Immense Subtlety of *Sir Gawain and the Green Knight*

Of shapes transformede to bodies strange, I propose to entreate.

Ovid, *Metamorphoses* (Golding translation)

Alchemy is only one of the ways medieval culture thought about the dramatically changeable. The influence of Ovid's *Metamorphoses* was persistent – bodies have been known to turn into very different bodies. *Sir Gawain and the Green Knight* invokes that notion as centrally as *Melusine* does, but the poem begins and ends otherwise, with a wide-angle overview of world history beginning with Troy. The first stanza of this anonymous poem begins, "When the siege and assault was ceased at Troy," and recounts the founding of Bretayn by Aeneas's supposed grandson Brutus, and the third zooms in on the Christmas festivities in King Arthur's court that will initiate Gawain's *aventure*.[1] For a fourteenth-century reader (this is a literary rather than an oral poem), this beginning conjured up associations from two of the respected "matters" of medieval storytelling: those of Troy/Greece and Britain. Since Geoffrey of Monmouth's influential *Historia Regum Britanniae* (Latin, ca. 1130–9), both the Trojan War and the Arthurian reign were regarded as historical verities and founding cultural myths.[2] The siege of Troy recurs in the last lines of the poem to place Gawain's tale alongside the *aventures* of Brutus, locating him among Britain's "national" heroes. Yet the poet also offers the tale as if it were an oral performance: "If ȝe wyl listen this laye bot on little quile [while], / I schal telle hit astit [right away] as I in toun herde, / With tonge" (29–31). "HONY SOYT QUI MAL PENCE" [Evil to him who thinks evil], the motto of the Order of the Garter, established by Edward III in 1348, was added to the manuscript by an unknown hand after the poet's "Amen," apparently in the belief that *Gawain and the Green Knight* relates to the founding of the order. The world-historical gravitas of the tale is endowed with an intimate twist. Brutus and Arthur belong to a broadly foundational history and the girdle (garter) to a narrower one; the town just down the road is still telling Gawain's story aloud.

As a late medieval English romance, the artistry of *Gawain and the Green Knight* is without peer for its intricate beauty. It is written in a north-west midlands dialect not easily read now, but available in many modern translations. Since it differs both orthographically and semantically from London English, it may have been difficult for Chaucer's Londoners too, although Richard II could understand it because his bodyguard spoke it.[3] Its particular poetic form is unique. It is untitled and consists of four parts, uneven in length, called fitts. The stanzas are constructed in an alliterative long-line form descended from Old English poetry (three or four stressed alliterated syllables, two on each side of a caesura), but each one ends with a "bob and wheel," a two-word phrase and then four short lines. Its dialect and prosody make the poem seem both archaic (in contrast with the growing influence of Chaucerian/London practices) and innovative. There is only one manuscript, dated about 1400, although the story it tells must have been fairly well known to have been retold in oral form later in the fifteenth century.[4]

This late-fourteenth-century narrative poem thrusts Sir Gawain from the Christmas festivities at the Arthurian court into his *aventure*, as a huge, green, axe-wielding rider on a huge green horse appears in the great hall, challenging Camelot's vaunted courage. As King Arthur's nephew, Gawain takes up the Green Knight's challenge, which is to cut off his head and accept a return blow in a year's time. Gawain promises to show up as the intruder picks up his severed head and rides off into the winter night. The next year Gawain faithfully seeks the green chapel that was given as the meeting place, passing through the wild wood of Wirral and arriving at a lovely castle, which seems as sumptuous and welcoming as Arthur's. Gawain is honoured there and joins a courtly game in which he and Bertilak, his host, vow to exchange each day's winnings at suppertime. The host goes hunting, first for a stag, then a boar, and finally a fox, which he yields to Gawain each evening. While he hunts, his lady tempts Gawain sexually, but he accepts only kisses, until on the third day she convinces him to wear her green girdle, which will protect him from death. He does not turn over the girdle to his host, but conceals it beneath his armour as he resolutely rides off to face the blow of the Green Knight the next morning. After two feints, the great axe wounds Gawain, but only slightly, and the giant reveals that he is really Bertilak under a spell cast by Morgan le Fay, who intended to scare Guinevere to death in the Christmas episode. Gawain's courage and chastity prevented this triumph over Arthur's court, but his *trawthe* was slightly compromised by his not exchanging the girdle, like his instinctive recoil from the axe that earned him the nick on his neck. On his return to Camelot, Arthur's people honour him by wearing such a girdle themselves as a sign of his renown, but for Gawain himself, it is a reminder of what he considers his shameful cowardice.

Gawain and the Green Knight makes good on romance *aventure* in all of its available meanings, as described by Michael Nerlich.[5] *Aventure* as "something that happens" is signalled by the Green Knight's intrusion at the outset (perhaps invited by Arthur's refusal to eat before he had seen a marvel "that he myȝt trawe [believe], 94)." It becomes something Gawain seeks, *his* quest to return the blow he had delivered in order to serve the king (who had failed to control the axe) and to keep his word, his *trawthe* (394, 403, 2348). Later the lady simply "bere on hym the belt" and he allowed it (1860), promising only not to reveal the gift to her husband. That was something that happened *to* him.[6] The plot describes the arc of quest romance – a journey into the unknown and return with a gift for his home, as outlined by Joseph Campbell[7] – but an ingeniously skewed one. The hero of medieval quest romance usually falls in love and through his courage and resolve wins his beloved and achieves his identity, but Gawain remains aloof from the lovely chatelaine and yet returns a Christian penitent, neither erotic nor heroic expectations for the genre completely met.[8] His commitments lie with loyalty to Arthur's dynasty, respect for his host's claim to his lady, Christian virtue (Mary's image on the inside of his shield), and the sanctity of his promise. Such gravitas activates the desire for understanding.

Aventure, by its nature, cannot be understood in advance. It means flinging oneself into an uncharted space, presumably under the aegis of blindfolded Lady Fortune. In this case, Gawain is propelled into the unknown by his loyalties as he meets the Green Knight's challenge, taking up his shield decorated on one side with the pentangle (an ancient symbol but here one of linked virtues), and an image of the Virgin on the other. Medieval Christian thought counters unpredictable Fortune with steadfast integrity.[9] Gawain's arms present him to others and perhaps to himself as the perfect Christian knight, a secular saint. His story might have been told that way, but it is not. A tiny flaw, a flaw Bertilak readily absolves him of and Arthur's court cannot even see, comes to dominate Gawain's self-understanding on his return from his *aventure*. As a result, Christian quest romance,[10] which produced the coherence expected of a successful work of art, is also skewed by the way his small imperfection frustrates closure for the poem. This is no problem for Kant's analysis of beauty: "The judgment of taste is entirely independent from the concept of perfection." Perfection depends on the demands of a concept, and genre is often treated as a concept, but the beautiful object escapes conceptual fixity. If *Gawain and the Green Knight* had completely fulfilled all the expectations of either popular love romances or saint's lives, it would have met the standard of what Kant calls "quantitative perfection," for which the abstract idea comes before the achieved work, close to beauty, but narrowly missing it.[11]

As the poem has come to us, though, its uncertain closure and its well-known "enigmas" are really there.[12] The most overarching of these is the status of magic as causality. The setting of the tale is the "central aristocratic society" which medieval romance takes as its "real" (as Jeff Rider has put it),[13] but crucial events are produced by Morgan le Fay. Magic operates in the plot: Bertilak's transformation into a green giant who rides off with his severed head beneath his arm, his castle, which may or may not be entirely illusory and does house Morgan as the old duenna – and perhaps the chatelaine too. The poem repeatedly acknowledges its events in terms of the marvellous. But much of its detail is anchored to medieval realities with such intricacy as to tether its drift towards fantasy or fairy tale. It therefore is, like *Troilus and Criseyde*, an early example of fictional realism, full of specific detail about courtly life, and a deeply imagined inner life for Gawain as well. Even some of its marvels are believed or known to have been present in that "central aristocratic" venue, although they must have seemed astonishing to untravelled readers. Perhaps the fearsome marvels (715–25) in the Wilderness of Wirral, the "wormez" [serpents, dragons] and "wodwos that woned in the knarrez [rocks]" – those threatening slithery types crawling out of the rocks or outlaws living among the rocks – were really there for all anybody knew, or knows, for that matter. The "magic" castle, if it is magic, seemed to Gawain "pared out of papure" (802), with its deep moat, walls rising above the water to high crenelated towers, and pinnacles all painted white. Such a wonderful sight, though, might have very well belonged to the real world. Much of the marvellous in the poem shades into the actual, but the Green Knight riding off with his head in his hand does not. We are forced to shift the gears of our generic and modal expectations as the poem goes on. A whirling hermeneutic circle intelligible one moment and mysterious the next can be aesthetically exhilarating. Gadamer would see the *energeia* of each succeeding scene formulated as contrast and echo, Kant as simultaneously exciting imagination and tantalizing understanding.

The narrative surface itself exhibits another kind of magic, as it weaves together three old stories: the "beheading game" from Irish folklore, told in both Bricriu's Feast and the First Continuation of Chrétien's *Perceval*,[14] the exchange of winnings with Bertilak, and the temptations offered by his lady. Together these narrative lines look more like a "tangled hierarchy," in Richard Hofstatder's terms, than the simpler bifurcation of *Melusine*'s reliance on history and folklore. The point where the three connect may be seen as a "vortex," a whirlpool that signals the self-referentiality of the poem while evading ordinary logic, a synthesis for exciting imagination and understanding.[15] In a more medieval frame of reference, *Gawain* looks like a Celtic interlace, an endless knot (like the pentangle), a teeming welter of detail, all of it intriguing, presumably important, but unmapped (like Gawain's path through Wirral).[16] Its obvious purposiveness as quest romance never comes to rest in a single purpose. Even its gravitas is enigmatically weighted: initially the poem seems grave about the history of Britain by setting this story among the founding legends back to Brutus and Troy, but later developments suggest that it probes the tensions between chivalry and Christian perfection. We will argue that its interrogative tone probes deeper yet, that it asks basic philosophical questions about time, reality, and possibility, as Gawain navigates between incompossible worlds.

Gawain's Times

Someone called Gawain had figured prominently in myth, history, and popular oral culture for centuries by the second half of the fourteenth century (the exact date of composition for the manuscript of *Gawain and the Green Knight* found on late-fourteenth-century vellum has not been established). The name of the hero would have been widely familiar in both English and French. Gawain is of course featured in the legends of the rise and fall of Arthur's earthly kingdom, as the king's nephew from the northern family of Lot, and as a brave and headstrong fighter in Geoffrey's account. His origins are Celtic and very old, mythically as a solar deity – Thomas Malory looks back to this origin in relating that his fighting powers reach their height at noon and wane as the day fades.[17] Thomas Hahn has brought together no less than eleven poems featuring Gawain in Middle English alone (not counting the best-known ones), some predating our poem, some contemporary with it, and still others later. He concludes that Gawain is more often featured in popular venues than any other hero, Arthurian or other, attesting to his "huge celebrity with an astonishing variety of audiences and across centuries of enormous cultural change."[18] The threads that run through the English popular tradition highlight both Gawain's bold prowess and the courtesy that sometimes restrains it, while his role in the French Arthurian tales is often that of a lover as well. Hahn finds him "a knight for all occasions rather than a hero shaped by distinctive drives or a particular destiny."[19] His is, therefore a familiar and revered *name*, but a name with no defining story, and certainly never before *this* story.

As a tale among tales about its protagonist, *Gawain and the Green Knight* reflects on its own intertextuality, but that does not diminish its romance energies.[20] Its interlace of motifs is matched by a similar interlace of gestures towards times past, other "Gawains," enhancing the sense of a "saturated world" by attributing causality to situations or events from other texts. One example is the chatelaine's knowledge (or pretence to knowledge) that Gawain's reputation as a lover precedes him, even though this poem has not even hinted at an erotic career for him. His penchant for courage and risk taking, however, is evident in both the poem and the intertexts; so are his courtesy and restraint, as in his clever, polite rebuffs to the chatelaine (1264–1304).[21] The sun-god motif of the mythic layer of this folded time is the most complex. Some traces of it may be seen in the description of Gawain and his armour as he sets off in fitt 2. In a single stanza (589–618) there are eleven words that refer to gleaming, shining, and gold, as well as the direct "glytered and glent as glem of the sunne" (604). Later, in the bedroom encounter, the trace belongs to a specifically Christian order: he is not a sun-god, but is associated with one through his mindfulness of Mary "myldest moder so dere" (754, also 1262, 1268), underscoring a religious piety absent or perfunctory in other Gawain tales. The poem denies any literal godlikeness in repeatedly calling attention to his mortality, as does Gawain himself: "Bot thaȝ my hede falle on the stonez / I con not hit restore" (2282–3). Concern for his life prompted him to accept the girdle and denies his power to return to this life as the Green Knight had. The inwardness so much in evidence in the tale balances the honour/shame culture of Arthur's court with a "guilt" culture, the belief that virtue is finally a matter between yourself and the judgment of God.[22] No Celtic sun god, but a bringer of light in another chapter of world history.

Unlike *Sir Orfeo, Troilus and Criseyde,* and *Melusine, Gawain and the Green Knight* has many translations (some illustrated), but no successors that play out its entangled themes. *The Green Knight* is a fifteenth-century tale intended for oral recitation, an instance of which, one Captain Cox reciting at Kenilworth Castle in 1575, has been documented.[23] It retells the beheading story in aabccb stanzas in a London dialect. It lacks the complication and the philosophical weight of *Gawain and the Green Knight*, but attests to the interest the main features of the tale continued to attract after perhaps two centuries.[24] Various modern versions of and allusions to it have taken advantage of the mysteriousness of the Green Man, most notably Iris Murdoch's *The Green Knight*.[25] Murdoch's book, though more obviously related to the narrative line, is less involved in the philosophical implications (natural/human/magical/divine) than Ronald Johnson's quest poem *The Book of the Green Man* (1967), and Russell Hoban's *Riddley Walker* (1980), a novel recounting wrongs against nature that destroy the civilization that intended to tame her. Neither Johnson nor Hoban, deeply as both have imagined the entanglement of human striving with natural process, can be said to have retold the narrative the *Gawain*-poet sets in motion.[26] The poem itself in its various translations has fascinated readers since the early twentieth century, when Israel Gollancz and others began to discuss the manuscript, but it has not spawned modern analogues that tell its story and reflect on the aesthetics of possibility in its distinctive manner.

Time is folded *within* the narrative. After the sweeping historical panorama of the Brutus/Arthur introduction, the first fitt presents a real-time, almost cinematic account of the Green Knight's visit, the place settings at the banquet table, the words and gestures of the principals in the scene. In the second fitt, the year passes as nature decrees, not a human word recorded until Gawain prepares to leave the court. The details of his arming are seen in real time, but his travel through Wirral is summarized until, while praying to Mary, he becomes aware of the imposing castle that will welcome him. Then time slows again as the third fitt presents Bertilak's three hunts and the three conversations between Gawain and the lady in fine detail. The *Gawain*-poet's clever management of the "meantime" structure of this section – alternating Gawain's bedroom *aventures* with Bertilac's hunting expeditions – makes his telling look novelistic.[27] Fitt 4 stays with Gawain as he faces the Green Knight, endures the axe feints, and finds out what it is that events have tested. This handling of temporal rhythms is not quite unique in the fourteenth century, since it can be found in Chaucer, but there is no evidence that either writer influenced the other; they look independently innovative. The *Gawain*-poet uses these techniques for pacing to heighten both the suspense surrounding events and the evocation of complex states of mind for Gawain, treating time as both objectively linear and humanly experienced.

Time figures in yet another way, which invites comparison with *Troilus and Criseyde* by suggesting a literary modality related to, but not identical with, modal logic. The first fitt presents the two title characters as belonging to incompossible domains of time. Gawain's story is located in Augustine's description of linear time, that of a mortal adventurer. The Green Knight, while he is the Green Knight, belongs to a different temporal order, cyclic rather than linear. The lovely stanzas chronicling the passing of the year that begins the second fitt (491–534) serve to both distinguish and link the two temporal worlds at stake in the tale, folding the two perspectives into a single, and singularly beautiful, evocation of the passing seasons. For Gawain the passage of time brings him closer to the death-dealing stroke he will almost certainly receive if he keeps his appointment. Well-known Arthurian figures (including Lancelot) show up to dissuade him from going (551–60), as well they might, since earthly lives begin with birth and end with death, like the swallow who flies into the hall and out again through time into eternity in Bede's metaphor.[28] In this, he is like everyman venturing into an unknown future, but his courage is impressive: "What may mon do bot fonde?" he says (565). That "fonde," a formation from "find" or "seek to perceive" likens him to an Odysseus sailing after knowledge, or an Orfeo boldly entering the passage in the hillside, resolutely facing whatever his destiny might bring (564) and striving to establish his identity as he meets it.

The passing year means something else for the Green Knight. He is presented in fitt 1, first as a human knight, a very large, green one (although no more outrageous in romance texts than a knight who rides invisible). He and his horse are well proportioned and accoutered with gold and precious stones, but an axe substitutes for a knightly sword and he is shoeless. He offers his challenge in formal, courtly language, but it is an incomprehensible challenge. What his axe and green-stockinged feet hint at will be made manifest by his picking up his severed head and riding off: he is not just a larger-than-life knight, but also a figure for Nature (capital letter). Like the green crops that are harvested each year, but appear again the next (the head cut off Mr Barleycorn), the Green Knight only *appears* to have received a mortal wound. The winter outside the castle, in which only the holly sprig he carries is green, will give way to the "solace of the softe somer" and then to harvest and the fading of the "gres that grene watz ere" (510, 527). The Green Knight will be back in business with his head attached next Christmas season, and Gawain has pledged to meet him at the Green Chapel. From this perspective, he is the force of Nature breaking into the fortified castle and orderly civilization Arthur had built as protection. Yet Nature is also the nourishing infrastructure for all human endeavour. And Arthur had, after all, expected a marvel and kept the dinner warm while he waited for one to appear.

In terms of literary modality, interpretation is challenged by the intrusion of a figure in the allegorical mode into a realistic fiction. A bona fide allegory identifies itself in two ways: (1) the text announces an underlying meaning, and/or (2) the literal level exhibits large-scale incoherence and surface clues hint at meaningful patterns. Fitt 1 delivers on the second count, and there is yet another (very subtle) clue in the seasons stanzas to the allegory in which Nature is personified and linked to the persona of the Green Knight. It comes down to the translation of the single word "ȝirnez." Arthur "ȝerned ȝelping [valiant boasting] to here," wanted to hear a great story before eating the holiday feast (492). This "ȝerned" means yearned, longed for, just as it does now. In the seasons passage "And thus ȝernez the ȝere in yesterdays mony" (529) the poet uses the same word in its continuing present form. The natural year itself, therefore, is presented as yearning. The year exhibits desire, like a creature. Although no translations put it that way,[29] the year and its avatar yearn for the passing of time, as mortal Gawain cannot. "Natural" means one thing for an allegorical figure and something quite different for an individual human being.

Detail, Super-real and Surreal

The apparent seamlessness of the ancient, Celtic, and feudal Christian elements in the poem exhibits Gadamer's "fusion of horizons," projecting into the future through countless details that constitute the "mysterious intimacy" of art.[30] In Kant's account, the experience of beauty fuses the sensible, which excites the imagination, with the intelligible, which summons understanding. Imagination is "our ability to take in and reproduce sensory impression and images."[31] *Gawain and the Green*

Knight stands alone among medieval romances for the clarity, richness, and subtlety with which images of the sights and sounds of the world of the poem are presented. In fact, the density and intricacy of realistic detail about its fictional world is unusual in any era. But Kant famously denied that *things in themselves*, rather than their appearances, can be known through perception.[32] The *Gawain*-poet presents a world heavy with things, but focuses on the perception of things, primarily by Gawain – his is the "central intelligence" of the poem as Hamlet is of his play and Emma is of her novel. In this poem the "sensible" component of Kant's sensible/intelligible pairing excites imagination through the interrelation of vivid realistic detail with incomprehensible marvel – the super-real and the surreal – such that no concept is adequate to contain them.[33] Yet they can be gathered to found apperceptions, although not necessarily the same ones for every reader.

Leibniz emphasizes perspective and "petite impressions." The pond Leibniz uses as an example and metaphor seems from a distance a serene surface, quite blank, but from above and up close it teems with smaller and yet smaller constituents. Closer perspective both reveals the source of "what is really there," like the breaking of individual waves that become the roar of the sea, and also redirects apperception, cognitive grasp.[34] Such apperception is not an aggregate or sum of all available detail, but emerges from it, becomes a "novel emergent" in modern philosophical parlance.[35] In a written tale, tiny verbal details are like the individual waves that produce the roar of the plot. This section's close account of some of the details in this richly detailed text was necessary because this dialect of Middle English is so unfamiliar today and because so much more of its aesthetic energy appears in its exact phrasings, its rich semantic texture. Most modern readers see its beauty in its structure, especially the suspense created by its uneasy tone and the rhythms of its repetitions and analogues, and they are right to do so. Looking at the kaleidoscopic detail of the textual pond under its surface, though, reveals the world of the poem as *saturated*.[36]

We will only be able to discuss a small subset of the tiny details that move the action from scene to scene, but these will serve to exemplify the remarkable tactic the poet uses throughout. In just three stanzas, fitt 1 turns from the fall of Troy to a tale heard in the town to a close-up of Arthur's banquet table at Christmas, exemplifying the poem's shifting perspective. The saturation of the world of the poem is focused first on the opulence of the Christmas feast – the fresh foods (in winter!) heaped on plates, the serving dishes covered with cloth, the twelve dishes each pair of diners shared, along with beer and wine both (122–9). We are asked to imagine the comfort and gaiety of the occasion at such close quarters that this culture appears our own; we are "here smelling the flowers," as David Lewis puts it.[37] When Arthur delays eating, we assume he awaits a striking entertainment, an *account* of an *aventure*, not the sort of intrusion that actually takes place when the Green Knight enters the hall. A Leibnizian take on real but unactualized possible worlds (those which the rest of the world has not allowed to become existent)[38] is given a distinctive twist in *Gawain and the Green Knight*, in that the wonder evoked by the intrusion of the "other world" is meshed with the wonder of the "real" feudal world so as to blur the line between them, far more than it is blurred in *Sir Orfeo* or Marie's *lais*.

Once a big green horseman enters the hall, we might expect the level of detail to change: *this*, surely, is a wonder that breaks the spell of cinematic realism. But instead the intruder is described in even closer and more intricate detail than the "real" aristocratic world. A whole stanza is devoted to the hair of the Green Knight and the mane of his horse, both of which were green (179–200). The man's tangled hair, clipped above his elbows, fanned out over his shoulders like a king's cape. His beard was like a bush covering his chest. But the horse's hair ("much to hit lyke" in being green) gets even more attention. It was crisped and curled, braided with gold thread ("fildore"), and bound up with precious stones, even the tail. The hair comes back into the picture when the Green Knight submits to Gawain's stroke; "His longe louelych lokkezhe layd ouer his crown" (419). The severed head "liyfte vp the yȝe-lyddez and loked ful brode" (445). When the horse and rider are *present* to imagination in such detail, where are we now in relation to the actual world? And where are Arthur, Gawain, and the rest of the court, who know they are experiencing a marvel (the word is all over the place in fitt 1)?

The fullness of detail seems to block recourse to a thoroughgoing allegory of Nature versus civilization, but clearly a world alien to the courtly idealization of medieval tradition has barged in. For the time being, understanding in general is frustrated, as we are asked to imagine in great detail an event that cannot be reconciled to its equally detailed setting. The court is astonished, of course, but they know what to do: they kick the severed head in an attempt to keep it from being reattached in order to prevent the promised return blow to Gawain's neck. Yet having failed, they quickly return to their festivities: Arthur, Gawain, and other zealous ("kene") knights serve everyone double portions and "mete and mynstralcie" resume. In terms of sense impressions, readers are repaid for their involvement with the hair and the food; they are asked to "see" one world of possibility superimposed on another, however unintelligible that may be. Only a small note in the last wheel of the fitt, one of the few interjected by the narrator's voice, takes stock of the stakes of the scene witnessed but not adequately apperceived.

> Now thenk wel, Sir Gawan,
> For wothe [danger] that thou ne wonde [hesitate]
> This aventure for to frayn [test]
> That thou hatz tan on honde. (486–90)

After these haunting lines, point of view lies almost entirely with Gawain, whose awareness of the danger incurred by his pledge (again the enigmatically binding, identity-defining promise) occupies the rest of the poem.

Fitt 2 continues that reflective tone with a wry comment that the men (Arthur and Gawain) have "sturne werk" in hand, more than they had asked for by yearning for *aventure*: "staf-ful" [crammed full] were their hands. This is followed by a suspense-producing "if" clause, "Bot thaȝ [if] the ende be heuy haf ȝe no wonder" (494–6), which serves to colour the notion of a "game" with more sombre tones. So often games and offhand bargains turn out to have serious consequences, as in the rash promises of the Fairie King in *Orfeo* and Dorigen in *The Franklin's Tale*. Yet the courtiers, Gawain included, are presented as returning to normal life. Then come the much-celebrated stanzas on the seasons. Their evocative account of the predictable cycles of the natural world coincides with the actual one we share with Gawain's Logres, but their urgent tone suggests the linear passage of time in an Augustinian mode, the present scarcely experienced before it becomes the past. For Gawain this year's earthly changes may be the last he witnesses. Watching him leave in his shining armour, the court blames Arthur for letting Gawain take on this onerous quest; proper counsel would have accounted it as a mere Christmas game (683–4), and were this a wholly "realistic" narrative, so would its readers.

The scene of Gawain's arming with its precise description of each item celebrates the customs and fashions of the military aristocracy (to which the seamstresses of the town contribute through winter work); everything gleams. Even his horse Gringolet's attire for the journey is described in detail. Yet behind these anchors for realism is the precaution this equipment provides (565–9). Everything the "wyȝtest [strongest] and the worthiest of the worldes kynde" (261) the knightly class had devised for their staying at the top of their game. But Gawain's arming implies another kind of protection in the shield with its ancient (perhaps pagan) pentangle and portrait of the Virgin Mary. Both medieval fashion and St Paul's admonition about the "whole armour of God" in Ephesians 6 are suggested. Analogues to this fullness of description are those of the Green Knight and his horse in fitt 1 and later Gawain's second arming, where the lace is emphasized instead of the pentangle and portrait (2011–45). Moreover, both Gringolet and the Green Knight's horse strike sparks from the "ston-fyr" as they leave the hall (459, 671).

The detailed itinerary to what turns out to be Hautdesert – North Wales with the Anglesey Islands on Gawain's left, to Holy Head, and through the Wilderness of Wirral – stands in sharp contrast to the usual romance vagueness about space and time. Gawain's journey through the lonely forest with its serpents and wild men and frozen waterfalls are specified, but not in real time. It would be too difficult, the narrator says, to describe the tenth part of these sufferings (719), and no one there knows God, or has ever heard of a Green Chapel (702–9), which hints at spookier suspicions. The castle that appears as he emerges from the wasteland strikes Gawain with awe; its moat is "wonderly depe" and its "chalk-wyt chymnees" make it look a "subtlety" decorating a fancy dessert.[39] His perspective at this point is the view of Leibniz's serene fishpond seen from a distance, and even inside the castle, its comforts bespeak a refined and perhaps hyperbolic example of feudal opulence. Lavish detail is accorded the brightly coloured tapestries and carpets, the cushioned chair before the blazing fire and ermine-lined robe "cast" upon Gawain, the board set with table linen and silver utensils, various preparations for the fish dishes, but again, Gawain saw much more than the poet could recount (1008). The scene is presented as too laden with detail either for Gawain to register or for the poet to convey. Mary has answered the prayer of her knight by allowing him to celebrate Christmas in such a household and observe Christian rites unhindered, and he is grateful for his arrival (754–62). Before his *aventure* is completed, though, his impressions of these details will be gathered into a different apperception.

This distant court seems to Gawain both homey, in being like the civilized court of his uncle, and marvellous, even uncanny, Freud's *unheimlich*.[40] The familiar, perhaps even heightened, comforts of the castle are further enhanced by the elaborate description of the beauty of the chatelaine, which contrasts with the simpler description of Guinevere, to whom she is favourably compared (945). The wasted demeanour of her old companion/duenna's unsightly face and misshapen body are equally explicit, but the embroidery on her wimple (960) marks her importance in the castle and reminds readers that the cover of Gawain's visor was similarly embroidered. The courtly customs in this new place that welcomes him so freely and the elaborate exchange of compliments between Gawain and his host are familiar too (1032–40). None of this deters Gawain from his quest, but it lightens his mood enough to allow him to join in yet another Christmas game, the exchange of winnings.

The particular unease both Gawain and readers experience in this section of the poem is registered as the deepening of detail about the hero's inner life as he responds to external events. The third fitt is characterized by a steady oscillation between the hunting expeditions from which Bertilak will take his winnings and the bedroom scenes that will yield what Gawain must exchange. Bertilak's hunting is called a quest (1150); it is an *aventure* in the sense of actively chosen risk. Gawain's, though, as the hunted in the curtained bed, is *aventure* in the sense of something unsought that happens, but there is risk in his position too, as he fully realizes. The tone for both is that of urgency, menace for the hunters and their animal prey, but especially for the hunted man in the bedchamber.

The fear the deer feel in attempting to evade the hunters and hounds is rendered so fully that they almost attain point of view (1150–71), and Bertilak gleefully hunts all day – "for blys abloy ["transported]" (1174). The fitt suggests a sense of emotional urgency even before its turn to Gawain, not fully awake, watching the morning light playing on the wall and hearing "a little din at his dor." He is on guard immediately, lifting up a corner of the curtain on his bed, seeing the chatelaine come in, and then feigning sleep (1178–1200). His "wonder" at this "marvel" is both implied by his actions and given as internal dialogue: "Bot ȝet he sayde in himself" (1198). A long, richly detailed scene follows, almost entirely presented in direct discourse (1208–1318).[41] The lady calls on the courtly trope of the lover as his beloved's prisoner in the game of erotic war, but she reverses the sexes and literalizes the metaphor by actually invading the space of his curtained bed and refusing to let him get up to dress (a glancing denial of his armour's protection). Gawain senses the threat her metaphor implies: he must embarrass her by direct refusal or betray his host. She presses him hard, telling him that she has bolted the door, and he is "welcum" to her "cors" (1237). Gawain, though, manages to reply as if an elaborate game were being played, agreeing to be her prisoner, vowing to be her servant, and craftily deflecting her obvious intentions without being insulting or haughty. Relieved when she seems about to leave, he agrees to receive a kiss for courtesy and happily goes off to mass. Ad Putter notes the subtlety of this passage in its use of pronouns: "I" accept the kiss lest "he" who is featured in your image of me disappoints (1303–4).[42] By this clever ploy, Gawain declines agency and denies his renown as a lover. He is shown doing a lot of receiving: the castle as a gift from Mary, the hospitality of the castle, this kiss, and the mass to which he immediately repairs.

The two stanzas that follow (1316–65) give an incredibly detailed account of the "breaking up" of the deer killed in the hunt. Every part of the carcass is accounted for, right down to the lungs and intestines mixed with blood and bread for the hounds and gristle for the crows. The description suggests a kind of ceremony and manual for aristocratic hunters.[43] It can be seen as one of many instances of the poem's being a kind of guidebook for honourmen, cementing bonds among a feudal landowning class, but our argument positions its welter of tiny details as a ballast for imagining a "real" location for Bertilak's behaviour, within a "central aristocratic society." A hunting party who knew how to butcher with such finesse belongs to *this* world (corroborated by extant hunting manuals), not an intrusive alternative. Throughout the second hunt, also called a quest (1421), sounds are emphasized; the landscape rings with the noise of the baying dogs and the cheers and horns of the men. The crags are called foes and the boar is seemingly cornered between an ominous fen and an overarching cliff: "Theras the rogh rocher [stone pile] vnrydely [confusedly] watz fallen" (1430–2). This hunt too is interrupted by the indoor (and interior) temptation of Gawain by the lady, from whom this time he received two kisses. The return to the boar hunt presents the only detailed account of sustained physical combat in the poem. In almost slow motion, Bertilak dismounts and ends up in a heap ("vpon hepez") with the now cornered animal, finally thrusting his blade into wily old boar's throat. As on the first day, the second exchange is festive, but this looks like the performance of a ceremony, as Bertilak tells his story and Gawain handles the huge head, praising his host's bravery.[44] After the evening's banquet, Gawain announces his intention to leave the next morning to find the green chapel, but Bertilak forbids it, promising him a guide to take him there well before prime to keep his bargain with the Green Knight.

The fox hunt of the third day is interrupted by the lady's third visit, this time with "Hir brest bare before, and bihinde eke" (1740) and words so obvious that he must either "lach [take] ther hir luf other lodly [with repugnance] refuse" (1772). Mary must come to his aid if he is to avoid scanting his obligation either to formal courtesy or to his own chastity – and she does.[45] With a finesse that matches the host's hunting skills, the hunted Gawain manages to lighten the mood and avoid direct insult. The tiniest detail here, though, is the word "lach" (1772): taking her love is taking the blow that nicks his neck (2499) and taking shame from the encounter (2507). The chatelaine lays yet another trap, though, by offering a gift. I'll give you a precious ring to remember me by, she says. Gawain again refuses, saying he has nothing to give in return. But when she takes the green girdle interlaced with gold from her waist and puts it on his, telling him that it can protect him from death, he does not refuse it. Her only condition is that he must not tell her husband. Gawain hides the girdle and hurries to a priest, making confession of "the more and the mynne [the greater and the lesser]" of his misdeeds. As a result, the priest "asoyled hym surely and sette hym so clene / As domezday schulde haf ben diȝt [arrive] on the morn" (1880–4). Gawain does not exchange the girdle for the fox he receives from his host that evening. Again, the emphasis has been on Gawain's receiving.

The linguistic detail that lurks everywhere in the poem, but especially in this fitt, is the recurrence of "fynde" and its variants. Gawain's "What may mon do bot fonde?" as he sets off to *find* his destiny in fitt 2 echoes later. There is a quite literal sense of "find" involved, since the Green Knight has given no directions to the chapel, but in the third fitt, the idea of seeking how the quest will manifest itself becomes more problematic for both Gawain himself and readers. Fitt 3 links the words "quest" and "find" through the motif of hunting; the animals were sought and found, the lady "fondet" (tried) Gawain (1549); Bertilak sought Gawain in the hall, "His feez [recompense] ther for to fonge" (1622); and Gawain hid the luf-lace where he could "eft [once more] fonde" it (1875). Lots of things are hiding or hidden in this longest of the four fitts.[46] The interconnected episodes interrupting each other risk being thought of as digressive, but ought to be seen as sharpening the vital question of what is meant by finding one's quest, while producing suspense about it. Gawain understands at this point that his commitment to chivalry involves contradictory duties, and he resolutely attempts to fulfil his promises, but he cannot see exactly what they will entail. That is the general human condition. But emerging from these details is a vague sense, for both the hero and the reader, that he is acting in another drama, directed by rules from another world.

Fitt 4 continues and exacerbates the suspense. The opening stanza folds back towards the passing of the seasons in fitt 2 in again personifying the warring winds and stinging snow, but here not distanced by the abstract idea of naturalness, "as the worlde askez" (590), but closer to his experience in Wirral when he slept in his armour with "iiseikkles" hanging over his head (726–31). It is Gawain who feels this cold and hears this howling wind. Yet he takes leave of Bertilak's castle with faultless courtesy, thanking everyone and commending them to God for their attention to his needs, especially the proper stabling and exercise of Gringolet and cleaning the rust from his armour. It is a sign of his peace of mind that he takes note of these kindnesses. As readers, we wonder whether his trust in the protection of the girdle, his faith that his soul had been cleansed by confession, or simply his customary faultless courtesy sustains him. As he dons his polished armour, though, the girdle is mentioned but the pentangle and portrait of Mary are not. Gawain's guide to the chapel offers to keep his secret if he turns back to avoid the Green Knight's stroke, but is refused. Gawain is decisive that he himself would be shamed even if no one ever found out that he had reneged on his promise. A guilt ethic has fully overshadowed mere shame, although shame is still felt in Bertilak's presence. Exterior conditions, interior perceptions, and big ideas are seamlessly blended in this final scene. The guide's directions to the chapel are extremely detailed, so detailed that Israel Gollancz thought the poet was describing a known place: Wetton Mill, Staffordshire.[47] Both the super-real and the surreal are suggested in this bleak, windswept scene where Gawain seeks his "wyrde" (2134). The poet's Old English "wyrde" conjoins the bygone heroic world with the Christian dispensation; it is translated by Borroff as "Fortune" and by Finch as "Providence."

The details of the meeting at the Green Chapel appear as Gawain experiences them from his Christian point of view. Instead of the sacred-looking place he sought, he finds an elaborately described mound in the hillside, "nobot an olde caue," where "aboute mydnyȝt / The Dele [devil] his matynnes telle!" (2183, 2187–8). Gawain must wait for the Green Knight to show up, listening to his axe being sharpened and feeling in his five wits that his oath has been sworn to the Fiend himself. Nonetheless, he keeps his date so he can be dealt his "destiné." He shrinks involuntarily from the first stoke but stands still as a stump with a hundred roots in the ground for the others. The third blow nicks him a bit, so he sees his blood on the snow and moves to arm himself for combat (2293–4). Only then does he *find* the meaning of his quest: the Green Knight is a shape taken by Bertilak de Hautdesert at the behest of Morgan le Faye, by whose power he holds his demesne. *Morgan's* power, in turn, comes from Merlin, that "conable klerk [excellent scholar]" (2450), from whom she had learned when they were lovers. At this point the uneasy familiarity, the uncanniness, of Bertilak's court becomes at least partly intelligible to Gawain, since Merlin, in the intertext to this poem, had engineered Arthur's kingship by disguising Uther as Igraine's husband, and Morgan is Arthur's half-sister and Gawain's aunt. He was, in a sense, near his dynastic home all along. As unlikely as Morgan's plot to scare Guinevere to death when the Green Knight picked up his severed head might seem, her role in the plot is far from gratuitous. Although her judgment is faulty in that Guinevere is hardier and Gawain braver than she predicted, she clearly has the power to manipulate appearances that make things happen in the "real" world. Bertilak, who is still the Green Knight under Morgan's spell in this final scene, nonetheless speaks in entirely Christian terms, accepting Gawain's confession and pronouncing him as "polysed" [cleansed] through the penance of his ordeal as if he had never sinned since the day he was born (2390–3).[48] The world that Morgan controls is called up intertextually through the way the poem casually alludes to the various Arthur/Gawain stories that contribute to its logic.

Gawain's (Leibniz's) Possible Worlds

Even more than most romances, *Gawain and the Green Knight* insists on our positing possible worlds. Fitt 1 positions readers as witnesses to events in Arthur's court during Christmas festivities, framed by the long history of the establishment of Britain by Brutus. Under that distancing lens, we see a splendid festivity in the actual world of Arthur's court impinged on by the appearance of a horse and rider from another realm altogether. Arthur's people know it is a marvel, but the poet's tactic of close, unexcited, almost cinematic description continues to prevail, presenting these green figures as fully available to sense perception. Once Gawain has accepted the Green Knight's challenge, though, we come to perceive the world of actuality as Gawain himself does. This world is continuous with Arthur's court, and we moderns can easily identify it with medieval beliefs (and with some of our own): the seasons follow predictably, wild things live in northern forests, hitherto unknown landlords preside over beautiful castles in distant places. The final scene, though, returns to the dilemmas posed in the first fitt. This poem is serious about alternative worlds – alternative and incompossible.

The poem presents its major figures as "real" in two rule-bound worlds, incompossible, but with enough overlap to allow the Green Knight (controlled by Morgan) and Gawain (pledged to the Virgin Mary) to be imagined as somehow co-present. When the Green Knight first shows up at Arthur's table, the poem presents all that specific detail about his clothing and his horse's trappings to suggest the appearance of a well-appointed, well-spoken emissary from another court, a *knight*, no more mysterious than the super-sized combatants in Chrétien's earlier or Malory's later tales. Arthur initially welcomes him and invites him to alight and stay awhile (252–4). Gawain will later be similarly welcomed at Bertilak's court. But, unlike Gawain, he does not make himself at home, and unlike most marvellous intruders, offers no violence to the assembly. He calls attention to his holly branch and lack of armour as proof that he means only a game. Although the exchange of blows is presented as a challenge to the court's pride in its courtesy and prowess, it would seem to end with the beheading of the Green Knight himself. That is, it would seem so if the rules of the actual world are in force. The fact that Arthur cannot strike with the axe is a clue that they are not, and when Gawain tactfully comes to his rescue and severs the head, which is recovered and speaks, the full force of an alternative world is made manifest. What is not manifested is why this marvel appeared amid Arthur's festivities. No one at the table is able to muster apperception from the game's confusion of details, the Green Knight gives no hint as to why Gawain and not Arthur can perform the exchange of blows or what, exactly, is at stake.

Readers, however, can reflect on this marvel. The Green Knight carries the only plant that is green in the winter (206), and of course he and his horse are green as well. The distance provided by the poet's narrative technique allows us to see him as a figure for the returning cycle of the natural year, renewed each year to begin again. The detail of his unshod feet allows him direct contact with the earth. In this light, he belongs to another possible world, that of allegory: Nature, cyclic and enduring, continually renewed, undermines the pride of Arthur's court, which is vulnerable to the "blysse and blunder" of historical time (18), and whose individuals die when their heads are cut off. The scene of Gawain's departure fully indulges the pathos of human limitation in general, against the background of the recurring seasons (516–65).

When they see him in his bright armour, the people even criticize Arthur for letting him go to what looks like his certain death (674). Allegory is an intellectual shape only invoked after the fact and is never apparent to the participants in an event. Nor would thinking allegorically have helped the courtiers to organize their impressions of these events, to apperceive their "true " meaning. What the people did suspect as the intrusion of an alternative world into their hall is magic. They kick the severed head to prevent the Green Knight from reattaching it to his body.

What readers (eventually) see is that the Green Knight is a shape-shifter, although we are not introduced to his fully human shape until the end of the second fitt and do not recognize it when we first see it.[49] He himself is not exactly a shape-shifter, though, because he does not control his manifestations. Morgan does, as we find out four stanzas from the end. He is "really" (i.e., in terms of the fictional realism of Gawain's world) Bertilak de Hautdesert, enchanted by Morgan, and possibly released from her power through Gawain's *trawthe*. Morgan and morganian *fées*, as Laurence Harf-Lancner has called fairies who, unlike melusines, do not marry humans and stay with them, are ubiquitous in the Middle Ages.[50] The figure is very old; R.S. Loomis has traced its origins from the ancient cult of Matrôna into Irish lore and then Geoffrey of Monmouth and the Matter of Britain. Always an enchantress and shape-shifter in the Arthurian tales, she is sometimes benign, but more often destructive. Her sometimes surpassing beauty, sometimes disgusting ugliness, her "multiple personality and infinite variety" allow her to be seen as "a female pantheon in miniature."[51] Edith Williams regards her role in *Gawain and the Green Knight* as an aspect of Gawain's psyche in a Jungian style, answering critics who find Morgan's role in the denouement of the poem a flaw in its design.[52] We do not regard the inclusion of Morgan as a flaw of any kind. It is the acknowledgment of the sudden intrusion of a possible world into the actualized one. There they are in Camelot, smelling the flowers (or roasted meats) waiting for a marvel to be told, when one comes in the door on horseback instead. The Green Knight, then, can be regarded as representing two quite different rule-bound systems, neither of which is fully apperceived in the banquet hall. Whether as an allegory of Nature or an emanation of magic, the Green Knight is wholly "other" to Arthur's court.

Gawain is an ordinary, though splendid, person. He is continuous with nature in that he lives a creaturely existence in linear time and has no signifying marks of allegory about him. Nor does he possess magical properties or devices. He is challenged by Nature in the form of the Green Knight, by the vicissitudes of the natural world in the Forest of Wirral, and by his natural physical selfhood (his sexual temptation by the lady, his survival instinct). He is aware of his vulnerability, and the poem points to his human limitations in both perception and power. He knows that if his head should fall on the stones he cannot replace it and resume his life (2283). He is also threatened by magic, but he stoically refuses to admit its power by regarding his bargain with the Green Knight as a courtly challenge that he must fulfil to avoid being a coward in others' eyes and his own. In his case a still larger pair of incompossibles describes his personhood: he grasps the idea of perfection and sets out to enact it by making the endless knot his emblem, but his path is filled with contingency and risk. This larger pair, perfection/contingency, encompass the Christian mystery itself: what is man, a little lower than the angels and yet a mere quintessence of dust, made in God's image, but fallen into the chaos of history. This is the essence of *aventure* in a Christian context. Bertilak is beholden to Morgan for his lands (2446), perhaps for his very existence. Gawain is upheld by Mary.

The Virgin Mary is central to Gawain's mental world, and his first recourse when he faces danger. Her image is painted on the inside of his shield, where he can see it for inspiration; it gives him strength (650). In Geoffrey of Monmouth, it is Arthur who carries a shield with her likeness on it, forcing him to be "thinking perpetually of her" (217). This may serve as another subtle identification of Gawain with the Arthurian dynasty, situating his identity in both the dynastic and religious worlds. He loves Mary and desires to emulate her piety, but he knows he is human and potentially flawed, continually second-guessing himself. Mary is, in another sense, a character in the story, one who comes to Gawain's aid when he needs a haven and a place to hear mass on Christmas (751–62) and when the chatelaine tempts him so aggressively that he almost loses the game (1769). Mary belongs to eternity, but she once belonged to linear time, like Gawain and all other humans. The late Middle Ages regarded her as the most important intercessor between the human and the divine. In the poem, she represents Gawain's commitment to the eternal. He strives to use his human time to serve Mary and eventually join her timeless company as a saved soul. The way Mary inhabits both time and eternity is clear in Christian doctrine and presents no problem for understanding *her*, although it contributes to the complexities of Gawain's ethical identity.

Gawain is, in the end, a saved Christian man who understands that in a contingent world, a world of accidents and appearances (often deceptive, like women), he cannot attain Mary's perfection or fully exhibit the linked virtues of the pentangle. He can, however, be a model of penitence and reflection in his actual, uncertain world. To arrive at this state of mind he undergoes an *aventure* that takes him into a second real world. This second world cannot be considered a creation of *his* mind, a nightmare, like Scrooge's visions of Christmases, or an illusion, like Lancelot's vision of the lions across the sword bridge. The Green Knight appears to Arthur's whole court; the tale must be seen as involving some sort of overlap between worlds.

Modal logicians have proposed two ways of considering overlap: (1) two possible worlds might overlap by sharing a particular part, like the intersection of two circles in a Venn diagram, or (2) some object (say a person) might exhibit "trans-world identity" by inhabiting two distinct worlds.[53] Since the question is still open philosophically, we will work from *Gawain and the Green Knight* itself and from the long history of romance writing. It might be said that the *Gawain*-poet himself raises the question of overlap in romance narrative, giving his strategy for storytelling a claim to be called "meta-romance."[54] The Green Knight obviously belongs to a different causal domain than Arthur's, but there he is in the dining hall picking up his head and riding off, his horse's hoofs striking sparks from the stone floor (459), just like those Gawain's horse sends up a year later (669).

The simplest way to account for the Green Knight is to imagine two worlds that overlap. Choosing that option, we could posit that the world of the Arthurian court is continuous with our general sense of how aristocratic life was imagined in Europe in the high Middle Ages (linear time for people, cyclic for nature), but with occasional pockets of overlap with Merlin's, and thus Morgan's, world of time/space, so that causality is sometimes disrupted. Of course it must be uncertain when and where the overlaps will appear. Consistently with this view, the Green Knight in fitt 1 enters the overlapping area and invites Gawain to seek him in a less known recess of that shared area. The whole *aventure* after Gawain emerges from the Wilderness of Wirral is set in an alternative world, but a world that mimics the appearances and customs of Arthur's court and seems continuous with it. To Gawain, Hautdesert is, in David Lewis's terms, "*epistemically accessible*"; it "might, for all he knows, be his world."[55] Gawain does make this assumption, but both he and readers are vaguely troubled by the tiny details of fitt 3 indicated in the previous section. From his vantage point there, he discovers his fallibilities, especially those of perception, and "recenters" himself, as Marie-Laure Ryan puts it.[56]

A solution using option 2 is that both the Green Knight and Gawain act in two different worlds and yet remain themselves; they exhibit trans-world identity. The second world, in each case, is made "real" when an important character enters it, real for the Green Knight and Gawain and real for readers.[57] Both the Green Knight/Sir Bertilak and Gawain himself exist in two worlds, incompossible with one another. The Green Knight's case might be given two interpretations. In one of them Bertilak might be taken as holding the northern territory of Hautdesert, who, for reasons unknown, had fallen under the power of Morgan in the normal feudal manner – she purchased or conquered his domain. Maintained in his estate by her "myȝt," this feudal lord is transformed by "Morgne the goddess" (2451), whom no one could or can resist. She endows him with powers from a world with different rules than Gawain's and from his own before he fell under her jurisdiction.

Especially in fitt 1, these powers seem to be the rules of a continuing, recurrent Nature, recovering from every year's harvest by blossoming into life in the spring. The strong suggestion that Nature is teaching Arthur's proud civilization a lesson is counteracted in fitt 4, when Morgan is called a goddess. Nature is God's creation and its rhythms are consistent. Morgan's use of its image is a trap, perhaps a lure for Gawain's acute ethical sensibilities, but a red herring in the unravelling of the mystery of the *aventure*. In this scenario, Morgan inhabits an alternative world, which has the power to intrude on Arthurian feudalism at will. She learned her craft from her lover Merlin, who had been regarded as having changed the course of ordinary history from Geoffrey of Monmouth's account onward. Her magical powers sustain Bertilak's identity in two worlds (he remembers his actions as both Green Knight and lord of Hautdesert when he catechizes Gawain in the Chapel scene). He is substantially the same man, although his accidents change. This vantage point would stress what seems his genuine admiration for Gawain and goodwill towards him. "I wol the as wel, wyȝe [sir], bi my faythe, / As any gome [man] vnder God, for thy grete trauthe" (2469–70). He seems fully conscious of having issued the challenge in fitt 1 and, having followed the events of the last few days, ready to be jealous had his wife's seductions succeeded.

In a second reading of the Green Knight's trans-world identity, Morgan conjured up both the Green Knight and Sir Bertilak, and inhabits his manor in both her ugly and beautiful manifestations; she apparently intends to be destructive to Gawain and Arthur, but ends up being inadvertently benign. In this reading Bertilak has no independent, substantial existence at all. Either conjecture about overlap might apply, but there is too little textual evidence to decide whether Bertilak was an ordinary feudal landlord before Morgan entered the picture or an emanation produced by her illusion-summoning powers. Although his discourse usually accords with Christianity, his referring to her as a goddess leaves open the possibility of either the creation or the transformation of "Bertilak" in the space shared by the two worlds. Gawain never discovers the nature of the world in which he has learned to be a penitent, nor do readers of the poem.

The overlap question makes more difference for our interpretation of Gawain, who is, in the end, a saved Christian soul living a life of continual penance. He comes to understand that in a world of accidents and appearances, he cannot attain Mary's changelessness or perfectly exhibit the linked virtues of the pentangle. He can, however be a model of penitence and reflection in his actual world. To arrive at this state of mind he undergoes an *aventure*, designed for him alone, that takes him into a second real world. When the Green Knight replaces his head and gallops off, everyone knows that another world has impinged on theirs, but Gawain insists on following the chivalric and Christian rules of his actual world. Except for his brief lapse in trusting the girdle (and not very deeply at that), he resolutely maintains his belief in that world and his identity in it, an identity that must be maintained even if no other being ever witnessed a falling off. His graciousness to the household as he leaves Hautdesert and his refusal to turn back when the guide (who may also be Bertilak) urges him to do so – "I were a knyȝt kowarde ... I myȝt not be excused" (2129–31) – are as marvellous as any of the other marvels in the poem. He travels to an incompossible world and returns without dissolving into dust, as Bran did in the Irish story. But he does return changed.

Gawain seems to inhabit both worlds with his essential qualities – courtesy, self-control, and courage – intact. Within the tale, it cannot be that Gawain's *aventure* exists only in a secondary mind-dependent sense.[58] The Green Knight, the axe, the blood on the snow are "really there," and Gawain shows off his scar and wears the green lace when he gets back to Camelot. (He gets back without incident, too, which suggests that Wirral resembles the portal between worlds we see in *Orfeo* and many other romances.) Marie-Laure Ryan's emphasis on the way readers can be instructed to re-centre their actual worlds by visiting fictional ones[59] may be used to apply both within the text and outside it. For Gawain, though, the timeless world of the Virgin Mary is even more pressingly real than when he first picked up his shield with her portrait on it. Gawain discovers that the true human Christian is penitent rather than perfect, but Arthur's court regards him as its best representative (2516). The medieval reader may have regarded both chivalric honour and spiritual humility as their home worlds, and taken them (perhaps discontinuously) as serious ideals; writing by Henry of Lancaster's *Livre de seintes medicines* strongly suggests that possibility.[60] The modern reader may see the dual ending of the poem as a reflection of and inspiration to serious lay thought. In many ways a guide to attainable civilized behaviour in matters of both truth telling and custom (how to hunt and butcher game, how to welcome guests and set a sumptuous table). But, by taking Gawain's point of view in the last fitt, it displays feelingly his dismay at his allowing the world of appearance, even social refinement, to hoodwink him, however briefly.

The rules by which an imagined world works is a key issue in all romances. Gawain sets off immediately for Arthur's court, which celebrates his return by adopting the girdle in his honour as a sign of brotherhood and writing his story in the "best boke of romaunce" as, like Brutus, part of British lore (2516–21). They accept a feudal, chivalric world intruded upon by magic, but Gawain will have none of it. His apperception of events produces a conception of testing, sin, and repentance, a thoroughly Christian salvation history. He will wear the green lace (itself a "falssyng" [2378], when he had sought *trawthe*) as a sign of his shame in taking it, his love of his earthly life (2506). The more important implication of his so-called anti-feminist tirade positions women, rather than just as sexual temptresses, as representatives of the physical world, the wiles of the apparent, in a judgment like Troilus's from the eighth sphere.[61] *Gawain and the Green Knight* sets the intelligible truth of the faith against Gawain's sensible experience produced by Morgan's machinations (as in the disappearance of the black rocks in the *Franklin's Tale,* even if the magic is an illusion, it has real-world effects). It's dual "conclusion" in the last few stanzas raises, but does not adjudicate, the rift between appearances and the intellectual grasp of who or what is responsible for them.

This accords with the treatment of historical time in the framing of the poem. The frame is the Troy story, incontrovertible for medievals and tied to the very real fact that Britain was founded and they are living there now. The poet presents it as both the event history of where we are now and a text "With lel [faithful] letteres loken" and also "in toun herde" (31–4). He ends it in the same way: Brutus came (2524), but we know it because it was written in the "best boke of romaunce" (2521), just like Gawain's coming back.

We would not, of course, expect a *concept* to become the organizing principle of a beautiful poem. Kant marks a serious, but subtle, distinction between a concept and an aesthetic idea. An aesthetic idea "occasions much thinking through without it being possible for any determinate thought, i.e., concept, to be adequate to it, which, consequently, no language fully attains or can make intelligible" (*CPJ*, 192). Imagination enjoys free play, but is organized by the sense of purposiveness produced by its form (108). The multitude of tiny perceptions are being presented to Gawain and to readers as a kind of kaleidoscope, continuously exciting to imagination, but both inviting and baffling understanding of the whole. Like the protagonist himself, the poem seems to be striving throughout to define its quest, reflecting on romance and heroism. In fitts 2, 3, and most of 4, it is very close to Gawain, but at the very end Arthur's court disputes his apperception. The modern reader is presented with a mystery that cannot be solved once and for all, yet begs to be pondered.

Gadamer's characterization of aesthetic "magic" as the transformation of *energeia* into form unites the realistic specificity of the poem with its handling of the genre romance (*TM*, 163). The *energeia* inheres in the tiny details, many so engaging as to invite reflection in their own right – the green horse's braided mane, the sight of the castle from the edge of the forest, man and the boar tussling in the stream. The poem exhibits too many of these centres of energy to be subsumed under a recognized form, even so capacious a form as romance, which it clearly both refers to at every turn and violates in important ways. This welter of detail can be organized in many ways to produce a reading, as the critical record bears witness. The hermeneutic circle, through which we move continually, formulating and then amending expectations for the whole, is put to the test by this poem. For the *magic* to work, a narrative needs coherence. The usual way of positing coherence in order to enter the circle is to identify genre, but *Gawain and the Green Knight* tantalizes with any number of generic markers. It presents both a national hero second only to Arthur himself, but one whose discretion and rectitude are celebrated above his prowess, and the legend of a secular saint whose triumph he himself regards as moral failure.

His quest is not entirely located in either the mythical Celtic forces called up by the identification of Morgan as feé (or "goddess," 2552), the national history of Britain, or the pattern of Christian salvation. The Green Knight's potential reading as a figure for Nature allows either an allegory of over-civilized medieval aristocratic culture confronted by natural forces or an account of the triumph of the values these "honour-men" share. The details of the telling do not arrange themselves into a fully readable shape even when the plot has completely unfolded, yet we are impelled to see them as somehow coherent.

There is no question that *Gawain and the Green Knight* carries its own history with it and includes future readers in its enchantment. In many ways it reveals aspects of the "real" world we moderns imagine medieval people to have lived in. It most certainly is part of a late medieval ideal that emphasized strict self-control, generosity, and even self-abasement in the service of social harmony. Perhaps it even predicts a pre-Calvinistic sensibility of ruthless self-examination. No subsequent work has been able to replicate or remediate its varied energies. *Sir Gawain and the Green Knight* may be the finest of all the medieval romances, but, like *Hamlet* and *Lear*, it challenges the boundaries of its genre.

Notes

Introduction

1 Cooper sees the realism of medieval romances in their detailed presentation of inner life. As for being too cheerful, many are amply furnished with the uglier aspects of both psychology and social behaviour; moreover, happiness is neither more nor less "realistic" than misery (*English Romances in Time* [Oxford: Oxford University Press, 2000], 361).

2 Jameson, "Magical Narratives: Romance as Genre," *New Literary History* 7 (1975), 153. Cf. Northrop Frye's influential assertion: "The romance is nearest of all literary forms to the wish-fulfillment dream"; *Anatomy of Criticism* (Princeton: Princeton University Press, 1957), 186. Adena Rosmarin's *The Power of Genre* (Minneapolis: University of Minnesota Press, 1985) provides a helpful commentary on genre in general.

3 See the *Cambridge Companion to Medieval Romance*, ed. Roberta Krueger (Cambridge: Cambridge University Press, 2000). In it Simon Gault discusses its general range in "Romance and Other Genres" (45–59), Christopher Baswell its oral and literary forms in "Marvels of Translation and Crises of Transition in the Romances of Antiquity" (29–44), and Sarah Kay its inclusion of women in "Courts, Clerks, and Courtly Love" (81–96).

4 Ludwig Wittgenstein, *Philosophical Investigations*, ed. G.E.M. Anscombe (Oxford: Blackwell, 2001), #67 (pp. 27–8e).

5 Michael Nerlich, *Ideology of Adventure: Studies in Modern Consciousness 1100–1750*, trans. Ruth Crowley (Minneapolis: University of Minnesota Press, 1987), esp. vol. 1.

6 Geraldine Heng regards the "structures of desire" exhibited by romance, especially female desire, as their defining feature. See *Empire of Magic* (New York: Columbia University Press, 2003), 3–4. The "feminization and domestication of affect" is hagiography's "gift" to narrative (201). Helen Cooper also places female desire as a central concern of the genre (ch. 4).

7 Jeff Rider defines the posited world of most romances as the "central aristocratic society which medieval romance takes as its 'real,'" and that "is in some sense 'our' society," but notes that most also contain other worlds "created to stand over and against the equally fictive world of its central aristocratic society." See "The Other Worlds of Romance," in the *Cambridge Companion to Medieval Romance*, ed. Roberta Krueger (Cambridge: Cambridge University Press, 2000), 116).

8 This reflection is largely internal to the texts themselves because, except for Chaucer, little is known about the authors biographically – *Orfeo* and *Gawain* are anonymous and few details about Marie or Jean d'Arras have been established.

9 *Heterocosmica: Fiction and Possible Worlds* (Baltimore: Johns Hopkins University Press, 1998), 22.

10 Neal Stephenson in his 2008 speculative novel *Anathem* (New York: HarperCollins) makes this point by acknowledging his debts to Thales, Plato, Leibniz, Kant, Gödel, and Husserl. Our list is pretty long too, but our central commitments are to Kant, Leibniz, and Gadamer.

11 "Monadology," "Discourse on Metaphysics," and "Preface to the New Essays" are quoted from *G.W. Leibniz: Discourses on Metaphysics and Other Essays*, ed. and trans. Daniel Garber and Peter Ariew (Indianapolis and Cambridge: Hackett Publishers, 1991); cited is "Preface to the New Essays," 55. Hereafter cited in the text.

12 Augustine, *Confessions*, trans. John K. Ryan (Garden City, NY: Doubleday, 1960), bk. 11, 16. 21 and 15. 18, pp. 288–90. See also Paul Ricoeur's discussion of this passage in *Time and Narrative* (3 vols, trans. Kathleen McLaughlin and David Pellauer [Chicago: University of Chicago Press, 1984]), 1: chap. 1.

13 In *Anathem*, Stephenson's characters discuss time and perception in much the same way, calling the past "a system of records encoded in our nerve tissue – records that tell a consistent story … It seems miraculous that our consciousness can do this" (731).

14 Deleuze, *The Fold: Leibniz and the Baroque* (1988), trans. Tom Conley (Minneapolis: University of Minnesota Press, 1993).

15 Ibid., 6.

16 Serres, *Rome: The Book of Foundations*, trans. Felicia McCarren (Stanford: Stanford University Press, 1991), 60 and 80–4.

17 Jonathan Gil Harris, in *Untimely Matter in the Time of Shakespeare* (Philadelphia: University of Pennsylvania Press, 2009), makes use of this position to explicate events and objects (like Desdemona's handkerchief) in early-modern works.

18 Latour, *We Have Never Been Modern*, trans. Catherine Porter (Cambridge, MA: Harvard University Press, 1993), 75.

19 *Time and Narrative*, 1: 72.

20 For Dinshaw, the "crowded now" is an aspect of queer temporality; *How Soon Is Now* (London and Durham: Duke University Press, 2012), 4.

21 Gadamer, *Truth and Method*, 2nd rev. ed., trans. Joel Weinsheimer and Donald Marshall (New York and London: Continuum Books, 2003); hereafter *TM* in the text.

22 Later readers are barred from authentic imaginative and judgmental participation in the texts of earlier generations because ideology insidiously infects the very language in which they were couched. See Habermas's review of Gadamer's *Truth and Method*, in *Understanding Social Inquiry*, ed. Fred Dallmayr and Thomas McCarthy (South Bend, IN: Notre Dame University Press, 1977). See also John Brenkman's *Culture and Domination* (Ithaca, NY: Cornell University Press, 1987) for a lucid account of the debate between Gadamer and Habermas.

23 *Time and Narrative*, 2: 158, 173–4, 220.

24 "Gadamer's Conversation: Does the Other Have a Say?" in *Feminist Interpretations of Hans-Georg Gadamer*, ed. Lorraine Code (University Park: Penn State University Press, 2003), 109–32.

25 "Gadamer's Feminist Epistemology," ibid., 231–58.

26 Ibid., 232.

27 "The Hermeneutic Conversation as Epistemological Model," ibid., 259–83.

28 Ibid., 266. See also Susan Hekman, "The Ontology of Change: Gadamer and Feminism (181–201) and Meili Steele, "Three Problematics of Linguistic Vulnerability: Gadamer, Benhabib, and Butler" (335–66).

29 Dionysios A. Anapolitanos, *Leibniz: Representation, Continuity and the Spatiotemporal* (Dordrecht, Boston, London: Kluwer Academic Publishers, 1999), 38. Discussing the importance of emergence in contemporary scientific knowledge, Sandra D. Mitchell, in *Unsimple Truths: Science, Complexity, and Policy* (Chicago: University of Chicago Press, 2009), describes a "deep uncertainty" in many complex natural systems, not unlike the complexity of literary works within history. Both resist predictable explanation (3–5, 25–44).

30 McRae, *Leibniz: Perception, Apperception, and Thought* (Toronto: University of Toronto Press, 1976), 38.

31 Leibniz, "Discourse on Metaphysics," in *Leibniz* (ed. Garber), 37.
32 *The Fold*, 78 and 86–7.
33 Bergson, *Time and Free Will* (1889), trans. F.L. Pogson (New York: Humanities Press, 1910), 186.
34 Deleuze, *The Fold*, 70–2. Bergson's comment on fiction continues: "The very fact that he [the novelist] spreads out our feeling in a homogeneous time, and expresses its elements by words, shows that he in his turn is only offering us its shadow: but he has arranged this shadow in such a way as to make us suspect the extraordinary and illogical nature of the object which projects it; he has made us reflect by giving outward expression to something of that contradiction, that interpenetration, which is the very essence of the elements expressed" (134).
35 Adorno, *Aesthetic Theory*, ed. Gretel Adorno and Rolf Tiedemann, trans. Robert Hullot-Kentor (Minneapolis: University of Minnesota Press, 1997), 358.
36 Doležel, *Heterocosmica*, 201.
37 Helen Cooper stresses throughout *English Romances in Time* the way romance as a genre (popular and literary) produces resonance by "recycling" motifs and details. She begins the book with a witty account of the intertextuality of actors in bear suits on the early-modern stage (1–2).
38 We agree with Lee Patterson's position, which argues that an ideology of individualism should not be allowed to define subjectivity itself, which "has always been part of our history, albeit in different configurations and with different powers and values" (*Chaucer and the Subject of History* [Madison: University of Wisconsin Press, 1987], 12). Carolyn Bynum locates an increased emphasis on "the inner mystery, the inner man, the inner landscape" in the twelfth century in *Jesus as Mother* (Berkeley: University of California Press, 1982), 106.
39 Solomon, "Emotions, Thoughts, and Feelings: Emotions as Engagements with the World," in *Thinking about Feeling*, ed. Robert Solomon (Oxford: Oxford University Press, 2004), 77. See also Ronald de Sousa, "Emotions: What I Know, What I'd Like to Think I Know, and What I'd Like to Think," ibid., 62–73.
40 The doubleness implied by the Middle English term *trouthe* as accuracy/ candour, or loyalty is discussed in Richard Firth Green's *A Crisis of Truth: Literature and Law in Richardian England* (Philadelphia: University of Pennsylvania Press, 1999).
41 G.W. Leibniz, *Theodicy: Essays on the Goodness of God, the Freedom of Man and the Origin of Evil* (New Haven: Yale University Press, 1952), 370. In *Fairies in Medieval Romance* (New York: Palgrave Macmillan, 2011), James Wade

uses the notion of possible worlds to delineate the narrative conventions that governed the various appearances of fairies in medieval romances.

42 Lewis, *On the Plurality of Worlds* (Oxford: Blackwell, 1986; repr. 2001), 2. Scientific discourse is also involved in discussions of multiple worlds; for example, physicist Lev Vaidman takes Lewis's arguments into account in "Many-Worlds Interpretation of Quantum Mechanics," in *The Stanford Encyclopedia of Philosophy* (2008).

43 Robert C. Stalnaker, "Possible Worlds," in *The Possible and the Actual: Readings in the Metaphysics of Modality*, ed. Michael J. Loux (Ithaca and London: Cornell University Press, 1979), 234 (hereafter, "in Loux").

44 Rescher, "The Ontology of the Possible," in Loux, 179.

45 Ryan, *Possible Worlds, Artificial Intelligence and Narrative Theory* (Bloomington: Indiana University Press, 1991), 21.

46 Lewis, *On the Plurality of Worlds*, 27. See also David J. Chalmers, "Epistemic Two-Dimensional Semantics," *Philosophical Studies* 118 (2004), 159, and Bruno Whittle, "Epistemically Possible Worlds and Propositions," *Noûs* 43, n. 2 (2009), 265.

47 Quilligan, "Allegory, Allegoresis, and the Deallegorization of Language," in *Allegory, Myth, Symbol*, ed. Morton Bloomfield (Cambridge, MA: Harvard University Press, 1981). The case is argued more expansively in *The Language of Allegory* (Ithaca: Cornell University Press, 1979).

48 Ryan, *Possible Worlds*, 32–41.

49 The term "encyclopedia" is discussed in Doležel's *Heterocosmica*, 177–8. Another congruence between Gadamer's position and modal logic is Doležel's discussion of the way fictional texts are performative, calling their worlds into existence, in *Possible Worlds of Fiction and History* (Baltimore: Johns Hopkins University Press, 2010), 42.

50 In modern philosophy, this is the debate about "trans-world identity," or TWI. See Roderick M. Chisholm, "Identity through Possible Worlds: Some Questions," 80–7; David Kaplan, "Transworld Heir Lines," 88–109; and Alvin Plantinga, "Transworld Identity or Worldbound Individuals?" 146–65. All three are in Loux.

51 "Letter to Louis Bourguet," in *Philosophical Papers and Letters*, ed. and trans. Leroy Loemker (Dordrecht-Holland and Boston: D. Reidel Publishing Co., 1969), 662.

52 For a more recent account of "thisness" or "haecceitism," see Penelope Mackie, *How Things Might Have Been: Individuals, Kinds, and Essential Properties* (Oxford: Clarendon Press, 2006), 150–68.

53 *Energeia* and *enargeia* both emerge from classical antiquity with slightly differing meanings. The former (from *ergon*, "work") was a technical term

from Aristotle translated as "activity" or "actuality," and used by Scaliger to mean "force." The latter (from *argos*, "bright, shining") was used by Cicero and Quintilian for figures that present something vividly to the mind's eye. See George Puttenham, *The Art of English Poesy*, ed. Frank Whigam and Wayne Rebhorn (Ithaca, NY: Cornell University Press, 2007), chap. 3, n. 1. The two terms were sometimes used interchangeably after Puttenham, and Gadamer seems to have fused vividness with efficacy in his usage.

54 Quoted in Michael J. Futch, *Leibniz's Metaphysics of Time and Space*, Boston Studies in the Philosophy of Science 258 (Spring 2008), 76.

55 *Critique of the Power of Judgment*, trans. Paul Guyer (Cambridge: Cambridge University Press, 2000), 238 and throughout. Kant argues his definition applies not to classes of things but to individual objects (116), and our argument is not for the beauty of romances as a class, but for particular fictions. Hereafter cited in the text as *CPJ*.

56 Elaine Scarry insists throughout *On Beauty and Being Just* (Princeton: Princeton University Press, 1999) that aesthetic experience involves placing oneself in the path of beauty, to be sure to be "looking in the right direction when a comet makes its sweep through a certain patch of sky" (7).

57 Bonaventure, *The Mind's Road to God*, trans. George Boas (Indianapolis: Bobbs-Merrill, 1953). For other congruences between Kant's thinking and that of other medieval writers, see Peggy A. Knapp, *Chaucerian Aesthetics* (New York: Palgrave, 2008), 17–42.

58 Kant, *CPJ*, 110. Kant's enigmatic "beauty is a symbol of the good" is a hot issue even now, and this is no place to attempt a full interpretation of it, except to say that the symbolism does not imply overt moral instruction. Jean-François Lyotard discusses this issue in *Lessons on the Analytic of the Sublime*, trans. Elizabeth Rottenberg (Stanford, CA: Stanford University Press, 1994), 159–90.

59 *The Critique of Judgement*, trans. James Creed Meredith (Oxford: Clarendon Press, 1962), 60); Guyer translates it as "animation" (104). Nicholas Rescher noted in a personal communication that "enliven" combines the idea of "endowing with life" and "rendering more lively."

60 In *Truth and Method*, we find "To seek the unity of the work of art solely in its form as opposed to its content is a perverse formalism, which moreover cannot invoke the name of Kant" (92). Adorno writes: "Closure for its own sake, independent of the truth content and what this closure is predicated on, is a category that in fact deserves the ominous name of formalism" (*Aesthetic Theory*, 159). Henry E. Allison puts it this way: a "subjective formal purposiveness" or "purposiveness of form" is a "non-restrictive conception of form" that combines conceptual content with the free play

of imagination. He is refuting Guyer's charge of "restrictive formalism" (*A Reading of the Critique of Aesthetic Judgment* [Cambridge: Cambridge University Press, 2001], 119).

61 Bonaventure's *The Mind's Road to God* insists on the shared human capacity to respond to beauty (18).

62 See Allison's discussion of the four moments as corresponding to "the division of the table of logical functions in the *First Critique*, where they are called "titles"; he describes them as "moments that judgment takes into consideration as it reflects" (*Kant's Theory of Taste*, 67, 74).

1 The Speculative Fiction of Marie de France

1 Jean Rychner, *Les Lais de Marie de France* (Paris: Éditions Champion, 1983). Verse translations are from Robert Hanning and Joan Ferrante, *The Lais of Marie de France* (Durham: The Labrynth Press, 1978).

2 Ibid., 28, n. 1.

3 Matilda Tomaryn Bruckner, *Shaping Romance: Interpretation, Truth, and Closure in Twelfth-Century French Fictions* (Philadelphia: University of Pennsylvania Press, 1993), 196.

4 Spitzer, "The Prologue to the *Lais* of Marie de France and Medieval Poetics," *Modern Philology* 41, no. 2 (November 1943), 98.

5 The term "encyclopedia" is discussed in Doležel's *Heterocosmica: Fiction and Possible Worlds* (Baltimore: Johns Hopkins University Press, 1998), 177–8.

6 Monica Brzezinski Potkay, "The Parable of the Sower and Obscurity in the Prologue to Marie de France's Lais," *Christianity and Literature* 57, no. 3 (Spring 2008), 359.

7 Ibid., 372.

8 Stephen G. Nichols, "Marie de France's Commonplaces," *Yale French Studies*, special issue, 1991, 147.

9 Mikhaïlova, "L'espace dans les Lais de Marie de France: Lieux, structure, rhétorique," *Cahiers de civilization médiévale* 40, no. 158 (April–June 1997), 157.

10 Rychner, "La présence et le point de vue du narrateur dans deux récits courts: Le Lai de Lanval et la Châtelaine de Vergi," *Vox Romanica* 39 (1980), 99–100.

11 Freeman, "Marie de France's Poetics of Silence: The Implications for a Feminine *Translatio*," *PMLA* 99, no. 5 (October 1984), 878.

12 Katherine McCloone, "Strange Bedfellows: Politics, Miscegenation and *Translatio* in Two Lays of Lanval," *Arthuriana* 21, no. 4 (Winter 2011), 3–22.

13 John Fowles, *The Ebony Tower* (New York: Signet, 1974), 10. Hereafter page numbers are cited in the text.

14 See Introduction above, 15–17.

15 Nelson, "Eliduc's Salvation," *The French Review* 55, no. 1 (October 1981), 37. Her allegorical reading follows the method of textual exegesis associated with D.W. Robertson, Jr, *A Preface to Chaucer* (Princeton: Princeton University Press, 1962).

16 Sharon Kinoshita, "Two for the Price of One: Serial Polygamy in the 'Lais' of Marie de France," *Arthuriana* 8, no. 2 (Summer 1998), 50.

17 In the textual notes to his edition of the *Lais*, Jean Rychner notes the scholarly dispute about whether *l'aventure* is the subject of *avenu*, or the object of *cunterai*. The syntax may not be decidable, but the change of title would seem to have greater significance if the *aventure* is something that happens to the women. *Les Lais de Marie de France* (Paris: Éditions Champion, 1983), 281, note to lines 25–7.

18 Mackie, *How Things Might Have Been* (Oxford: Clarendon Press, 2006) and Kripke, *Naming and Necessity* (Oxford: Blackwell, 1980).

19 Leibniz, see Introduction, 12.

20 Ludwig Wittgenstein, *Philosophical Investigations*, ed. G.E.M. Anscombe (Oxford: Blackwell, 2001), 159–60.

21 David Lewis, "Counterpart Theory and Quantified Modal Logic" and Alvin Plantinga, "Transworld Identity or Worldbound Individuals?"; both are in *The Possible and the Actual: Readings in the Metaphysics of Modality*, ed. Michael J. Loux (Ithaca and London: Cornell University Press, 1979), 110–28 and 146–65, respectively.

22 As Leibniz put it, "I call possible anything which is perfectly conceivable and which, as a result, has an essence or an idea, without raising the question of whether the rest of the world permits it to become existent." *Philosophical Papers and Letters*, ed. and trans. Leroy Loemker (Dordrecht-Holland and Boston: D. Reidel Publishing Co., 1969), 662. See Introduction, 19–20.

23 Bruckner, *Shaping Romance*, 4.

24 Keith Nickolaus surveys marriage reform in the twelfth century in *Marriage Fictions in Old French Secular Narratives, 1170–1250: A Critical Re-Evaluation of the Courtly Love Debate* (New York and London: Routledge, 2002), 131–52, and discusses literary examples criticizing coercive aristocratic marriage not based on consent and affection. For an account of aristocratic marriage practices, see Georges Duby, *Love and Marriage in the Middle Ages*, trans. Jane Dunnett (Chicago: University of Chicago Press, 1994), 22–35.

25 As E. Jane Burns writes, "We have known for some time that important alternative configurations of female desire, pleasure, and subjectivity

are articulated by female authors such as the women troubadours (or *trobairitz*) in the southern French (Occitan) tradition, by women *trouvère* poets in the north, and by the Anglo-Norman author Marie de France, among others." "Courtly Love: Who Needs It? Recent Feminist Work in the Medieval French Tradition," *Signs* 27, no. 1 (Autumn 2001), 26.

26 Ramm, "Making Something of Nothing: The Excesses of Storytelling in the Lais of Marie de France and La Chastelaine de Vergi," *French Studies* 60, no. 1, 12.

27 Nickolaus, *Marriage Fictions*, and Duby, *Love and Marriage in the Middle Ages*, note 23.

28 Sharon Kinoshita, *Medieval Boundaries: Rethinking Difference in Old French Literature* (Philadelphia: University of Pennsylvania Press, 2006); Seeta Chaganti, "The Space of Epistemology in Marie de France's 'Yonec,'" *Romance Studies* 28, no. 2 (April 2010), 71–83.

29 Kinoshita, *Medieval Boundaries*, 113–19.

30 Ibid., 123–4.

31 Boyd, "The Ring, the Sword, the Fancy Dress and the Posthumous Child: Background to the Element of Heroic Biography in Marie de France's *Yonec*,' *Romance Quarterly* 55, no. 3 (Summer 2008), 207.

32 Sylvia Huot, "Others and Alterity," in *The Cambridge Companion to Medieval French Literature*, ed. Simon Gaunt and Sarah Kay (Cambridge: Cambridge University Press, 2008), 239.

33 Chaganti, "Space of Epistemology," 75.

34 Denyse Delcourt, "Oiseaux, ombre, désir: Écrire dans les Lais de Marie de France," *MLN* 120, no. 4, French issue (September 2005), 814.

35 Bruckner, *Shaping Romance*, 4.

36 See Introduction, 7–8.

37 Bloch, *The Anonymous Marie de France* (Chicago and London: University of Chicago Press, 2003), 28.

2 Perception and Possible Worlds in *Sir Orfeo*

1 Surviving references to Orpheus date from the sixth-century BCE poet Ibykos and include Aeschylus, Plato, and Aristotle. Versions of his story are told by Virgil, Ovid, and Boethius, and depicted on many physical objects. The Orphic legacy is linked variously with Apollonian and Dionysian strands of Greek thought. See W.K.C. Guthrie, who writes: "Famous he was at the first date at which we hear of him, and famous he has been ever since" (*Orpheus and Greek Religion* [New York: Norton, 1966], 1).

2 Although the best-known Roman versions (Virgil's and Ovid's) emphasize the look back and the second loss of Eurydice, some Greek sources tell of her successful return (Charles Segal, *Orpheus: The Myth of the Poet* [Baltimore: Johns Hopkins University Press, 1989], 8, and Guthrie, *Orpheus and Greek Religion*, 25–68).

3 For a thorough account of the poem's Celtic elements, see A.J. Bliss, ed., *Sir Orfeo.* (Oxford: Clarendon Press, 1966), xxvii–xli. We have cited this edition of the Auchinleck manuscript by line number throughout the text.

4 Steele Nowlin uses the anthropological notions of Victor Turner to define a zone of "liminality" within the Breton lay where "cultural paradigms can be engaged, explained, and re-conceived" ("Between Precedent and Possibility: Liminality, Historicity, and Narrative in Chaucer's The Franklin's Tale," *Studies in Philology* 103, no. 1 [Winter 2006], 48–9).

5 Orfeo's descent is traced from Juno and Pluto, rather than Calliope, as Boethius and others claim, but this detail acknowledges the Greco-Roman roots of the tale.

6 "As for my own opinion, I have said more than once that I hold space to be something purely relative, as time is – that I hold it to be an order of coexistences, as time is an order of successions." Leibniz, in *G.W. Leibniz and Samuel Clarke: Correspondence*, ed. and intro. Roger Ariew (Indianapolis: Hackett Publishing Co., 2000), 14.

7 Riddy, "The Uses of the Past in *Sir Orfeo*," *Yearbook of English Studies*, 6 (1976), 15.

8 Friedman, *Orpheus in the Middle Ages* (Cambridge, MA: Harvard University Press, 1970), 167.

9 Helen Cooper, *The English Romance in Time: Transforming Motifs from Geoffrey of Monmouth to the Death of Shakespeare* (Oxford: Oxford University Press, 2004), 16.

10 Fletcher, "*Sir Orfeo* and the Flight from the Enchanters," *Studies in the Age of Chaucer* 22 (2000), 143.

11 Hynes-Berry, "Cohesion in *King Horn* and *Sir Orfeo*," *Speculum* 50, no. 4 (October 1975), 663.

12 The framing contention of Battles's argument is that *Sir Orfeo* reflects the continuing memory of conflict between Norman and Anglo-Saxon after the conquest, and that Orfeo's exile is more like that of the Anglo-Saxon poems than it is like the wilderness sojourn of a hero of French romance such as Yvain. "*Sir Orfeo* and English Identity," *Studies in Philology* 107, no. 2 (Spring 2010), 199.

13 Andrea G. Pisan Babich, "The Power of the Kingdom and the Ties That Bind in *Sir Orfeo*," *Neophilologus* 82 (1998), 480.

14 Letter to Arnaud, 14 July 1686.
15 Alvin Plantinga, "Transworld Identity or Worldbound Individuals?" in *The Possible and the Actual: Readings in the Metaphysics of Modality*, ed. Michael J. Loux (Ithaca and London: Cornell University Press, 1979), 165.
16 Plantinga quotes the following passage of Boethius: "For let the incommunicable property of Plato be called 'Platonity.' For we can call this quality 'Platonity' by a fabricated word, in the way in which we call the quality of a man 'humanity.' Therefore, this Platonity is one man's alone, and this not just anyone's, but Plato's. For 'Plato' points out a one and definite substance, and property, that cannot come together in another"; "Actualism and Possible Worlds," in Loux, ed., *The Possible and the Actual*, 262. See also Chaucer, *Boece*, book 2, pr 4.
17 Leibniz uses the example of Alexander, who, as a subject, contains all the predicates that may be attributed to him, versus Alexander as king, which is only an accident of his being, "not determinate enough to constitute an individual"; "Discourse on Metaphysics," 8.
18 Dickson, "Verbal and Visual Disguise: Society and Identity in Some Twelfth-Century Texts," in *Medieval Insular Romance: Translation and Innovation*, ed. Judith Weiss at al. (Cambridge: D.S. Brewer, 2000), 41–54.
19 Friedman, *Orpheus in the Middle Ages*, 193.
20 Longworth, "'Sir Orfeo,' the Minstrel, and the Minstrel's Art," *Studies in Philology* 79, no. 1 (Winter 1982), 7.
21 Cartlidge, "Sir Orfeo in the Otherworld: Courting Chaos?" *Studies in the Age of Chaucer* 26 (2004), 195–226.
22 See Derek Pearsall, "Madness in *Sir Orfeo*," in *Romance Reading on the Book: Essays in Medieval Narrative Presented to Maldwyn Mills*, ed. Jennifer Fellows, Rosalind Field, Gillian Rogers, and Judith Weiss (Cardiff: University of Wales Press, 1996, 51–63. James Wade invokes Giorgio Agamben's theory of "sovereign exception" to characterize the frightening incomprehensibility introduced by the Fairy King; *Fairies in Medieval Romance* (New York: Palgrave Macmillan, 2011), 74, 79–80.
23 Friedman, *Orpheus in the Middle Ages*, 191.
24 James F. Knapp, "The Meaning of Sir Orfeo," *Modern Language Quarterly* 29 (1968), 263–73. Seth Lerer has noted that the earliest commentator to understand the poem in conceptual terms might be the narrator in the Ashmole manuscript's variant of the text, whose coda is specifically eschatological; "Artifice and Artistry in *Sir Orfeo*," *Speculum* 60 (January 1985), 106).
25 *Sir Orfeo* is widely admired by modern scholars, but most have attended primarily to its address to medieval audiences and how later writers like

Shakespeare have appropriated various of its elements. Our concern, finally, is with the *presence* of its beauty, weathered as it is by the passage of time and linguistic change.

26 Rainer Maria Rilke, *Orpheus. Eurydike. Hermes* (1904).

27 There are many ways of constituting generic categories: (1) verse and prose; (2) tragedy, comedy, romance, and their combinations (see Polonius's comments to the actors in *Hamlet* 2.2.379–82); (3) "realism" and allegory – strictly, a mode, rather than a genre, but a feature of formal shaping.

28 Hans-Georg Gadamer, *Truth and Method*, 2nd rev. ed., trans. Joel Weinsheimer and Donald Marshall (New York and London: Continuum Books, 2003), 110.

29 Friedman links the abduction at noon to Celtic lore, but also to Psalm 90's "deliver me ... from the noon-day demon"; *Orpheus in the Middle Ages*, 187–8.

30 Among English poems, *Sir Gawain and the Green Knight* comes closest in threatening the hero's death in a strange Celtic landscape, but at the last minute, it introduces Morgan's influence as a (partial?) explanation for events. A close French analogue is the failure to specify the nature of Bagdamagu's realm in Chrétien's *Lancelot*.

31 Works that are clearly announced allegories, whose "second meanings" are apparent, do not require allegorization, which Maureen Quilligan (*The Language of Allegory: Defining the Genre* [Ithaca: Cornell University Press, 1979]) and others call "allegoresis."

32 John of Garland's *Integumenta Ovidii* presents a stark version of the allegorical method: "Field is Pleasure, wife is Flesh, Viper is Poison, / Man is Reason, Styx is Earth, Lyre is Speech" (quoted in Friedman, *Orpheus in the Middle Ages*, 121). On the general issue, see Jeff Rider, *Cambridge Companion to Medieval Romance*, ed. Roberta Krueger (Cambridge: Cambridge University Press, 2000), 115–31.

33 Both Guthrie (*Orpheus and Greek Religion*, 265) and Friedman (*Orpheus in the Middle Ages*, 58) present an image of it and regard it as a sign of the syncretism of Orphic and early Christian beliefs.

34 Guthrie, *Orpheus and Greek Religion*, 265.

35 Aeschylus simply regards Orpheus as turning away from Dionysus to Apollo (Segal, *Orpheus: The Myth of the Poet*, 156). Guthrie describes the Orphic bible as a loose collection of writings (*Orpheus and Greek Religion*, 41 and 159) that move from a superstitious to a more orderly account of the cult, and cites F.M. Cornford on the transmission to St Paul (195). The *Testament of Orpheus*, a forged document from the middle of the third

century CE, claims that Orpheus was converted to monotheism by the teaching of Moses. Used by Eusebius, it contributed to Judeo-Christian interest in Orpheus (Friedman, *Orpheus in the Middle Ages*, 13–37).

36 Rushdie, *The Ground beneath Her Feet* (New York: Henry Holt, 1999).

37 Berman, *All That Is Solid Melts into Air* (New York: Viking Penguin, 1988).

3 Capturing Beauty: Chaucer's *Troilus and Criseyde*

1 Its association with epic concerns no doubt served to elevate the literary seriousness of *Troilus and Criseyde*. Gordon Teskey argues that English Renaissance classical (read "higher") forms incorporated romance elements so pervasively that the genres became mutually implicated; the connection seems to us to have started in the Middle Ages. See "Introduction" to *Unfolded Tales: Essays on Romance*, ed. George M. Logan and Gordon Teskey (Ithaca: Cornell University Press, 1989), 1–3.

2 Chaucer's precedents for the story of the war are Virgil and Ovid, together with two accounts that claimed to be translations into Latin from what was claimed to be Greek eyewitness testimony: Dictys (fourth century C.E., the Greek side, originally a Phoenician record buried with Dictys and ordered to be copied into Greek by Nero) and Dares (sixth century C.E., the Trojan side, which includes the detail that Briseida [Criseyde] had joined eyebrows). H.A. Kelly suggests that Chaucer may have used Boccaccio's version without knowing the author's name; see *Chaucerian Tragedy* (Woodbridge, Suffolk: D.S. Brewer, 1977), 40.

3 Boethius, *The Consolation of Philosophy*, trans. P.G. Walsh (Oxford: Clarendon Press, 1999); when *Boece*, *Troilus and Criseyde*, and *The Canterbury Tales* are quoted in the text, it is from the *Riverside Chaucer*, ed. Larry Benson et al., 3rd ed. (Boston: Houghton Mifflin, 1987).

4 The result of such autonomy, he argues, is that art becomes socially oppositional whatever its content, by foregrounding subjective experience. Adorno here speaks for many modern theorists in thinking of medieval as "other." Theodor Adorno, *Aesthetic Theory*, ed. Gretel Adorno and Rolf Tiedemann, trans. Robert Hullot-Kentor (Minneapolis: University of Minnesota Press, 1997), 225. We agree with Maura Nolan that Adorno's position in this book looks more directly Kantian than is usually assumed, and also that his choice of Cervantes as the break with the medieval is arbitrary and easily countered. See Maura Nolan, "Making the Aesthetic Turn: Adorno, the Medieval, and the Future of the Past," *Journal of Medieval and Early Modern Studies* 34, no. 3 (Fall 2004), 549–75.

5 Donaldson, *The Swan at the Well* (New Haven: Yale University Press, 1985), 9; Aers, *Community, Gender and Individual Identity* (New York: Routledge, 1988), 129; Dinshaw, *Chaucer's Sexual Poetics* (Madison: University of Wisconsin Press, 1989). These readings from different vantage points converge in that they take Criseyde's life-world as a serious feature of the poem and read the poem in terms of its social and psychological realism.

6 D.W. Robertson, Jr, *A Preface to Chaucer* (Princeton: Princeton University Press, 1962), 473. We refer to this passage because Robertson's is the most fully argued of many positions that take Criseyde as a figure for the seductiveness of this unstable world, her apparent loveliness an illusion.

7 De Man, *The Resistance to Theory* (Minneapolis: University of Minnesota Press, 1986), 64. Geoffrey Galt Harpham critiques his position in "Aesthetics and the Fundamentals of Modernity," in George Levine, *Aesthetics and Ideology* (New Brunswick: Rutgers University Press, 1994), 131–3.

8 Introduction to *Troilus and Criseyde*, ed., Stephen Barney (New York: Norton Critical Edition, 2006), ix.

9 *Critique of the Power of Judgment*, trans. Paul Guyer (Cambridge: Cambridge University Press, 2000), 97–8. A beautiful object can of course also be good, but the classification of the two qualities arises from a different mode of judgment. Kant's enigmatic "beauty is a symbol of the good" (225–8) is a hot issue even now, and this is no place to attempt a full interpretation of it, except to say that the symbolism occurs on a high level of abstraction. See Jean-François Lyotard, *Lessons on the Analytic of the Sublime*, trans Elizabeth Rottenberg (Stanford, CA: Stanford University Press, 1994), 159–90.

10 The injunction against invoking formal rules is found throughout the treatise, but is especially clear on page 126. The quotation is from *Critique of the Power of Judgment*, trans. Paul Guyer (Cambridge: Cambridge University Press, 2008), 185.

11 Dennis Donoghue writes, "It is not that words correspond to the previously felt; the words make feeling possible"; *Speaking of Beauty* (New Haven: Yale University Press, 2003), 107.

12 Gadamer, *Truth and Method*, 2nd rev. ed., trans. Joel Weinsheimer and Donald Marshall (New York and London: Continuum Books, 2003), 110–18.

13 Leibniz, *The Monadology*, §57. Considering genre involves taking a perspective, like looking across and then into Leibniz's pond teeming with immensely subtle things. "Discourse on Metaphysics," 57, and "Monadology," §67 in *Discourses on Metaphysics and Other Essays*, ed.

and trans. Daniel Garber and Peter Ariew (Indianapolis and Cambridge: Hackett Publishers, 1991). Wittgenstein's aspect recognition (*Philosophical Investigations* 2.11 (pp. 165–93) also comes to mind on this issue. We are using G.E.M. Anscombe's German/English facing-pages edition (Oxford: Blackwell, 2001).

14 McAlpine, *The Genre of* Troilus and Criseyde (Ithaca: Cornell University Press, 1978); Windeatt, *Oxford Guide to Chaucer: Troilus and Criseyde* (Oxford: Clarendon Press, 1992), 138–79. Helen Cooper emphasizes Chaucer's interest in the genres in the *Canterbury Tales*: an "overt generic label [is] attached to almost all of the stories in the links, a process that first introduces into English the idea of genre as the key to both writing and to hermeneutics" ("Responding to the Monk," *Studies in the Age of Chaucer* 22 [2000], 432).

15 Giancarlo, "The Structure of Fate and the Devising of History in Chaucer's *Troilus and Criseyde*," *Studies in the Age of Chaucer* 26 (2004), 230.

16 The proheme to book 1 announces the subject as Troilus's *aventures* in love. There is a "goodly aventure" in store for Criseyde too, as Pandarus tells her (2.281) and she is advised not to let "aventure slake" (2.291). By the end of book 2 she refers to "myn aventure" (742). In book 3 the lovers speak of their mutual commitment as "this aventure" (1367), and finally, in book 5, Troilus understands his abandonment and endures ("drieth forth") his *aventure* (1540).

17 Kelly calls this "instinctive" rather than "Aristotelian" because he does not find Troilus guilty of a "tragic flaw," either for letting Criseyde go to the Greek camp or in the allegory for loving her in the first place (*Chaucerian Tragedy*, 40–1). He has some scathing things to say about the criticism that pinpoints Troilus's failings of intellect and morality (117). Instead, he finds Troilus's love "innocently sought and virtuously attained," not "immoral and idolatrous" (104). He does not examine the case for Criseyde as a potential tragic heroine, as Monica McAlpine does in *The Genre of* Troilus and Criseyde.

18 The story of Antenor conniving to steal the Palladium, which ensured the safety of Troy is told in Benoît and Guido, but not Boccaccio. Chaucer does not tell this part of Antenor's history, but emphasizes the tragic irony of the prisoner exchange as an "ensample" of a "cloude of errour" (4.200–1).

19 In Kant's view, even the creator of art does not know his idea as a concept, nor does he know where it came from (*CPJ*, 187). As Henry E. Allison writes, glossing Kant: "Texts can nevertheless combine with conceptual representations to form a complex, only partly aesthetic, type of judgment, which is still a judgment of beauty in the broad sense"; *Kant's Theory of*

Taste: A Reading of the Critique of Aesthetic Judgment (Cambridge: Cambridge University Press, 2001), 120.

20 Natalie Suzelis regards Criseyde's wish for death on account of the world's untrustworthiness (2.409–10) as an anticipation of "Troilus's journey to the eighth sphere as true freedom from the inconstancy and faithlessness of worldly desire … a freedom she wishes to preserve for herself" (unpublished paper, 2014).

21 Elizabeth Allen's "Flowing Backward to the Source: Criseyde's Promises and the Ethics of Allusion," *Speculum* 88 (July 2013), 681–720, regards Criseyde's promises of fidelity as bold and sincere attempts to perceive and resist malign historical forces; see especially 683–5. See also Monica McAlpine's essay on the passage: "Criseyde's Prudence," *Studies in the Age of Chaucer* 25 (2003), 199–224.

22 Jill Mann takes this view: Chaucer's aim "is to show human change in its fully tragic dimensions, and for this Criseyde's loss is not enough: we need to see the deformation of her personality"; "Feminizing Chaucer," in Barney's Norton Critical Edition of *Troilus and Criseyde*, 618.

23 Poirion, "Mask and Allegorical Personification," in *Rereading Allegory*, ed. Sahar Amer and Noah D. Guynn, Yale French Studies 95 (New Haven and London, 1999), 7.

24 Kitto, *Form and Meaning in Drama* (Oxford: Methuen, 1956), ch. 1.

25 This detached, orderly world of divine creation is of course Boethius's, but linked to later thought though Leibniz's *Theodicy* (New Haven: Yale University Press, 1952). The point is made by Giancarlo, "Structure of Fate," 262.

26 Modal literary claims (distinguishing realistic fictions from *exempla*, parables, and allegories) are not strictly identical to the way modal logic addresses truth claims under conditions of necessity and possibility. Leibniz's reflections on modality, developed by Saul Kripke's discussion of modal logic, overlaps with the realism/allegory problem; see "Semantical Considerations on Modal Logic," *Acta Philosophica Fennica* 16 (1963), 83–94.

27 Doležel, *Heterocosmica: Fiction and Possible Worlds* (Baltimore: Johns Hopkins University Press, 1998), 14 (italics in original). In "Introduction: Modality and Metaphysics," Michael Loux discusses the notion that "our access to possible worlds is effectively stipulative," a viewpoint appropriate to fictions; Loux, *The Possible and the Actual: Readings in the Metaphysics of Modality* (Ithaca and London: Cornell University Press, 1979), 44.

28 Marie-Laure Ryan, *Possible Worlds, Artificial Intelligence, and Narrative Theory* (Bloomington: Indiana University Press, 1991), 32–41.

29 Ibid., 57. From the literary side, Northrop Frye makes a similar argument by including allegory among the thematic modes; *Anatomy of Criticism* (Princeton: Princeton University Press, 1957), 52.

30 Gadamer, *Truth and Method*, 291. Elizabeth Allen identifies a common misstep in the recursive reading of the poem: "Detractors and defenders [of Criseyde] alike tend to view her from the perspective of her betrayal of Troilus, a 'view from the end' that much of the poem actively discourages" ("Flowing Backward to the Source," 683).

31 Doležel, *Heterocosmica*, 32.

32 Mann, "Feminizing Chaucer," 611.

33 Poirion, *Rereading Allegory*, 14.

34 David Lewis, *On the Plurality of Worlds* (Oxford: Blackwell, 1986, repr. 2001), discussed in the introduction, 16.

35 Peggy A. Knapp, "Criseyde's Beauty," in *New Perspectives on Criseyde*, ed. Cindy Vitto and Marcia Smith Marzec (Asheville, NC: Pegasus Press, 2004), 242–7.

36 As Jeff Rider, suggests, we should assume neither complete continuity between medieval methods of signification nor total alterity; see "The Inner Life of Women in Medieval Romance Literature," in *The Inner Life of Women in Medieval Romance Literature*, ed. Rider and Jamie Friedman (New York: Palgrave, 2011), 1–9.

37 Solomon, "Emotions, Thoughts, and Feelings: Emotions as Engagements with the World," in *Thinking about Feeling*, ed. Robert Solomon (Oxford: Oxford University Press, 2004), 71. See also Ronald de Sousa, "Emotions: What I Know, What I'd Like to Think I Know, and What I'd Like to Think," ibid., 62–73. Linda Martin Alcoff links feminist thinking about "immanent" understanding, as opposed to "human independent" epistemological knowledge, to Gadamer's description of the emergence of truth. Her account of mental life, with its emphasis on "relations of involvement" matches Solomon's on "engagement." See "Gadamer's Feminist Epistemolgy," in *Feminist Interpretations of Hans-Georg Gadamer*, ed. Lorraine Code (University Park: Penn State University Press, 2003), 244 and 250–1.

38 Barney, "Troilus Bound," *Speculum* 47 (1972), 446.

39 Dinshaw, *Chaucer's Sexual Poetics*, 28–64.

40 Examples of this case appear in Stephen Barney's "Troilus Bound" and Davis Taylor's "The Terms of Love: A Study of Troilus's Style," in the Norton Critical Edition of *Troilus and Criseyde*, 503–22.

41 Deleuze, following Leibniz, calls these movements of mind "microconceptions," some conscious, some below the threshold of consciousness:

"Representatives of the world are these little folds that unravel in every direction, folds in folds, following folds … And these are minute, obscure, confused perceptions that make up our macroperceptions, our conscious, clear, and distinct apperceptions"; *The Fold: Leibniz and the Baroque*, trans. Tom Conley (Minneapolis: University of Minnesota Press, 1993), 86–7.

42 The narrator announces that he "shal yow devyse" Troilus's anguish at the prisoner exchange (4.259) and again Criseyde's (4.735), suggesting "show the details of." Giancarlo discusses "devise" in its meanings "structure," "perceive," and "plan" as key to the way history is presented in the poem in "Structure of Fate," 229–39.

43 Robertson: "The ironic pun in line 543 is a bitter comment on what it is that Troilus actually misses"; see "Chaucerian Tragedy," *English Literary History* 19 (1952), 35; repr. *Chaucer Criticism: Troilus and Criseyde and the Minor Poems*, ed. Richard Schoeck and Jerome Taylor (Notre Dame, IN: University of Notre Dame Press, 1961), 116.

44 "The idea of a structure of feeling can be specifically related to the evidence of forms and conventions – semantic figures – which in art and literature are often among the very first indications that such a new structure is forming"; Raymond Williams, *Marxism and Literature* (Oxford: Oxford University Press, 1977), 133.

45 In *Chaucer and the Poets* (Ithaca: Cornell University Press, 1984), Winthrop Wetherbee places Criseyde in a "realistic" world of time and circumstance, while Troilus's innocence and integrity locate him in a different world (180); by book 5 he sees that no "real being" could reciprocate his love on this level (221). Criseyde also senses the realism/allegory divide too. In praising Troilus (4.1674–8), she regards him "as enshrined and imprisoned by his virtues"; he has therefore "ceased to be wholly real for her" (190).

46 For Lewis allegory underlies "the very nature of thought and language to represent what is immaterial in picturable terms"; to express inner life, metaphor is necessary, and "every metaphor is an allegory in little" (*The Allegory of Love* [New York: Oxford University Press, 1936]), 44, 60. Similarly, Frye writes in *Anatomy* that "all commentary is allegorical interpretation, an attaching of ideas to the structure of poetic imagery" (89); he calls formal allegory a thematic mode (53–4). Joel Fineman also treats allegory as criticism through its desire to read itself ("The Structures of Allegorical Desire," in *Allegory and Representation*, ed. Stephen Greenblatt, English Institute Essays, 1979–80 [Baltimore and London: Johns Hopkins University Press, 1981], 27).

47 Teskey, *Allegory and Violence* (Ithaca: Cornell University Press, 1996). Hereafter cited parenthetically as *AV*.

48 The term "allegory" does not appear in Chaucer's poetry, but "amphibologies" (*TC*, 4.1406) (a form of the word is also used by Kant in the *First Critique* [A.1.3]) and "ambages" (*TC*, 4.97–9) gesture beyond simple ambiguity toward the substitution of one *level* of significance for another in the manner of Augustinian interpretation of the Old Testament in terms of the New.

49 Quilligan, *The Language of Allegory: Defining the Genre* (Ithaca: Cornell University Press, 1979) argues that "true allegory" (as a genre) occurs rarely.

50 Nolan, "Making the Aesthetic Turn," 566.

51 Daniel Selcer, *Philosophy and the Book* (London: Continuum, 2010), 40. Selcer quotes Jon Whitman on this point.

52 This is, of course, a commonplace of medieval thought. Joel Fineman puts it to use in treating the *General Prologue* to the *Canterbury Tales* in "The Structures of Allegorical Desire."

53 Sashi Nair argues that Criseyde's "Boethian pragmatism" is a feature of her characterization all along, particularly in her distrust of Fortune, contrasted with Troilus's confidence that his joy will and should last ("'O brotel wele,'" *Paregon* 23 [2006], 36 and 49).

54 In *Troilus and the Poets*, Wetherbee argues for an even stronger connection with the *Commedia*, especially *Purgatorio*, featuring Troilus as the pilgrim Dante, Pandarus as his "false Vergil," and Criseyde as "pseudo-Beatrice." In this reading, "Troilus's virtue remains the poem's central concern." His decisive experience in the temple transports him beyond the world of the rest of Troy, placing him among Platonic ideas. "His" Criseyde is the unchanging deity to whom his service is plighted. It is as if Troilus inhabits an allegorical space (one he only comes to understand in book 5), detached from the "real" Troy (179–80).

55 This point is made by Peter Haidu in "Repetition: Modern Reflections on Medieval Aesthetics," *Modern Language Notes* 92 (December 1977), 875–87.

56 Barney, "Troilus Bound," 446. Nearly all the capture imagery is added to Boccaccio's poem by Chaucer. Although the general idea of love as binding can be found in *Filostrato*, the recurrent imagery of the trays, the fishing net, and the birdlime is Chaucer's.

57 Troilus's inability to solve the puzzle of freedom and predestination should not, we think, be taken as a flaw in his mental make-up. His seriousness is indicated by his anguished attempt to find the radical causes of events; he is, after all, a pagan until he transcends history after his death.

58 Augustine, *On Christian Doctrine*, trans. D.W. Robertson (Indianapolis, IN: Bobbs-Merrill, 1958), 2.6.7; p. 37.
59 Angus Fletcher, *Allegory: Theory of a Symbolic Mode* (Ithaca: Cornell University Press, 1964), 174–80.
60 Kittredge, *Chaucer and His Poetry* (Cambridge: Harvard University Press, 1915; repr. 1970), 109; Baugh, *Chaucer's Major Poetry* (New York: Appleton Century Crofts, 1963), 81.
61 Wetherbee, "Criseyde Alone," in *New Perspectives on Criseyde*, ed. Vitto and Marzec, 300. Later in the essay, Wetherbee compares Pandarus and Criseyde to Osmond and Madam Merle in Henry James's *Portrait of A Lady* (312).
62 Doležel, *Heterocosmica*, 201.
63 See Kelly's conclusion to this effect in *Chaucerian Tragedy* and above, 93.
64 The phrase is from Leibniz's *The Monadology*, §22, the result of his strong sense of temporal causality: "And since every present state of a simple substance is a natural consequence of its preceding state, the present is pregnant with the future."
65 Williams, *Marxism and Literature*, 126. Every apperception is a "novel emergent," an interpretation, rather than a mere gathering of details. Robert McRae, *Leibniz: Perception, Apperception, and Thought* (Toronto: University of Toronto Press, 1976), 38.
66 *The Poems of Robert Henryson*, ed. Robert Kindrick (Kalamazoo, MI: Medieval Institute Publications, 1997). Henryson may be relying on Benoît, in whose account Cresseid "finds pleasure in the trade of love" (19) and, though sorry to leave Troy, would have joy again tomorrow (9–10).
67 *Troilus and Cressida*, ed. Anthony B. Dawson, New Cambridge Edition (Cambridge: Cambridge University Press, 2003).
68 In addition, Shakespeare's Pistol in *Henry V* refers to a "lazar kite of Cressid's kind," seeming to acknowledge Henryson's plotting.
69 Dawson, "Introduction" to New Cambridge Edition, 3. We would add that this "philosophical" language is located in intimate or self-reflective moments (4.4.98).
70 James, *Shakespeare's Troy* (Cambridge: Cambridge University Press, 1997), 89. James quotes Charnes.
71 Ibid., 2, 36. She argues that this debunking registers Shakespeare's coolness towards empire, perhaps even providing a "capitalist" moment (113).
72 The quoted phrase is from Doležel, *Heterocosmica*, 201.
73 James, *Shakespeare's Troy*, 98.

74 "Genius is the talent (natural gift) that gives the rule to art … That it cannot itself describe or indicate scientifically how it brings its product into being, but rather that it gives the rule as nature" (*CPJ*, 186–7).

75 Cavell's "The Avoidance of Love: A Reading of *King Lear*," in *Disowning Knowledge in Six of Shakespeare's Plays* (Cambridge University Press, 1987), 112.

4 Melusine's *Aventure* among the Humans

1 *Melusine* was translated into Middle English in 1500; it is available as EETS, e.s. 68, trans. A.K. Donald (London: Kegan, Paul, Trench, Trübner, 1895). John Gower's late-fourteenth-century writing was done in English, French, and Latin.

2 Jean d'Arras, *Melusine; or, The Noble History of Lusignan*, translated into modern English by Donald Maddox and Sara Sturm-Maddox (University Park: Pennsylvania State University Press, 2012); hereafter cited parenthetically in the text as *M*. Middle French passages quoted are from *Mélusine, Roman du XIVe siècle*, ed. Louis Stouff (Geneva: Slatkine Reprints, 1974), cited as *FM*. We have also consulted *Mélusine ou La noble histoire de Lusignan*, ed. with facing pages of modern French by Jean-Jacques Vincensini (Paris: Librairie Générale Française, 2003) and Couldrette's *Mélusine or Le roman de Parthenay*, a bilingual edition edited by Matthew W. Morris (Lewiston, NY: Edwin Mellen Press, 2003). The use of *parfaire* as finished, complete in terms of an idea, is discussed by Donald Maddox, "Configuring the Epilogues," in *Melusine of Lusignan: Founding Fiction in Late Medieval France*, ed. Maddox and Sara Sturm-Maddox (Athens: University of Georgia Press, 1996), 268–9.

3 E. Jane Burns locates "Albanie" as an Albania located in the Mediterranean, rather than Scotland (Albion). If she is Melusine of Albania, her two names mean "marvellous" and "trustworthy" (from the Greek), and her father's realm gives the tale greater geographical reach. See "Magical Politics from Poitou to Armenia: Mélusine, Jean de Berry, and the Eastern Mediterranean," *Journal of Medieval and Early Modern Studies* 43, no. 2 (Spring 2013), 276. Burns stresses Melusine's trustworthiness: "a steadfast and politically adept mother" (278) and the "ever steady Melusine" (281), without neglecting her marvellous otherworldly inheritance.

4 Marie-Laure Ryan discusses genre in terms of accessibility in *Possible Worlds, Artificial Intelligence, and Narrative Theory* (Bloomington: Indiana University Press, 1991), 32–41.

5 Nonetheless, many "historical" episodes – unlikely military victories and the rescue of captive or threatened princesses – considered in themselves, look a good deal like romances. Chrétien's "Eric and Enid" and "Yvain" come easily to mind.
6 Dinshaw, *How Soon Is Now* (Durham and London: Duke University Press, 2012), 4 and passim.
7 Maddox and Sturm-Maddox, "Introduction," *Melusine*, 1–3.
8 Sylvia Huot, "Others and Alterity," in *Cambridge Companion to Medieval French Literature*, ed. Simon Gault and Sarah Kay (Cambridge: Cambridge University Press, 2008), 242.
9 Jane H.M. Taylor, "Mélusine's Progeny and Perplexities," in *Founding Fiction*, ed. Maddox and Sturm-Maddox, 166 and 173, and Burns, "Magical Politics," 278.
10 Taylor, "Mélusine's Progeny," constructs a genealogy that connects Raymondin's family with St Guillaume, "a conflation of several saints of the name," and Melusine's father Elinas to Alexander (168). Harf-Lancner, too, notes that it is advantageous to have someone supernatural connected with your line; *Les fées au Moyen Age: Morgane et Mélusine. La naissance des fées* (Paris: Champion, 1984), 172, and Burns, "Magical Politics," 278.
11 Maddox and Sturm-Maddox, "Introduction," *Melusine*, 2.
12 Douglas Kelly describes the "signe" that mark all but the two youngest sons. Fathers in mixed marriages contribute the seed and mothers the blood (fairy blood is blue). Melusine's children carry very noticeable signs of the supernatural parentage, sometimes considered "marks of royalty." See "The Domestication of the Marvelous in the Melusine Romances," in Maddox and Sturm-Maddox, eds, *Melusine: Founding Fiction*, 40.
13 The letter is quoted in the Middle English *Melusine* in a note to page 340, p. 385.
14 Serres, *Rome: The Book of Foundations*, trans. Felicia McCarren (Stanford: Stanford University Press, 1991), 60, and Latour, *We Have Never Been Modern*, trans. Catherine Porter (Cambridge: Harvard University Press, 1993), 75. Leibniz lurks behind these formulations; see above, p. 9.
15 *Melusine*, 20 and nn. 6 and 7. This appeal may seem strained, but Aristotle was writing to reconcile observational with rational (for example, numerical) modes of inquiry. Jean entered an old debate in a surprising way, but so did other medieval writers.
16 "[P]lus sera deliee de engine at de science naturelle et plustost y aura affection que ce soit chose faisable combien que les choses secretes de Dieu ne puet nulz savior au cler"; *FM*, 311.

17 Burton concludes: "Many thousands took notice of the fact, for it was done in the midst of Greece."*Anatomy of Melancholy*, ed. Floyd Dell and Paul Jordan-Smith (New York: Tudor Publishing Co., 1948), 648. This observation is echoed in the public nature of Melusine's departure from the fortress: she flew above the town, circling it three times, "but not so high that the people below could not see her clearly and hear her from even farther away … They never found out what had become of her" (*M*, 195). We are grateful to Jon Klancher for alerting us to the fact that Burton's account appeared with Keats's poem.

18 Harf-Lancner uses "Morganian" and "Melusianian" as categories in major strands of folkloric structure with variants across the world; *Les fées*, 8. Heurodis, although not a fairy, also returns to Ofeo's mortal world from a timeless realm in which she does not age.

19 Ana Pairet outlines three potential endings for this story type: the fairy mistress leaves the human world, her children must do so, or, as in this case, she leaves and the children remain. This third ending enables dynastic founding legends like Jean d'Arras's. See "Melusine's Double Bind: Foundation, Transgression, and Genealogical Romance," in *Reassessing the Heroine in Medieval French Literature*, ed. Kathy M. Krause (Gainesville: University Press of Florida, 2001), 71.

20 Harf-Lancner argues for a general acceptance of three types of supernatural activity: Christian miracle, Satanic magic, and paisano marvel (*Les fées*, 7). What Harf-Lancner calls "paisano," James Wade calls "adoxic," and links fairy magic to Giorgio Agamben's idea of the "state of exception" existing "outside orthodoxy without also being strictly unorthodox" (*Fairies in Medieval Romance* [New York: Palgrave Macmillan, 2011], 15).

21 But that same epilogue is readable as a topical political allegory in that Armenia was taken over by Mamluk Turks and the ousted king wanted French and English forces to make peace and launch a crusade against the Turks. The episode thus connects with other aspects of the tale in alluding to the well-known crusading expeditions Lusignans were known to have pursued. Burns describes these complicated real-world scenarios in detail ("Magical Politics," 280). Stephen Nichols concludes that "no other late romance so persistently interweaves real historical markers" and that *Melusine* may be the first instance in the European vernacular to present "the fairy realm joined to the contemporary, political world for the purpose of making political allegory"; "Melusine between Myth and History: Profile of a Female Demon," in Maddox and Sturm-Maddox, eds, *Founding Fiction*, 161 and 162. In *Empire of Magic*, Geraldine Heng

has traced the practice of mixing tales of love and adventure with sober historical accounts to Geoffrey of Monmouth's *Historia Regum Britanniae* in the twelfth century, arguing that romance (cultural fantasy) "does not evade but confronts history" (14).

22 Maddox and Maddox, "Introduction," 10, and Nichols, "Melusine between Myth and History," in *Melusine of Lusignan: Founding Fiction*, 138.

23 Rabinowitz, *Before Reading: Narrative Conventions and the Politics of Interpretation* (Ithaca: Cornell University Press, 1987), 148.

24 For Boethius, a "thisness" representing a subject's essential selfhood can be indicated by a name, while some philosophers stress that while "accidental" properties may change when someone crosses into another world, "essential" properties persist.

25 Sara Sturm-Maddox asserts that readers cannot expect access to the subjectivity of fairies: "These creatures, who appear to act according to the promptings of their own sovereign will, often seem curiously impassive"; "Alterity and Subjectivity in the *Roman de Melusine*," in *The Court and Cultural Diversity*, ed. E. Mullally and J. Thompson (Woodbridge and Rochester NY: D. S. Brewer, 1997), p. 123.

26 Ryder, "The Other Worlds of Romance," in *Cambridge Companion to Medieval Romance*, ed. Roberta Kreuger (Cambridge: Cambridge University Press, 2000), 115. Subtle shades of emotional states are absent from *fées* who fit the "morgan" pattern. The fairy princess in Marie's "Lanval" is a positive version of the morgan type who spirits her human lover away from his world, but whose motivations remain unstated.

27 "Emotions, Thoughts, and Feelings: Emotions as Engagements with the World," in *Thinking about Feeling*, ed. Robert Solomon (Oxford: Oxford University Press, 2004), 77 (italics in original). See also Ronald de Sousa, "Emotions: What I Know, What I'd Like to Think I Know, and What I'd Like to Think," ibid., 62–73.

28 Maddox and Sturm-Maddox, "Introduction," 15. They have translated using a wider range of terms when appropriate.

29 The illustration is reproduced in Tanya M. Colwell's "Gesture, Emotion: Depictions of Mélusine in the Upton House Bearsted Fragments," in *The Inner Life of Women in Medieval Romance Literature: Grief, Guilt, Hypocrisy*, ed. Jeff Rider and Jamie Friedman (New York: Palgrave, 2011), 118, fig. 5.4.

30 In "Alterity and Subjectivity" Sturm-Maddox uses the phrase for Melusine, but concludes (as we do not) that it mars the fiction's attempt to celebrate the legacy of the Lusignanian line and foretells its decline (129). Ana Pairet agrees that Melusine's hybrid body becomes a negative political allegory, "an emblem of political instability"; "Melusine's

Double Bind: Foundation, Transgression, and Geneological Romance," in Kathy M. Krause, ed., *Reassessing the Heroine in Medieval French Literature* (Gainesville: University Press of Florida, 2001), 71.

31 Certain self-contained episodes lend themselves to allgoresis, like Geoffroy's defeat of the giant Grimaut in Albany, freeing prisoners long held, as predicted by astronomers, a link with Count Aimery at the beginning of the narrative. It recalls Chrétien's *Knight of the Cart*, with its fitfully suggested allegory of Christ's harrowing of Hell as Lancelot travels to the realm of the dead to rescue Guinevere and release the captives from Logres.

32 In chapter 3, we saw this assessment of Criseyde connected with Boethius's attack on Lady Fortune, and references to Fortune are also prominent in *Melusine.* Raymondin frequently remonstrates against her, and in his rage at having been goaded into breaking his promise to his wife, his tirade (against his intention) seems to elide Melusine's having "raised [him] to high estate" and Fortune's having cast him down (*M*, 182).

33 In *On Christian Doctrine*, trans. D.W. Robertson (Indianapolis, IN: Bobbs-Merrill, 1958), Augustine provides an extended defence of Christian uses for pagan thought, justified by God's command to the Israelites to take gold from Egypt in their exodus (2.40.60; pp. 75–6).

34 Harf-Lancner concludes that Jean d'Arras has refused to demonize her, that she is as sincerely Christian as she says she is, "creature de Dieu at bonne Catholique" (*Les fées*, 165). Tanya Colwell argues that the presentation of her motherhood is modelled on the ideal of the Virgin Mary; "Mélusine: Ideal Mother or Inimitable Monster," in *Love, Marriage, and Family Ties in the Later Middle Ages*, ed. Isabel Davis, Miriam Müller, and Sarah Rees Jones (Turnhout, Belgium: Brepols, 2003), 181–203. Stephen Nichols, by contrast, interprets all Melusine's acts, "even those seemingly most benevolent," as shaded with "a strong sense of illusion" ("Between Myth and History," 151).

35 Page 22. Morris calls Count Aimery's killing a "murder" (10) and argues that the "mother's marks" that appear on the faces of the sons are punishments for Raymondin's sin in killing his uncle instead of evidences of Melusine's fairy world, as Raymondin himself assumes (38).

36 Teskey, *Allegory and Violence* (Ithaca: Cornell University Press, 1996), 24.

37 Colwell, "Gesture, Emotion," 109. W.J.T. Mitchell comments in *Iconology* that imagination works by "accepting the fact that we create much of our world out of the dialogue between verbal and pictorial images"; *Iconology: Image, Text, Ideology* (Chicago: University of Chicago Press, 1986), 46.

38 Monette's *Mélusine* (New York: Ace Books, 2005).

39 Byatt, *Possession: A Romance* (New York: Random House, 1990), winner of the 1990 Booker Prize for Fiction; hereafter cited in the text.
40 A good example is the "long Chinese dragon" on Maud's kimono with its reminiscence of medieval depictions of Melusine as a courtly lady with a tiny dragon somewhere in the scenes. Roland sees the kimono when he stoops to look through the bathroom keyhole in the Bailey House bathroom and gets a "galvanic" charge as Maud opens the door, a glancing, comic allusion to Raymondin's glimpse of Melusine bathing (162–3).
41 Ash, a medievalist, has researched *Melusine* and during Christabel's childhood in Brittany, her father, at work on a *Mythologie Française*, told her various versions of Melusine's history.
42 One image depicts Melusine directing stone workers at the foot of a ladder, which suggests that medieval illustrators took her skill in construction literally (cover illustration).
43 Maud hides her "yellow hair" lest it be seductive for men, but rejects vigorous lesbian overtures from her American colleague.
44 For all the scholars involved, careers are at stake and money (especially money from the United States) comes to account for a great deal. Even genealogy comes into the picture, as Maud discovers herself to be distantly related to Christabel.
45 The novel may, therefore, illuminate its ancestor, exhibiting the bidirectional intertextuality Lubomír Doležel invokes in *Heterocosmica: Fiction and Possible Worlds* (Baltimore: Johns Hopkins University Press, 1998), 201; or, as Hawthorne puts it, "truth of the human heart" presented "under circumstances … of the writer's own choosing or creation."

5 Romance by Other Means: The *Canterbury Tales*

1 Kant, *Critique of the Power of Judgment*, trans. Paul Guyer (Cambridge: Cambridge University Press, 2008), 185; hereafter *CPJ* in the text.
2 Three of the tales we will consider here are set in a fictionally real world of "central aristocratic society," as Jeff Rider has argued most romances are ("Other Worlds of Romance," in *Cambridge Companion to Medieval Romance*, ed. Roberta Krueger [Cambridge: Cambridge University Press, 2000], 115–31), but the frame story and many others, including the Canon's Yeoman's, posit a much more inclusive social world.
3 Leibniz, *Monadology*, §57 in "*Discourses on Metaphysics and Other Essays*," ed. and trans. Daniel Garber and Peter Ariew (Indianapolis and Cambridge: Hackett Publishers, 1991).

4 D.W. Robertson in *A Preface to Chaucer* (Princeton: Princeton University Press, 1962) and Bernard Huppe in *A Reading of the* Canterbury Tales (New York: SUNY Press, 1964) begin the pan-allegorical interpretive tradition; Hope Phyllis Weisman treats feminist issues in "Antifeminism and Chaucer's Characterizations of Women," in *Geoffrey Chaucer*, ed. George Economou (New York: McGraw Hill, 1975), 93–110; and Mary Carruthers in "The Wife of Bath and the Painting of Lions," *PLMA* 94 (1979), 209–22 makes the case for Alisoun as a medieval businesswoman. In the meantime criticism attests to scores of closely reasoned and nuanced accounts of the Wife's representation, far too many to be cited here.

5 All quotations of the *Canterbury Tales* are from the *Riverside Chaucer*, ed. Larry Benson et al., 3rd ed. (Boston: Houghton Mifflin, 1987).

6 In Shakespeare's source for *Hamlet*, the Ophelia character is a hired prostitute in a test for whether Hamlet's madness is an act, since a sane man would sleep with a willing woman.

7 Some of Alisoun's interpretations of scripture appear as parody but, as Lawrence Besserman points out, some of her biblical allusions are quite straightforward, and in any case she can cite amply; see *Chaucer's Biblical Poetics* (Norman: University of Oklahoma Press, 1998), 106.

8 Ovid's story goes on to have the reeds publicize the king's ears, but Alisoun breaks off without reporting this detail; read Ovid, she says, to learn the rest.

9 The last division, called "Part 6," is regarded as a scribal addition (Cooper, *Oxford Guide to the* Canterbury Tales [Oxford University Press, 1989], 192).

10 "Corage" took on many implications from bravery to sexual appetite in Middle English and in the *Canterbury Tales*, and in this passage its sexual suggestion is clear. See Peggy A. Knapp, *Time-Bound Words* (New York: Palgrave, 2000).

11 Mitchell, "Chaucer's *Clerk's Tale* and the Question of Ethical Monstrosity," *Studies in Philology* 102 (Winter 2005), 25. Mitchell's essay gives a full and judicious account of those decades of scholarship on this issue. On alternating force fields in allegory generally, Gordon Teskey writes of oscillation between a "project of reference [in this case the domestic tale] and a project of capture" by allegory (*Allegory and Violence* [Ithaca: Cornell University Press, 1996], 9).

12 Heng, *Empire of Magic* (New York: Columbia University Press, 2003), 201–2.

13 Teskey, *Allegory and Violence*, 17.

14 Most notes gloss this as "intolerable"; but the *OED* gives two meaning for that word – 1. Not endurable; intolerable: insupportable mental anguish,

and 2. Lacking grounds or defence; unjustifiable: an insupportable claim. Most critics regard the Clerk as saying that no woman would be able to bear such suffering, but sense 2 suggests that because of the Clerk's study of logic, "unjustified" is a better gloss.

15 *Gesta Romanorum*, trans. Charles Swan (London: Routledge, n.d.), 132. Similar allegorizations of the Orpheus legends, in *Ovid Moralisé*, for example, are discussed in chapter 2.

16 This phasing refers to Harriet Hawkins's brilliant article "The Victim's Side: Chaucer's *Clerk's Tale* and Webster's *Duchess of Malfi*," *Signs* 1 (1975), 339–61. Hawkins argues that judicious medieval readers could see, just as we can, that the vehicle for the Clerk's allegory was, and was meant to be, repugnant.

17 Cooper, *Oxford Guide*, 198. See also the *Riverside* note on "Lenvoy."

18 Teskey, "Irony, Allegory, and Metaphysical Decay," *PMLA* 109 (1994), 402b. A similar passage occurs in *Allegory and Violence*, 67, but the book leaves out the role of history, which we think is important in this logic. See also Larry Scanlon's discussion of this issue: "The Authority of Fable: Allegory and Irony in the *Nun's Priest's Tale*," *Exemplaria* 1, no. 1 (March 1989), 43–68.

19 *The Winter's Tale* comes to mind here too, as Hermione answers Polixenes's "I may not, veriliy" with "A lady's 'verily's' / As potentent as a lord's" (1.46, 51–2).

20 Critical appraisals of the ethics of this scene have been sharply divided for over a century. G.L. Kittredge set the discussion in motion by arguing that the problem of *maistry* posed by the "marriage group" is solved by Arveragus and Dorigen's accord and the patience with which they carry it out ("Chaucer's Discussion of Marriage," *Modern Philology* 9 [1911–12], 435–67). D.W. Robertson disagrees profoundly, finding Arveragus "not much of a husband," having given his authority away in the marriage contract (*A Preface to Chaucer*, 272). Mary Carruthers, by contrast, calls Arveragus's respect for Dorigen's integrity an act of moral courage that "costs him dearly" ("The *Gentilesse* of Chaucer's Franklin," *Criticism* 23 [1981], 295). Steele Nowlin argues that Arveragus's response represents "forgiveness," moving the tale entirely into a late medieval Christian ethos ("Between Precedent and Possibility: Liminality, Historicity, and Narrative in Chaucer's *The Franklin's Tale*," *Studies in Philology* 103 [2006], 53–5). Our reading regards Arveragus's decision as an enlarged vision of ethical responsibility.

21 Richard Firth Green's illuminating *A Crisis of Truth: Literature and Law in Richardian England* (Philadelphia: University of Pennsylvania Press, 1999) lays out the linguistic and social details of this usage.

22 In "'The Road Not Taken': Virtual Narratives in *The Franklin's Tale*," *Poetics Today* 31 (2013), 53–113, Anna Narinsky uses Marie-Laure Ryan's narrative theory to discuss possible worlds as those mentioned as alternative courses of action in the text, but not represented – a "branching" model of possibility (see chapter 1, p. 36). There are, of course, a great many of these (creating a densely figured telling), but none that consider worlds with different rules (metaphysical otherness). We consider the intrusion of a metaphysically possible world in which a rocky coast is cleared through magic, as well as a merely convincing illusion that the characters in the tale take as what may be true *as far as they know* (epistemic possibility).

23 Nowlin, "Between Precedent and Possibility," 48 and 53.

24 The Yeoman describes his boss as "Lurkynge in hernes and in lanes blynde, / Whereas thise robbours and thise theves by kynde / Holden hir pryvee fereful residence" (V3.658–60).

25 In Chaucer's work, "apparence" turns up only rarely (the other instance is the *House of Fame*, 265), and elsewhere in Middle English almost never. It seems not to have been used to mean simply "appearance," but may have some connection with "apparent," in its sceptical sense.

26 Robert Solomon, "Emotions, Thoughts, and Feelings: Emotions as Engagements with the World," in *Thinking about Feeling*, ed. Robert Solomon (Oxford: Oxford University Press, 2004), 77.

27 The Franklin's phrasing "jupartie" suggests that he, and presumably Arveragus, understand that this legalistic rape will injure Dorigen. In a reading that coarsens the moral tone and denies the pathos of the situation, Bernard Huppé thinks of his decision as entirely self-serving: he gets back "a slightly used wife, perhaps, but a live one"; *A Reading of the* Canterbury Tales (New York: SUNY Press, 1964), 169. In choosing between saving her life and integrity and causing both of them humiliation and suffering, Averagus is valuing her faithful mind over her unsullied body.

28 The charlatans and "puffers" who read alchemical treatises in the hope of changing base metal to gold are generally distinguished from the true philosophers who understand that the names of materials are only "cover-names or symbols to preserve truth from the vulgar." In this tradition, words, and the bits of matter they name, are always only windows through which a transcendent truth may be read. John Reidy, "Chaucer's Canon and the Unity of the Canon's Yeoman's Tale," *PMLA* 80, no. 1 (March 1965), 34.

29 David Raybin, "'And Pave It All of Silver and of Gold': The Humane Artistry of the Canon's Yeoman's Tale," in *Rebels and Rivals: The Contestive Spirit in The Canterbury Tales*, ed. Susanna Greer Fein, David Raybin, and Peter C. Braeger (Kalamazoo: Medieval Institute Publications, 1991), 193.

30 Quoted in Edgar H. Duncan, "The Literature of Alchemy and Chaucer's Canon's Yeoman's Tale: Framework, Theme, and Characters," *Speculum* 43, no. 4 (October 1968), 648.
31 Nagel, "Shadows and Ephemera," *Critical Inquiry* 28, no. 1 (Autumn 2001), 24.

6 The Immense Subtlety of *Sir Gawain and the Green Knight*

1 *The Poems of the Pearl Manuscript: Pearl, Cleanness, Patience, Sir Gawain and the Green Knight*, ed. Malcolm Andrew and Ronald Waldron, rev. ed. (Exeter: University of Exeter Press, 1987). Line numbers are hereafter cited in the text from this edition. We have also consulted various modern English translations, often Marie Borroff's (Norton, 2001) and Casey Finch's facing-page edition *The Complete Works of the Pearl Poet* (Berkeley: University of California Press, 1993).
2 Geraldine Heng begins *Empire of Magic* (New York: Columbia University Press, 2003) by crediting Geoffrey's *Historia* with allowing historical record and fantasy to "collide and vanish, each into the other" and thus inaugurate the tradition of medieval romance (2). Helen Cooper agrees that Geoffrey supplies a "myth of origin" in Brutus, repeated by Holinshed and many others; *The English Romance in Time: Transforming Motifs from Geoffrey of Monmouth to the Death of Shakespeare* (Oxford: Oxford University Press 2004), 24.
3 Ad Putter, Sir Gawain and the Green Knight *and French Arthurian Romance* (Oxford: Clarendon Press, 1995), 193.
4 The Percy Folio, ca. 1500, contains an 86-stanza poem said to have been recited at Kennilworth Castle. *The Green Knight* is reprinted in Thomas Hahn, ed., *Sir Gawain: Eleven Romances and Tales*, TEAMS Middle English Text Series (Kalamazoo, MI: Medieval Institute Publications, 1995).
5 Nerlich, *Ideology of Adventure: Studies in Modern Consciousness 1100–1750*, trans. Ruth Crowley (Minneapolis: University of Minnesota Press, 1987), 1: 3–6.
6 Ad Putter emphasizes the way the *Gawain*-poet crafts the scene to show Gawain's passivity in accepting the girdle; *Introduction to the Gawain-poet* (London and New York: Longmans, 1996), 92.
7 "A hero ventures forth from the world of common day into a region of supernatural wonder: fabulous forces are there encountered and a decisive victory is won: the hero comes back from this mysterious adventure with the power to bestow a boon on his fellow man"; Campbell, *The Hero with a Thousand Faces* (Princeton: Princeton University Press, 1971), 30.

8 Northrop Frye's definition of quest romance is straightforward: "The reward of the quest usually is or includes a bride"; in dream terms, the desiring self receives a "fulfillment that will deliver it from the anxieties of reality but will still contain that reality"; in ritual terms, it is "the victory of fertility over the wasteland." *Anatomy of Criticism* (Princeton: Princeton University Press, 1957), 193. Gawain refuses a love affair, remains anxious, and does not, as he sees it, successfully refresh his home court.

9 In Boethius's *Consolation*, Lady Philosophy (taken in the Middle Ages to be articulating Christian doctrine) demonstrates that loyalty to her produces happiness in spite of Lady Fortune's command over the contingencies of sublunary life; *The Consolation of Philosophy*, trans. P.G. Walsh (Oxford: Clarendon Press, 1999) and Chaucer's *Boece* in *Riverside Chaucer*.

10 Geraldine Heng in *Empire of Magic*, 183–4, argues for the continuity between romance and saint's legends.

11 "Quantitative perfection, as the completeness of any thing in its own kind, is entirely distinct from this, and is a mere concept of magnitude (of totality), in which what the thing is supposed to be is thought of as already determined and it is only asked whether everything requisite for it exists"; *Critique of the Power of Judgment*, trans. Paul Guyer (Cambridge University Press, 2008), 70–1 (hereafter cited as *CPJ* in the text).

12 Derek Brewer, for one, lists the poem's various anomalies on the "manifest level," convincing him that realism is "beside the point" and concluding that the poem is an elaborately disguised family romance in the Freudian style – both Bertilak and Arthur are father figures and both Morgan (as the host's wife and the lady's duenna) and Mary mother figures; *Symbolic Structures* (New York: Rowan and Littlefield, 1980), 80–91.

13 Rider, "The Other Worlds of Romance," in *Cambridge Companion to Medieval Romance*, ed. Roberta Krueger (Cambridge: Cambridge University Press, 2000), 115–16. This literary piece treats the aristocratic as real, but the story is heard "in toun" (30), and the intricate embroidery on Gawain's gear as he arms appeared to have taken seamstresses "in toune" seven long winters to complete (613–14). These acknowledgements of the commerce between town and court further enhance the fictive realism of the poem.

14 Putter, *Introduction*, makes this point and tells the story of Carados, which is a close analogue (41–2).

15 Hofstatder, *Gödel, Escher, Bach: An Eternal Golden Braid* (New York: Vintage Books, 1979), 713–19.

16 The classic essay on the interlace aesthetic is John Leyerle's "The Interlace Structure of *Beowulf*," *University of Toronto Quarterly* 37 (1967), 1–17.

17 *Malory: Works*, ed. Eugène Vinaver (London: Oxford University Press, 1971), 704.

18 Hahn, *Sir Gawain: Eleven Romances and Tales*, 306.

19 Hahn, "Gawain," in Roberta Krueger, ed., *Cambridge Companion to Medieval Romance* (Cambridge: Cambridge University Press, 2000), 221. However, in *Gawain and the Green Knight*, Gawain is aware that he has a particular destiny, using the word itself at crucial times (564, 2285), at least once as a synonym of *wyrd* (2134).

20 John Finlayson, "Expectation of Romance," *Genre* 12 (1979), 1–24, seems to imply that "meta" tendencies would disqualify it. Instead, the poem presents a prominent example of intertextuality in Lubomír Doležel's sense: distant texts brought together "in a relationship of mutual semantic illumination" (*Heterocosmica: Fiction and Possible Worlds* [Baltimore: Johns Hopkins University Press, 1998]), 201.

21 Hahn, "Gawain," points out that in four of the popular romances, Gawain finds himself in bed with his hostess, but stresses his "courteous and rule-bound exchange of women among men" (224).

22 Helen Cooper makes this observation about inward-looking romances in general; *English Romance in Time*, 25.

23 Hahn, *Eleven Romances*, 14–15.

24 *The Green Knight* appears in Hahn, *Eleven Romances*, 310–37.

25 Murdoch, *The Green Knight* (New York: Viking Press, 1994).

26 James F. Knapp and Peggy A. Knapp, "Found in Translation," in *The Medieval Translator* 12, Brepols English Language Series, ed. Denis Renevey and Christiana Whitehead, 339–49 (Turnhout, Belgium: Brepols, 2009).

27 Benedict Anderson considers the "meantime" a resource of "modern" storytelling that signals the imagined community of the absolutist state; see *Imagined Communities* (London: Verso, 1983), esp. 28–36.

28 Bede, *Ecclesiastical History of the English People* (London: Penguin, 1955), 2.13, pp. 129–30.

29 Most translations give something like "run," and Ad Putter traces the similarity of the Old English root of "ȝerne" to Latin "currant," used for the seasons (*Introduction to the* Gawain-*poet*, 9–10). We discuss our position on the meaning of ȝerne in "Found in Translation."

30 "Fusion of horizons" appears throughout Gadamer's *Truth and Method*, 2nd rev. ed., trans. Joel Weinsheimer and Donald Marshall (New York and London: Continuum Books, 2003); for the "mysterious intimacy of art" see *Philosophical Hermeneutics*, trans. David E. Linge (Berkeley: University of California Press, 1976), 95.

31 Paul Guyer's introduction to *Critique of the Power of Judgment* consolidates several passages from Kant's own introductions; xxvi.
32 A helpful recent account of Leibniz's "deep and lasting" influence on Kant appears in Anja Jauernig's "Kant, the Leibnizians, and Leibniz," in *The Continuum Companion to Leibniz*, ed. Brandon Look (London and New York: Continuum Press, 2011), 33. The essay makes clear that Kant did not fully accept Leibniz on the sensible and intelligible, but their differences do not bear heavily on our interpretation of the poem.
33 Kant refers to a "multitude of related representations" (*CPJ*, 193).
34 This line of reasoning appears in *The Monadology* (§ 67) and "Discourse on Metaphysics" (37). See *Discourses on Metaphysics and Other Essays*, ed. and trans. Daniel Garber and Peter Ariew (Indianapolis and Cambridge: Hackett, 1991).
35 Robert McRae, *Leibniz: Perception, Apperception, and Thought* (Toronto: University of Toronto Press, 1976), 38. See above, p. 13.
36 No fiction (and for that matter no one's working notion of the actual world) can stipulate all its features completely, but realistic fictions come close, often eliciting emotional experience; Doležel, *Heterocosmica* (Baltimore: Johns Hopkins University Press, 1998), 165–7. A related idea is Adorno's that in artworks that refuse to become archaic, "thought [is] saturated with experience"; *Aesthetic Theory*, ed. Gretel Adorno and Rolf Tiedemann, trans. Robert Hullot-Kentor (Minneapolis: University of Minnesota Press, 1997), 349.
37 Lewis, *On the Plurality of Worlds* (Oxford: Blackwell, 1986; repr. 2001), 2.
38 Leibniz, "Letter to Louis Bourguet," in *Philosophical Papers and Letters*, ed. and trans. Leroy Loemker (Dordrecht, Holland, and Boston: D. Reidel Publishing Co., 1969), 662.
39 Constance Hieatt and Sharon Butler describe recipes of culinary practices in *Pleyn Delit* (Toronto: University of Toronto Press, 1977; repr. 1996), including how subtleties were made and used in formal medieval banquets. We are reading the phrase "pared out of paper" as a doubly "realistic" detail – a realistic account of how the castle struck Gawain and a reference to the culinary subtlety. For John Ganim the passage "emphasizes the paradox, which is part of the paradox of the plot, the seeking for purity, spirituality, abstraction, in a world earthbound and material"; *Style and Consciousness in Middle English Narrative* (Princeton: Princeton University Press, 1983), 58.
40 "*Unheimlich* is in some way or other a sub-species of *Heimlich*" (Complete *Psychological* Works *of Sigmund* Freud, Standard Edition, ed. James Strachey, vol. 17, 225). In "The Uncanny" (218–52), Freud observes that this

effect is strongest in narrative when "the writer pretends to move in the world of common reality" and yet allows the supernatural to bring about "events that would never or very rarely happen in fact" (250).

41 The long speeches of this sustained dialogue are highly uncommon in medieval literature generally. The nearest analogues are the conversations between Troilus and Criseyde, especially in book 4 of Chaucer's poem. Internal dialogue also occurs there and throughout the *Clerk's Tale* and in a particularly important instance in the *Knight's Tale* ("but softe unto himself he seyde," 1.1773).

42 Putter, *Introduction*, 92.

43 A similarly detailed passage occurs in Gottfried's *Tristan* – when the very young hero is cast ashore in Cornwall, he teaches this advanced art to the hunters he meets and wins favour at Mark's court for his sophistication. These accounts are largely in agreement with each other and with hunting manuals from the period.

44 Andrew and Waldron gloss line 1634 as Gawain making "a show of abhorrence" of the huge head, intended to compliment his host.

45 In what Carolyn Dinshaw would call a "dense, crowded now," the Virgin Mary and the chatelaine are both present to Gawain at the same event, as Christ is to Margery Kemp in Norwich; *How Soon Is Now?* (Durham and London: Duke University Press, 2012), 105–7.

46 Fitt 1 has 490 lines; fitt 2, 634; fitt 3, 871; and fitt 4, 530.

47 Andrew and Waldron trace the history of this identification in their note to line 2221.

48 Marie Borroff's note on the puzzle of the confession to the priest at Bertilak's court (1880–1) concludes: "However Gawain's confession and absolution at Hautdesert are to be interpreted, it is fair to say that the absolution that strikes most readers of the poem as 'real' is the secular one Sir Gawain receives later from the Green Knight" (2391–4).

49 Among our students, few first-time readers of the poem firmly identify Bertilak before he reveals his identity to Gawain, though they may have dawning suspicions.

50 Harf-Lancner, *Les fées au Moyen Age: Morgane et Mélusine. La naissance des fées* (Paris: Champion, 1984).

51 Loomis, "Morgain La Fee and the Celtic Goddesses," *Speculum* 20 (1945), 200.

52 Williams agrees with Laura Hubbard Loomis that Morgan is both the old and the young woman in Bertilak's castle; see "Morgan La Fee as Trickster in *Sir Gawain and the Green*," *Knight Folklore* 96 (1985), 38–56. Although we have no particular investment in the Jungian view as an overall account

of the poem, Williams does illuminate lines 1885–8, in which Gawain becomes free-hearted and merry after accepting the girdle; she calls it a "sudden freeing of energy" resulting from his having kept his "instinctual drives" under control in his dealings with the lady (51).

53 Thorough discussion of both kinds of overlap are presented in David Lewis, *On the Plurality of Worlds* (Oxford: Basil Blackwell, 1986) and Penelope Mackie, *How Things Might Have Been* (Oxford: Clarendon, 2006), who come to different conclusions.

54 We do not regard the "meta" tendencies of the poem to be in any way dismissive of the genre – all the romances in our study probe the nature and limits of the genre. Like Ad Putter, we consider the poet to have chosen Arthurian romance because its ethos was "compatible" with his own "assumptions and ambitions." See "Sir Gawain and the Green Knight *and French Arthurian Romance*, 4.

55 Lewis, *On the Plurality of Worlds*, 27.

56 Ryan, *Possible Worlds, Artificial Intelligence, and Narrative Theory* (Bloomington: Indiana University Press, 1991), 21.

57 Ibid.

58 Rescher, whose position on possible worlds is referenced here, would consign the whole fiction to mind-dependence; "The Ontology of the Possible," in *The Possible and the Actual: Readings in the Metaphysics of Modality*, ed. Michael J. Loux (Ithaca and London: Cornell University Press, 1979), 179.

59 Ryan, *Possible Worlds*, 32–41.

60 Henry of Lancaster, *Livre de seintes medicines*, ed. J. Arnould, Anglo-Norman Text Society (Oxford: Blackwell, 1940; repr. New York: Johnson Reprints, 1967).

61 Gawain's examples are all biblical, but Bertilak reveals an Arthurian analogue in Morgan's betrayal of Merlin, which of course bears directly on this tale.

References

Adorno, Theodor. *Aesthetic Theory*. Ed. Gretel Adorno and Rolf Tiedemann, trans. Robert Hullot-Kentor. Minneapolis: University of Minnesota Press, 1997.

Aers, David. *Community, Gender and Individual Identity*. New York: Routledge, 1988.

Allen, Elizabeth. "Flowing Backward to the Source: Criseyde's Promises and the Ethics of Allusion." *Speculum* 80 (July 2013), 681–720.

Allison, Henry E. *Kant's Theory of Taste: A Reading of the Critique of Aesthetic Judgment*. Cambridge: Cambridge University Press, 2001.

Anapolitanos, Dionysios. *Leibniz: Representation, Continuity and the Spatiotemporal*. Dordrecht, Boston, and London: Kluwer Academic Publishers, 1999.

Anderson, Benedict. *Imagined Communities*. London: Verso, 1983.

Aristotle. *The Metaphysics*. Trans. Hugh Lawson-Tancred. London: Penguin Books, 1998.

Auerbach, Erich. *Mimesis: The Representation of Reality in Western Literature*. Trans. Willard R. Trask. Princeton: Princeton University Press, 1953.

Augustine. *The Confessions*. Trans. John K. Ryan. Garden City, NY: Doubleday, 1960.

– *On Christian Doctrine*. Trans. D.W. Robertson. Indianapolis, IN: Bobbs-Merrill, 1958.

Babich, Andrea G. Pisani. "The Power of the Kingdom and the Ties That Bind in *Sir Orfeo*." *Neophilologus* 82 (1998), 477–86.

Barney, Stephen. "Troilus Bound." *Speculum* 47 (1972), 445–58.

Barney, Stephen, ed. *Troilus and Criseyde with facing-page Il Filostrato*. New York: Norton Critical Edition, 2006.

Baswell, Christopher. "Marvels of Translation and Crises of Transition in the Romances of Antiquity." In *Cambridge Companion to Medieval Romance*, ed. Roberta Krueger, 29–44. Cambridge: Cambridge University Press, 2000.

Battles, Dominique. "*Sir Orfeo* and English Identity," *Studies in Philology* 107, no. 2 (Spring 2010), 179–211.

Baugh, Albert C. *Chaucer's Major Poetry*. New York: Appleton Century Crofts, 1963.

Bede. *Ecclesiastical History of the English People*. London: Penguin, 1955.

Bergson, Henri. *Time and Free Will*. Trans. F.L. Pogson. New York: Humanities Press, 1910 (French 1889).

Berman, Marshall. *All That Is Solid Melts into Air*. New York: Viking Penguin, 1988.

Besserman, Lawrence. *Chaucer's Biblical Poetics*. Norman: University of Oklahoma Press, 1998.

Bloch, Howard. *The Anonymous Marie de France*. Chicago and London: University of Chicago Press, 2003.

Boethius. *The Consolation of Philosophy*. Trans. P.G. Walsh. Oxford: Clarendon Press, 1999.

– As *Boece*. Trans. Geoffrey Chaucer. In Chaucer, *The Riverside Chaucer*.

Bonaventura. *The Mind's Road to God*. Trans. George Boas (Indianapolis: Bobbs-Merrill, 1953.

Borroff, Marie, ed. *Sir Gawain and the Green Knight, Patience, Pearl: Verse Translations*. New York: Norton, 2001.

Boyd, Mathieu. "The Ring, the Sword, the Fancy Dress and the Posthumous Child: Background to the Element of Heroic Biography in Marie de France's *Yonec*.' *Romance Quarterly* 55, no. 3 (Summer 2008), 205–30.

Brenkman, John. *Culture and Domination*. Ithaca: Cornell University Press, 1987.

Brewer, Derek. *Symbolic Structures*. New York: Rowan and Littlefield, 1980.

Brooks, Peter. *Reading for the Plot*. New York: Alfred Knopf, 1984.

Bruckner, Matilda Tomaryn. *Shaping Romance: Interpretation, Truth, and Closure in Twelfth-Century French Fictions*. Philadelphia: University of Pennsylvania Press, 1993.

Burgess, Glyn S. *Marie de France: Text and Context*. Athens: University of Georgia Press, 1987.

Burns, E. Jane. "Courtly Love: Who Needs It? Recent Feminist Work in the Medieval French Tradition." *Signs* 27, no. 1 (Autumn 2001), 23–57.

– "Magical Politics from Poitou to Armenia: Mélusine, Jean de Berry, and the Eastern Mediterranean." *Journal of Medieval and Early Modern Studies* 43, no. 2 (Spring 2013), 275–301.

Byatt, A.S. *Possession: A Romance*. New York: Random House, 1990.

Bynum, Caroline Walker. *Jesus as Mother: Studies in the Spirituality of the High Middle Ages*. Berkeley: University of California Press, 1982.

Campbell, Joseph. *Hero with a Thousand Faces*. Princeton: Prince University Press, 1987.

Caputo, John D., and Michael J. Scanlon, eds. *Augustine and Postmodernism: Confessions and Circumfession*. Bloomington: Indiana University Press, 2005.

Carruthers, Mary. "The Gentilesse of the Franklin." *Criticism* 23 (1981), 283–300.

– "The Wife of Bath and the Painting of Lions." *PLMA* 94 (1979), 209–22.

Cartlidge, Neil. "Sir Orfeo in the Otherworld: Courting Chaos?" *Studies in the Age of Chaucer* 26 (2004), 195–226.

Cavell, Stanley. "The Avoidance of Love: A Reading of *King Lear*." In *Disowning Knowledge in Six of Shakespeare's Plays*. Cambridge: Cambridge University Press, 1987.

Chaganti, Seeta. "The Space of Epistemology in Marie de France's 'Yonec.'" *Romance Studies* 28, no. 2 (April 2010), 71–83.

Chalmers, David J. "Epistemic Two-Dimensional Semantics." *Philosophical Studies* 118 (2004), 153–226.

Chaucer, Geoffrey. *The Riverside Chaucer*. Ed. Larry Benson et al. 3rd ed. Boston: Houghton Mifflin, 1987.

Chisholm, Roderick M. "Identity through Possible Worlds: Some Questions." In *The Possible and the Actual*, ed. Michael Loux, 80–7. Ithaca and London: Cornell University Press, 1979.

Code, Lorraine, ed. *Feminist Interpretations of Hans-Georg Gadamer*. University Park: Penn State University Press, 2003.

Colwell, Tania. "Gesture, Emotion: Depictions of Mélusine in the Upton House Bearsted Fragments." In *The Inner Life of Women*, ed. Jeff Rider, 107–27. New York: Palgrave, 2011.

– "Mélusine: Ideal Mother or Inimitable Monster." In *Love, Marriage, and Family Ties in the Later Middle Ages*, ed. Isabel Davis, Miriam Müller, and Sarah Rees Jones, 181–203. Turnhout, Belgium: Brepols, 2003.

Cooper, Helen. *English Romances in Time: Transforming Motifs from Geoffrey of Monmouth to the Death of Shakespeare*. Oxford: Oxford University Press, 2004.

– *Oxford Guide to the* Canterbury Tales. Oxford: Oxford University Press, 1989.

– "Responding to the Monk." *Studies in the Age of Chaucer* 22 (2000), 425–33.

Cooper, Pamela. *The Fictions of John Fowles: Power, Creativity, Femininity*. Ottawa: University of Ottawa Press, 1991.

Couldrette. *Mélusine or Le Roman de Parthenay* (1401). Bilingual edition, ed. Matthew W. Morris. Lewiston, NY: Edwin Mellen Press, 2003.

Crane, Susan. "The Franklin as Dorigen." *Chaucer Review* 24 (Winter 1990), 236–52.

– *Gender and Romance in Chaucer's* Canterbury Tales. Princeton: Princeton University Press, 1994.

– *Insular Romance.* Los Angeles: University of California Press, 1986.

Cummings, Brian, and James Simpson, eds. *Cultural Reformations: Medieval and Renaissance in Literary History.* Oxford: Oxford University Press, 2010.

d'Arras, Jean. *Mélusine, Roman du XIVe Siècle* (1393). Ed. Louis Stouff. Geneva: Slatkine Reprints, 1974.

– *Melusine; or, the Nobel History of Lusignan.* Trans. and intro. Donald Maddox and Sara Sturm-Maddox. University Park: Penn State University Press, 2012.

– *Mélusine ou La Noble Histoire de Lusignan.* Ed. (with facing pages of modern French) Jean-Jacques Vincensini. Paris: Librairie Générale Française, 2003.

Davis, Isabel, et al., eds. *Love, Marriage, and Family Ties in the Later Middle Ages.* Turnhout, Belgium: Brepols, 2003.

Dawson, Anthony B. "Introduction." New Cambridge Edition of *Troilus and Cressida.* Cambridge: Cambridge University Press, 2003.

Delany, Sheila. "Techniques of Alienation in *Troilus and Criseyde.*" In Norton Critical Edition of *Troilus and Criseyde,* ed. Stephen A. Barney, 487–503. New York: Norton, 2006.

Delcourt, Denyse. "Oiseaux, ombre, désir: Écrire dans les Lais de Marie de France." *Modern Language Notes* 120, no. 4, French issue (September 2005), 807–24.

Deleuze, Gilles. *The Fold: Leibniz and the Baroque.* Trans. Tom Conley. Minneapolis: University of Minnesota Press, 1993.

de Looze, Laurence. "'La fourme du pie toute escripte': Melusine and the Entrance into History." In *Melusine: Founding Fiction,* ed. D. Maddox and S. Sturm-Maddox, 125–36.

de Sousa, Ronald. "Emotions: What I Know, What I'd Like to Think I Know, and What I'd Like to Think." In *Thinking about Feeling,* ed. Robert Solomon, 62–73. Oxford: Oxford University Press, 2004.

Dickson, Morgan. "Verbal and Visual Disguise: Society and Identity in Some Twelfth-Century Texts." In *Medieval Insular Romance,* ed. Judith Weiss, Jennifer Fellows, and Morgan Dickson, 41–54. Cambridge: Boydell & Brewer, 2000.

Dinshaw, Carolyn. *Chaucer's Sexual Poetics.* Madison: University of Wisconsin Press, 1989.

– *How Soon Is Now?* London and Durham: Duke University Press, 2012.

Doležel, Lubomír. *Heterocosmica: Fiction and Possible Worlds.* Baltimore: Johns Hopkins University Press, 1998.

– *Possible Worlds of Fiction and History: The Postmodern Stage.* Baltimore: Johns Hopkins University Press, 2010.

Donaldson, E. Talbot. *The Swan at the Well.* New Haven: Yale University Press, 1985.
Donoghue, Denis. *Speaking of Beauty.* New Haven: Yale University Press, 2003.
Doran, Madeleine. *Endeavors of Art: A Study of Form in Elizabethan Drama.* Madison: University of Wisconsin Press, 1954.
Dronke, Peter. "The Return of Eurydice." *Classica et Mediaevalia* 23 (1962), 108–25.
Duby, Georges. *Love and Marriage in the Middle Ages.* Trans. Jane Dunnett. Chicago: University of Chicago Press, 1994.
Duncan, Edgar H. "The Literature of Alchemy and Chaucer's Canon's Yeoman's Tale: Framework, Theme, and Characters. *Speculum* 43 (1968), 633–56.
Eagleton, Terry. *Sweet Violence.* Oxford: Oxford University Press, 2003.
Evans, Ruth. "*Sir Orfeo* and Bare Life." In *Medieval Cultural Studies: Essays in Honor of Stephen Knight*, ed. Ruth Evans, Helen Fulton, and David Matthews, 198–206. Cardiff: University of Wales Press, 2006.
Fawkner, H.W. *The Timescapes of John Fowles.* Madison, NJ: Fairleigh Dickinson University Press, 1984.
Finch, Casey, ed. and trans. *The Complete Works of the Pearl Poet.* Facing-page edition. Berkeley: University of California Press, 1993.
Fineman, Joel. "The Structures of Allegorical Desire." In *Allegory and Representation*, ed. Stephen Greenblatt, 26–60. English Institute Essays, 1979–80. Baltimore and London: Johns Hopkins University Press, 1981.
Finlayson, John. "Definitions of Medieval Romance." *Chaucer Review* 15 (Summer 1980), 48–62.
– "Expectation of Romance." *Genre* 12 (1979), 1–24.
Fitz, Brewster E. "The Storm Episode and the Weasel Episode: Sacrificial Casuistry in Marie de France's *Eliduc*." *Modern Language Notes* 89, no. 4, French issue (May 1974), 524–49.
Fleming, John V. "Sacred and Secular Exegesis in the Wyf of Bath's Tale." In *Rereading Tales*, ed. Thomas Hahn and Alan Lupack, 73–90. Rochester, NY: D.S. Brewer, 1997.
Fletcher, Alan J. "*Sir Orfeo* and the Flight from the Enchanters," *Studies in the Age of Chaucer* 22 (2000), 141–77.
Fletcher, Angus. *Allegory: Theory of a Symbolic Mode.* Ithaca: Cornell University Press, 1964.
Fowles, John. *The Ebony Tower.* New York: Signet, 1974.
– *Wormholes: Essays and Occasional Writings.* Ed. Jan Relf. New York: Henry Holt, 1988.
Freeman, Michelle A. "Marie de France's Poetics of Silence: The Implications for a Feminine *Translatio*." *PMLA* 99, no. 5 (October 1984), 860–83.

Freud, Sigmund. "The Uncanny." In Complete *Psychological* Works *of Sigmund* Freud, Standard Edition, ed. James Strachey, vol. 17, 218–52.

Friedman, John Block. *Orpheus in the Middle Ages*. Cambridge, MA: Harvard University Press, 1970.

Frye, Northrop. *Anatomy of Criticism*. Princeton: Princeton University Press, 1957.

Futch, Michael J. *Leibniz's Metaphysics of Time and Space*. Boston Studies in the Philosophy of Science 258. Heidelberg: Springer Verlag, 2008.

Gadamer, Hans-Georg. *Philosophical Hermeneutics*. Trans. David E. Linge. Berkeley: University of California Press, 1976.

– *Truth and Method*. 2nd rev. ed. Trans. Joel Weinsheimer and Donald Marshall. New York and London: Continuum Books, 2003.

Ganim, John. *Style and Consciousness in Middle English Narrative*. Princeton: Princeton University Press, 1983.

Gault, Simon, and Sarah Kay, eds. *Cambridge Companion to Medieval French Literature*. Cambridge: Cambridge University Press, 2008.

– "Romance and Other Genres." In *Cambridge Companion to Medieval Romance*, ed. Roberta Krueger, 45–59. Cambridge: Cambridge University Press, 2000.

Gesta Romanorum. Trans. Charles Swan. London: Routledge, n.d.

Giancarlo, Matthew. "The Structure of Fate and the Devising of History in Chaucer's *Troilus and Criseyde*." *Studies in the Age of Chaucer* 26 (2004), 227–66.

Gil Harris, Jonathan. *Untimely Matter in the Time of Shakespeare*. Philadelphia: University of Pennsylvania Press, 2009.

Gordon, R.K. *The Story of Troilus*. Toronto: University of Toronto Press, 1978.

Green, Richard Firth. "Changing Chaucer." *Studies in the Age of Chaucer* 25 (2003), 25–52.

– *A Crisis of Truth: Literature and Law in Ricardian England*. Philadelphia: University of Pennsylvania Press, 1999.

Greene, Virginie, ed. *The Medieval Author in Medieval French Literature*. New York: Palgrave, 2006.

Guthrie, W.K.C. *Orpheus and Greek Religion*. New York: Norton, 1966.

Guyer, Paul. *Kant and the Claims of Taste*. Cambridge, MA: Harvard University Press, 1979.

Habermas, Jürgen. "A Review of Gadamer's Truth and Method." In *Understanding and Social Inquiry*, ed. Fred Dallmayr and Thomas McCarthy, 335–63. South Bend, IN: Notre Dame University Press, 1977.

Hahn, Thomas. "Gawain." In *Cambridge Companion to Medieval Romance*, ed. Roberta Krueger, 218–34. Cambridge: Cambridge University Press, 2000.

– *Retelling Tales: Essays in Honor of Russell Peck*. Rochester, NY: D.S. Brewer, 1997.

– *Sir Gawain: Eleven Romances and Tales.* TEAMS Middle English Text Series. Kalamazoo, MI: Medieval Institute Publications, 1995.

Haidu, Peter. "Repetition: Modern Reflections on Medieval Aesthetics." *Modern Language Notes* 92 (December 1977), 875–87.

Hanson, Elaine. *Chaucer and the Fictions of Gender*. Berkeley: University of California Press, 1992.

Harf-Lancner, Laurence. *Les fées au Moyen Age: Morgane et Mélusine. La Naissance des fées.* Paris: Champion, 1984.

Harpham, Geoffrey Galt. "Aesthetics and the Fundamentals of Modernity." In *Aesthetics and Ideology*, ed. George Levine, 124–49. New Brunswick, NJ: Rutgers University Press, 1994.

Hawkins, Harriet. "The Victim's Side: Chaucer's *Clerk's Tale* and Webster's *Duchess of Malfi.*" *Signs* 1 (1975), 339–61.

Heng, Geraldine. *Empire of Magic: Medieval Romance and the Politics of Cultural Fantasy*. New York: Columbia University Press, 2003.

Henry of Lancaster. *Livre de Seintes Medicine.* Ed. J. Arnould. Anglo-Norman Text Society. Oxford: Blackwell, 1940; repr. New York: Johnson Reprints, 1967.

Henryson, Robert. *The Poems of Robert Henryson*. Ed. Robert Kindrick. Kalamazoo, MI: Medieval Institute Publications, 1997.

Hieatt, Constance, and Sharon Butler. *Pleyne Delit*. Toronto: University of Toronto Press, 1977; repr. 1996.

Hofstatder, Douglas. *Gödel, Escher, Bach: An Eternal Golden Braid.* New York: Vintage Books, 1979.

Hume, Kathryn. "Why Chaucer Calls the Franklin's Tale a Breton Lai." *Philological Quarterly* 51 (1972), 365–74.

Huot, Sylvia. "Others and Alterity." In *Cambridge Companion to Medieval French Literature*, ed. Simon Gaunt and Sarah Kay, 238–50. Cambridge: Cambridge University Press, 2008.

Huppé, Bernard. *A Reading of the* Canterbury Tales. New York: SUNY Press, 1964.

Hynes-Berry, Mary. "Cohesion in *King Horn* and *Sir Orfeo.*" *Speculum* 50, no. 4 (1975), 652–70.

James, Heather. *Shakespeare's Troy: Drama, Politics, and the Translation of Empire.* Cambridge: Cambridge University Press, 1997.

Jameson, Fredric. "Magical Narratives: Romance as Genre." *New Literary History* 7 (1975), 135–63.

Jauernig, Anja. "Kant, the Leibnizians, and Leibniz." In *The Continuum Companion to Leibniz*, ed. Brandon Look, 289–309. London and New York: Continuum, 2011.

Jauss, Hans Robert. *Question and Answer: Forms of Dialogic Understanding*. Ed. and trans. Michael Hays. Minneapolis: University of Minnesota Press, 1989.

Jean d'Arras. *Melusine; or, The Noble History of Lusignan*. Trans. (into modern English) Donald Maddox and Sara Sturm-Maddox. University Park: Penn State University Press, 2012.

– *Mélusine, Roman du XIVe siècle*. Ed. and trans. Louis Stouff. Geneva: Slatkine Reprints, 1974.

– *Mélusine ou La Noble Histoire de Lusignan*. Ed., with facing pages of modern French, Jean-Jacques Vincensini. Paris: Librairie Générale Française, 2003.

Kant, Immanuel. *The Critique of Judgment* (1790). Trans. James Creed Meredith. Oxford: Clarendon Press, 1962.

– *Critique of the Power of Judgment*. Trans. Paul Guyer. Cambridge: Cambridge University Press, 2008.

Kaplan, David. "Transworld Heir Lines." In *The Possible and the Actual*, ed. Michael Loux, 88–109. Ithaca and London: Cornell University Press, 1979.

Kay, Sarah. "Courts, Clerks, and Courtly Love." In *Cambridge Companion to Medieval Romance*, ed. Roberta Krueger, 81–96. Cambridge: Cambridge University Press, 2000.

Kelly, Douglas, "The Domestication of the Marvelous in the Melusine Romances." In *Melusine of Lusignan: Founding Fiction*, ed. D. Maddox and S. Sturm-Maddox, 32–47.

Kelly, Henry Ansgar. *Chaucerian Tragedy*. Woodbridge, Suffolk: D.S. Brewer, 1977.

Kinoshita, Sharon. *Medieval Boundaries: Rethinking Difference in Old French Literature*. Philadelphia: University of Pennsylvania Press, 2006.

– "Two for the Price of One: Serial Polygamy in the 'Lais' of Marie de France." *Arthuriana* 8, no. 2 (Summer 1998), 35–55.

Kitto, H.D. *Form and Meaning in Drama*. Oxford: Methuen, 1956.

Kittredge, G.L. "Chaucer's Discussion of Marriage." *Modern Philology* 9 (1911–12), 435–67.

– *Chaucer and His Poetry*. Cambridge, MA: Harvard University Press, 1915; repr. 1970.

Knapp, James F. "The Meaning of Sir Orfeo." *Modern Language Quarterly* 29, no. 3 (September 1968), 263–73.

Knapp, James F. and Peggy A. "Found in Translation." In *The Medieval Translator* 12, ed. Denis Renevey and Christiana Whitehead, 339–49. Turnhout, Belgium: Brepols, 2009.

Knapp, Peggy A. *Chaucerian Aesthetics*. New York: Palgrave, 2008.

– "Criseyde's Beauty." In *New Perspectives on Criseyde*, ed. Cindy Vitto and Marcia Smith Marzec, 231–54. Asheville, NC: Pegasus Press, 2004.

– *Time-Bound Words: Semantic and Social Economies from Chaucer's England to Shakespeare's*. New York: Palgrave, 2000.

Krause, Kathy, ed. *Reassessing the Heroine in Medieval French Literature*. Gainesville: University Press of Florida, 2001.

Kripke, Saul. *Naming and Necessity*. Oxford: Blackwell, 1980.

Krueger, Roberta, ed. *Cambridge Companion to Medieval Romance*. Cambridge: Cambridge University Press, 2000.

Kubler, George. *The Shape of Time: Remarks on the History of Things*. New Haven and London: Yale University Press, 1962.

Latour, Bruno. *Politics of Nature: How to Bring the Sciences into Democracy*. Cambridge: Harvard University Press, 2004.

– *We Have Never Been Modern*. Trans. Catherine Porter. Cambridge: Harvard University Press, 1993.

Latour, Bruno, and Michel Serres. *Conversations on Science, Culture, and Time*. Trans. Roxanne Lapidus. Ann Arbor: University of Michigan Press, 1995.

Le Goff, Jacques, and Emmanuel Le Roy Ladurie. "Mélusine maternelle et défricheuse." *Annales: Économies, Sociétés, Civilisations* 26, no. 3 (May–August 1971), 587–622.

Leher, Seth. "Artifice and Artistry in *Sir Orfeo*." *Speculum* 60 (January 1985), 92–109.

– *Inventing English: A Portable History of the Language*. New York: Columbia University Press, 2007.

Leibniz, G.W. "Discourse on Metaphysics," "Monadology," and "Preface to the New Essays." In *Discourses on Metaphysics and Other Essays*. Ed. and trans. Daniel Garber and Peter Ariew. Indianapolis and Cambridge: Hackett Publishers, 1991.

– *G. W. Leibniz and Samuel Clarke: Correspondence*. Ed. and intro. Roger Ariew. Indianapolis: Hackett Publishing Co., 2000.

– "Letter to Louis Bourguet." In *Philosophical Papers and Letters*, ed. and trans. Leroy Loemker. Dordrecht, Holland and Boston: D. Reidel Publishing Co., 1969.

– *Theodicy: Essays on the Goodness of God, the Freedom of Man and the Origin of Evil*. New Haven: Yale University Press, 1952.

Leicester, H. Marshall. *The Disenchanted Self: Representing the Subject in the* Canterbury Tales. Berkeley and Los Angeles: University of California Press, 1990.

Levine, George. "Introduction: Reclaiming the Aesthetic." In *Aesthetics and Ideology*, ed. George Levine. New Brunswick: Rutgers University Press, 1994.

Lewis, C.S. *The Allegory of Love*. New York: Oxford University Press, 1936.

Lewis, David. "Counterpart Theory and Quantified Modal Logic." In *The Possible and the Actual*, ed. Michael J. Loux, 110–28. Ithaca and London: Cornell University Press, 1979.

– *On the Plurality of Worlds*. Oxford: Blackwell, 1986; repr. 2001.

Leyerle, John. "The Interlace Structure of *Beowulf*." *University of Toronto Quarterly* 37 (1967), 1–17.

Logan, George M., and Gordon Teskey. *Unfolded Tales: Essays on Renaissance Romance*. Ithaca: Cornell University Press, 1989.

Longworth, Robert. "'Sir Orfeo,' the Minstrel, and the Minstrel's Art." *Studies in Philology* 79, no. 1 (Winter 1982), 1–11.

Loomis, R.S. "Morgain La Fee and the Celtic Goddesses." *Speculum* 20 (1945), 183–203.

Loux, Michael J., ed. *The Possible and the Actual: Readings in the Metaphysics of Modality*. Ithaca and London: Cornell University Press, 1979.

Lucas, Peter J. "An Interpretation of Sir Orfeo." *Leeds Studies in English*, n.s. 6 (1972), 1–9.

Lyotard, Jean-François. *Lessons on the Analytic of the Sublime*. Trans. Elizabeth Rottenberg. Stanford, CA: Stanford University Press, 1994.

Mackie, Penelope. *How Things Might Have Been: Individuals, Kinds, and Essential Properties*. Oxford: Clarendon Press, 2006.

Maddox, Donald. "Configuring the Epilogues." In *Melusine of Lusignan: Founding Fiction*, ed. D. Maddox and S. Sturm-Maddox, 267–87.

Maddox, Donald, and Sara Sturm-Maddox, eds. *Melusine of Lusignan: Founding Fiction in Late Medieval France*. Athens: University of Georgia Press, 1996.

Malory, Thomas. *Works*. Ed. Eugène Vinaver. London: Oxford University Press, 1971.

Mann, Jill. "Feminizing Chaucer." In Norton Critical Edition of *Troilus and Criseyde*, ed. Stephen A. Barney, 606–22. New York: Norton, 2006.

Marechal, Chantal, ed. *In Quest of Marie de France, a Twelfth-Century Poet*. Lewiston, NY: Edwin Mellen Press, 1992.

Marie de France. *Les Lais de Marie de France*. Ed. Jean Rychner. Paris: Éditions Champion, 1983.

– *The Lais of Marie de France*. Trans. Robert Hanning and Joan Ferrante. Durham, NC: Labyrinth Press, 1978.

McAlpine, Monica. "Criseyde's Prudence." *Studies in the Age of Chaucer* 25 (2003), 199–224.

– *The Genre of* Troilus and Criseyde. Ithaca: Cornell University Press, 1978.

McCloone, Katherine. "Strange Bedfellows: Politics, Miscegenation and *Translatio* in Two Lays of Lanval." *Arthuriana* 21, no. 4 (Winter 2011), 3–22.

McRae, Robert. *Leibniz: Perception, Apperception, and Thought*. Toronto: University of Toronto Press, 1976.

Mehl, Dieter. *The Middle English Romances of the Thirteenth and Fourteenth Centuries*. New York: Barnes and Noble, 1969.

Mikhaïlova, Milena. "L'espace dans les Lais de Marie de France: Lieux, structure, rhétorique." *Cahiers de civilization médiévale* 40, no. 158 (April–June 1997), 145–57.

Mitchell, Allan. "Chaucer's *Clerk's Tale* and the Question of Ethical Monstrosity." *Studies in Philology* 102 (Winter 2005), 1–26.

Mitchell, Sandra. *Unsimple Truths: Science, Complexity, and Policy*. Chicago: University of Chicago Press, 2009.

Mitchell, W.J.T. *Iconology: Image, Text, Ideology*. Chicago: University of Chicago Press, 1986.

Monette, Sarah. *Mélusine*. New York: Ace Books, 2005.

Mootz, Francis, III, and George H. Taylor, eds. *Gadamer and Ricoeur: Critical Horizons for Contemporary Hermeneutics*. London and New York: Continuum Books, 2011.

Mueller, Janel. *The Native Tongue and the Word: Developments in English Prose Style 1380–1500*. Chicago: University of Chicago Press, 1984.

Mullally, E., and J. Thompson, eds. *The Court and Cultural Diversity*. Woodbridge, Suffolk, and Rochester, NY: D.S. Brewer, 1997.

Murdoch, Iris. *The Green Knight*. New York: Viking Press, 1994.

Muscatine, Charles. "The Canon's Yeoman's Tale." In *Chaucer Criticism*, vol. 1, *The Canterbury Tales*, ed. Richard J. Schoeck and Jerome Taylor, 259–67. Notre Dame, IN: University of Notre Dame Press, 1960.

Nagel, Sidney R. "Shadows and Ephemera." *Critical Inquiry* 28 (Autumn 2001), 23–39.

Nair, Sashi. "'O brotel wele of mannes joie unstable!' Gender and Philosophy in *Troilus and Criseyde*." *Paregon* 23 (2006), 35–56.

Narinsky, Anna. "'The Road Not Taken': Virtual Narratives in *The Franklin's Tale*." *Poetics Today* 31 (2013), 53–113.

Nelson, Deborah. "The Implications of Love and Sacrifice in *Fresne* and *Eliduc*." *South Central Bulletin* 38, no. 4 (Winter 1978), 153–5.

Nerlich, Michael. *Ideology of Adventure: Studies in Modern Consciousness 1100–1750*. Trans. Ruth Crowley. Minneapolis: University of Minnesota Press, 1987.

Nichols, Stephen. "Marie de France's Commonplaces." *Yale French Studies* (1991), 134–48.

– "Melusine between Myth and History: Profile of a Female Demon." In *Melusine of Lusignan: Founding Fiction*, ed. D. Maddox and S. Sturm-Maddox, 137–64.

Nickolaus, Keith. *Marriage Fictions in Old French Secular Narratives, 1170–1250: A Critical Re-Evaluation of the Courtly Love Debate.* New York and London: Routledge, 2002.

Nolan, Maura. "Making the Aesthetic Turn: Adorno, the Medieval, and the Future of the Past." *Journal of Medieval and Early Modern Studies* 34, no. 3 (Fall 2004), 549–75.

Nowlin, Steele. "Between Precedent and Possibility: Liminality, Historicity, and Narrative in Chaucer's *The Franklin's Tale.*" *Studies in Philology* 103 (2006), 47–67.

Ovid. *Metamorphoses.* Trans. Charles Martin. New York: Norton, 2004.

Owst, G.R. *Literature and the Pulpit in Medieval England.* New York: Barnes and Noble, 1961.

Pairet, Ana. "Medieval Bestsellers in the Age of Print: *Melusine* and *Olivier de Castille.*" In *The Medieval Author*, ed. Virginie Greene, 189–204. New York: Palgrave, 2006.

– "Melusine's Double Bind: Foundation, Transgression, and Genealogical Romance." In *Reassessing the Heroine*, ed. Kathy Krause, 71–86. Gainesville: University Press of Florida, 2001.

Patterson, Lee. *Chaucer and the Subject of History.* Madison: University of Wisconsin Press, 1991.

– "'For the Wyves love of Bathe': Feminine Rhetoric and Poetic Resolution in the *Roman de la Rose* and the *Canterbury Tales.*" *Speculum* 58 (1983), 656–95.

– *Negotiating the Past.* Madison: University of Wisconsin Press, 1987.

– "Perpetual Motion: Alchemy and the Technology of the Self." *Studies in the Age of Chaucer* 15 (1993), 25–57.

Pearsall, Derek. "Madness in *Sir Orfeo.*" In *Romance Reading on the Book: Essays in Medieval Narrative Presented to Maldwyn Mills*, ed. Jennifer Fellows, Rosalind Field, Gillian Rogers, and Judith Weiss, 51–63. Cardiff: University of Wales Press, 1996.

– *Sir Gawain and the Green Knight*: An Essay in Enigma." *Chaucer Review* 46 (2011), 248–58.

Plantinga, Alvin. "Actualism and Possible Worlds." In *The Possible and the Actual*, ed. Michael J. Loux, 253–73. Ithaca and London: Cornell University Press, 1979.

– "Transworld Identity or Worldbound Individuals?" In *The Possible and the Actual*, 146–65.

Poirion, Daniel. "Mask and Allegorical Personification." In *Rereading Allegory*, ed. Sahar Amer and Noah D. Guynn, 13–32. Yale French Studies 95. New Haven and London, 1999.

Potkay, Monica Brzezinski. "The Parable of the Sower and Obscurity in the Prologue to Marie de France's Lais." *Christianity and Literature* 57, no. 3 (Spring 2008), 355–78.

Powers, Richard. *Plowing in the Dark.* New York: Farrar, Strauss and Giroux, 2000.

Puttenham, George. *The Art of English Poesy.* Ed. Frank Whigam and Wayne Rebhorn. Ithaca, New York: Cornell University Press, 2007.

Putter, Ad. *Introduction to the* Gawain-*poet.* London and New York: Longman, 1996.

– Sir Gawain and the Green Knight *and French Arthurian Romance.* Oxford: Clarendon Press, 1995.

Putter, Ad, and Jane Gilbert, eds. *The Spirit of Medieval Popular Romance.* Harlow: Longman, 2000.

Quilligan, Maureen. "Allegory, Allegoresis, and the Deallegorization of Language." In *Allegory, Myth, Symbol,* ed. Morton Bloomfield, 163–85. Cambridge, MA: Harvard University Press, 1981.

– *The Language of Allegory: Defining the Genre.* Ithaca: Cornell University Press, 1979.

Rabinowitz, Peter. *Before Reading: Narrative Conventions and the Politics of Interpretation.* Ithaca: Cornell University Press, 1987.

Ramm, Ben. "Making Something of Nothing: The Excesses of Storytelling in the Lais of Marie de France and La Chastelaine de Vergi." *French Studies,* 60, no. 1 (2006), 1–13.

Raybin, David. "'And Pave It All of Silver and of Gold': The Humane Artistry of the Canon's Yeoman's Tale." In *Rebels and Rivals: The Contestive Spirit in The Canterbury Tales,* ed. Susanna Greer Fein, David Raybin, and Peter C. Braeger, 189–212. Kalamazoo: Medieval Institute Publications, 1991.

Reidy, John. "Chaucer's Canon and the Unity of 'The Canon's Yeoman's Tale.'" *PMLA* 180, no. 1 (March 1965), 31–7.

Rescher, Nicolas. "The Ontology of the Possible." In *The Possible and the Actual,* ed. Michael J. Loux, 166–81. Ithaca and London: Cornell University Press, 1979.

Ricoeur, Paul. *Time and Narrative.* 3 vols. Trans. Kathleen McLaughlin and David Pellauer. Chicago: University of Chicago Press, 1984.

Riddy, Felicia. "The Uses of the Past in *Sir Orfeo.*" *The Yearbook of English Studies* 6 (1976), 5–15.

Rider, Jeff. "The Other Worlds of Romance." In *Cambridge Companion to Medieval Romance,* ed. Roberta Krueger, 115–31. Cambridge: Cambridge University Press, 2000.

– "Receiving Orpheus in the Middle Ages: Allegorization, Remythification and *Sir Orfeo.*" *Papers on Language* 24 (1988), 343–66.

Rider, Jeff, and Jamie Friedman, eds. *The Inner Life of Women in Medieval Romance Literature*. New York: Palgrave, 2011.

Rilke, Rainer Maria. *Orpheus. Eurydike. Hermes*. 1904.

Robertson, D.W., Jr. "Chaucerian Tragedy." *English Literary History* 19 (1952); repr. in *Chaucer Criticism: Troilus and Criseyde and the Minor Poems*, ed. Richard Schoeck and Jerome Taylor, 86–121. Notre Dame, IN: University of Notre Dame Press, 1961.

– *A Preface to Chaucer*. Princeton: Princeton University Press, 1962.

Rosmarin, Adena. *The Power of Genre*. Minneapolis: University of Minnesota Press, 1985.

Rushdie, Salman. *The Ground beneath Her Feet*. New York: Henry Holt, 1999.

Ryan, Marie-Laure. *Possible Worlds, Artificial Intelligence, and Narrative Theory*. Bloomington: Indiana University Press, 1991.

Rychner, Jean. "La présence et le point de vue du narrateur dans deux récits courts: Le Lai de Lanval et la Châtelaine de Vergi." *Vox Romanica* 39 (1980).

Scanlon, Larry. "The Authority of Fable: Allegory and Irony in the *Nun's Priest's Tale*." *Exemplaria* 1, no. 1 (March 1989), 43–68.

Scarry, Elaine. *On Beauty and Being Just*. Princeton: Princeton University Press, 1999.

Segal, Charles. *Orpheus: The Myth of the Poet*. Baltimore: Johns Hopkins University Press, 1989.

Selcer, Daniel. *Philosophy and the Book*. London: Continuum, 2010.

Serres, Michel. *Rome: The Book of Translations*. Trans. Felicia McCarren. Stanford, CA: Stanford University Press, 1991.

Serres, Michel, and Bruno Latour. *Conversations on Science, Culture, and Time*. Trans. Roxanna Lapidus. Ann Arbor: University of Michigan Press, 1995.

Shakespeare, William. *The Riverside Shakespeare*. Ed. G. Blakemore Evans. Boston: Houghton Mifflin, 1974.

Shepherd, Stephen H.A., ed. *Middle English Romances*. New York: Norton, 1995.

"Sir Gawain and the Green Knight." From *The Poems of the Pearl Manuscript*, ed. Malcolm Andrew and Ronald Waldron. Rev. ed. Exeter: University of Exeter Press, 1987.

Sir Orfeo. Ed. A.J. Bliss. Oxford: Clarendon Press, 1966.

Solomon, Robert, ed. *Thinking about Feeling*. Oxford: Oxford University Press, 2004.

Spearing, A.C. "Interpreting a Medieval Romance." In *Readings in Medieval Poetry*. Cambridge: Cambridge University Press, 1987.

– *Textual Subjectivity: The Encoding of Subjectivity in Medieval Narratives and Lyrics*. Oxford: Oxford University Press, 2005.

Spitzer, Leo. "The Prologue to the *Lais* of Marie de France and Medieval Poetics." *Modern Philology* 41, no. 2 (November 1943), 96–102.
Stalnaker, Robert C. "Possible Worlds." In *The Possible and the Actual*, ed. Michael J. Loux, 225–34. Ithaca and London: Cornell University Press, 1979.
Stephenson, Neal. *Anathem*. New York: HarperCollins, 2008.
Strohm, Paul. *Theory and the Premodern Text*. Minneapolis: Minnesota University Press, 2000.
Sturm-Maddox, Sara. "Alterity and Subjectivity in the *Roman de Melusine*." In *The Court and Cultural Diversity*, ed. E. Mullally and J. Thompson, 121–9. Woodbridge, Suffolk, and Rochester, NY: D.S. Brewer, 1997.
– "Crossed Destinies: Narrative Programs in the *Roman de Mélusine*." In *Melusine of Lusignan: Founding Fiction*, ed. D. Maddox and S. Sturm-Maddox, 12–31.
Taylor, Davis. "The Terms of Love: A Study of Troilus's Style." In Norton Critical Edition of *Troilus and Criseyde*, ed. Stephen A. Barney, 503–22. New York: Norton, 2006.
Taylor, Jane. "Mélusine's Progeny." In *Melusine of Lusignan: Founding Fiction*, ed. D. Maddox and S. Sturm-Maddox, 165–84.
Teskey, Gordon. *Allegory and Violence*. Ithaca: Cornell University Press, 1996.
– "Introduction." In *Unfolded Tales: Essays on Renaissance Romance*, ed. George M. Logan and Gordon Teskey, 1–15. Ithaca: Cornell University Press, 1989.
– "Irony, Allegory, and Metaphysical Decay," *PMLA* 109 (1994), 397–408.
Virgil. *The Georgics of Virgil*. Trans. David Ferry, 2005.
Wade, James. *Fairies in Medieval Romance*. New York: Palgrave Macmillan, 2011.
Weisman, Hope Phyllis. "Antifeminism and Chaucer's Characterizations of Women." In *Geoffrey Chaucer: A Collection of Original Articles*, ed. George Economou, 93–110. New York: McGraw Hill, 1975.
Weiss, Judith, et al., eds. *Medieval Insular Romance*. Cambridge: Boydell & Brewer, 2000.
Wetherbee, Winthrop. *Chaucer and the Poets*. Ithaca, NY: Cornell University Press, 1984.
– "Constance and the World in Chaucer and Gower." In *John Gower: Recent Readings*, ed. R.F. Yeager, 65–93. Kalamazoo, MI: Medieval Institute Publications, 1989.
– "Criseyde Alone." In *New Perspectives on Criseyde*, ed. Cindy Vitto and Marcia Smith Marzec, 229–332. Asheville, NC: Pegasus Press, 2004.
Whalen, Logan. *Marie de France and the Poetics of Memory*. Washington, DC: Catholic University Press of America, 2008.
Whittle, Bruno. "Epistemically Possible Worlds and Propositions." *Noûs* 43, no. 2 (2009).

Williams, Edith. "Morgan la Fée as Trickster in *Sir Gawain and the Green Knight*." *Folklore* 96 (1985), 38–56.

Williams, Raymond. *Marxism and Literature.* Oxford: Oxford University Press, 1977.

Witmore, Michael. *Shakespeare and Metaphysics.* London and New York: Continuum, 2008.

Wittgenstein, Ludwig. *Philosophical Investigations.* Ed. G.E.M. Anscombe. Oxford: Blackwell, 2001.

Yeager, R.F., ed. *John Gower: Recent Readings.* Kalamazoo, MI: Medieval Institute Publications, 1989.

Index

www.ingramcontent.com/pod-product-compliance
Lightning Source LLC
LaVergne TN
LVHW040150080826
844660LV00014B/910/J
* 9 7 8 1 4 8 7 5 0 1 9 1 4 *